Praise for *The Heart Is a Shifting Sea*

"The book not only charts the winding course of three marriages in one of the world's largest and fastest-growing metropolises, but also provides a detailed portrayal of a rapidly changing India. Flock's telling of these six middle-class lives is deeply sympathetic but un-sentimental." —*NPR*

"Fascinating." —*People*

"The three real-life couples in journalist Elizabeth Flock's *The Heart Is a Shifting Sea*, a fascinatingly intimate study of India's progres-sive new generation, illuminate the distance between our romantic imaginings and reality." —*Vogue*

"In *The Heart Is a Shifting Sea*, Flock seeks to understand the evo-lution of Indian marriage. . . . What unfolds is a book that truly is impossible to put down." —*Washington Post*

"People come together, grow apart, struggle to hold on to love and family. It's an old story, of course, but a new book offers an unusu-ally intimate focus in a place where tradition is colliding with twen-ty-first-century global culture: Mumbai, India." —*PBS NewsHour*

"In the mode of Katherine Boo and Adrian Nicole LeBlanc, Flock absents herself from the narrative, allowing us to enter the lives of her subjects and witness moments of almost unbearable intimacy. . . . A small armada of books have explored the aspirations of India's booming middle class. . . . What distinguishes Flock's take is her interest in and access to the inner lives of married women who face particular constraints." —*New York Times*

"Among the book's many strengths, Flock abstains from generalizing about India or Indian marriages. Instead, she nimbly captures the interiority of her subjects. . . . Although they are imperfect people in imperfect marriages, in these resplendent passages their humanity shines through." —*Minneapolis Star Tribune*

"While this book is a nonfiction look at love, marriage, and shifting cultural norms in Mumbai, specifically tracking three married couples through a span of about a decade, it reads like a novel. Thoroughly researched, it's also haunting and lovely. You'll find yourself strangely riveted as you follow the lives of each couple."

—*New York Post,* "This Week's Must-Read Books"

"Elizabeth Flock takes us on an intimate cruise on the shifting sea of the heart, in the best book set in Bombay that I've read in years. Flock's total access to her characters, and her highly sympathetic and nonjudgemental gaze, prove that love and literature know no borders. Easily the most intimate account of India that I've read, and of value to anybody that believes in love and marriage."

—Suketu Mehta, author of *Maximum City*

"An intimate portrait of three marriages. . . . Because Flock goes deep, rather than broad . . . she makes readers feel as though they are peering through a window into these couples' lives. . . . Flock writes about . . . sensitive topics with generosity and empathy in this beautifully rendered, intricate, and human exploration of love and marriage." —*Library Journal*

"*The Heart Is a Shifting Sea* is an intimate look at life in India, yet its intricately reported, novelistic portraits of marriage will resonate regardless of where you live. This book will keep you up reading deep into the night; it will make you ignore your loved ones, shirk your responsibilities. It is that good."

—Peggy Orenstein, author of *Girls & Sex*

"Flock writes about her subjects with omniscient authority. . . . Distilling large swaths of culture and history into brief, well-deployed asides, she keeps her focus on the couples themselves. It's a good strategy. What's extraordinary about *The Heart Is a Shifting Sea* is the apparent ease with which Flock has unlocked these marriages."

—*New York Times Book Review*

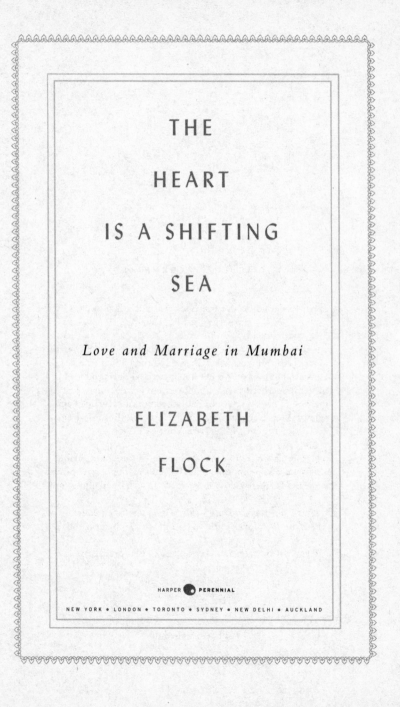

THE

HEART

IS A SHIFTING

SEA

Love and Marriage in Mumbai

ELIZABETH

FLOCK

HARPER ● PERENNIAL

NEW YORK ● LONDON ● TORONTO ● SYDNEY ● NEW DELHI ● AUCKLAND

HARPER ● PERENNIAL

HarperCollins books may be purchased for educational, business, or sales promotional use. For information, please e-mail the Special Markets Department at SPsales@harpercollins.com.

Excerpts from *Kamala Das: Selected Poems* published courtesy of Penguin Random House India and Dr. Devinder Kohli.

FIRST HARPER PERENNIAL EDITION PUBLISHED 2019.

Designed by Fritz Metsch
Maps by James Sinclair

Library of Congress Cataloging-in-Publication Data has been applied for.

ISBN 978-0-06-245649-6 (pbk.)

19 20 21 22 23   LSC   10 9 8 7 6 5 4 3 2 1

To my dad and stepdad

HERMIA: O hell! to choose love by another's eyes.

LYSANDER: Or, if there were a sympathy in choice,
           War, death, or sickness did lay siege to it,
           Making it momentary as a sound,
           Swift as a shadow, short as any dream . . .
           The jaws of darkness do devour it up.
           So quick bright things come to confusion.

—William Shakespeare, *A Midsummer Night's Dream*

CONTENTS

AUTHOR'S NOTE

NINE YEARS AGO, at the age of twenty-two, I moved from Chicago to Mumbai in search of adventure and a job, knowing no one in the city. I lived there for nearly two years. During that time—because I was restless and homesick—I stayed with half a dozen couples and families across the city and met many more. This is where my interest in the Indian love story began.

In Mumbai, people seemed to practice a showy, imaginative kind of love, with an eye toward spectacle. Relationships were often characterized by devotion, even obsession, especially if two people could not be together. This kind of love played out on the movie screens, but it was also deep in the bones of India's stories, in the Hindu scriptures and the Bhakti and Sufi devotional poems. I was young, and drawn to the drama.

It was also a kind of love I admired, because it seemed more honest and vulnerable than what I knew. My parents divorced when I was very young, and after watching my father's two subsequent marriages fall apart, I thought that perhaps this devotional quality was what they'd been missing. When I arrived in Mumbai after my dad's third divorce, the city seemed to hold some answers.

Out of all the people I met in Mumbai, three couples stood out from the rest. I liked them because they were romantics and rule breakers. They dreamed of being married for seven lifetimes, but they didn't follow convention. They seemed impatient with the old middle-class morals. And where the established rules for love did not fit their lives, they made up new ones.

I began asking them questions about their marriages. I had no defined goal at first. Eventually, though, I quit my job at an Indian business magazine to write about them, drawn in by their love stories. I wanted to write about them to understand how their marriages worked.

❦❦❦❦❦

The American journalist Harold Isaacs, who chronicled Asian life in the mid-twentieth century, once complained that Americans had only a few impressions of Indian people: as exotic (snake charmers and *maharajahs*), mystical (holy men and palmists), heathen (cow and idol worshippers), and pitiful (leprous beggars and slum dwellers).

Isaacs was writing fifty years ago, but it seems that not much has changed since. The same tired stereotypes are still trotted out by Westerners. With a country as large as India, it is tempting to oversimplify. And in Mumbai, City of Dreams, it is easy to overromanticize.

In reality, India is too big and diverse for generalities. It is home to a sixth of everyone on Earth and a bewildering array of languages, religions, castes, and ethnicities. And Mumbai is an unpredictable city. I was reminded of this when I returned and found things were not as I remembered.

At home in Washington, DC, I had regularly questioned whether I was fit to write a book about Indian marriages. I wasn't Indian, or married. But as the years passed, I saw that the book I wanted to read about India—that I wanted Americans to read about India—did not exist. Ultimately I decided to approach the subject the only way, as a reporter, I knew how: to go back to Mumbai armed with a dozen notebooks, a laptop, and a recorder.

When I landed in Mumbai in 2014, the city, save for its skyline—which had more malls and high-rises—looked much the same. The people I knew did not. Their marriages did not. They were calling old lovers. They were contemplating affairs and divorce. And the desperate attempts they were making to save their marriages, by having children, in at least one instance, were efforts I recognized from my own family.

Within each couple, one partner had begun dreaming of a different life while the other was still moved by old ideas. Where before their love stories had dazzled me, now they struck me as uncertain. I tried to make sense of what had changed. "Cities don't change," an editor in Mumbai told me with a sigh. "People do."

It was not just them. Indian historian Ramachandra Guha said that India is undergoing not one, but multiple revolutions: political, economic, urban, social, and cultural. In Europe and America, these revolutions were staggered. In India, these changes in cities and in people are happening all at once. And they seem to be upending the Indian marriage.

Nowhere are these shifts happening faster than in Mumbai, India's most frenetic city. And in no part of society is it causing more pain than among India's middle class, which does not have the moral freedom of the very rich or very poor. Certainly, for all three couples I followed, the opinions of family, friends, and neighbors mattered very much. *People will talk* was a phrase I often heard when I asked why they didn't do what they wanted.

That, and: *What you dream doesn't happen.* And yet I found our conversations would often end in dreaming, as they spoke of hopes for a bigger house, a better job, a trip to Kashmir, getting pregnant, falling in love again, or moving somewhere far away. Or they spoke of how their dreams had been deferred but would surely someday belong to their children.

ଓଓଓଓଓ

This is a work of nonfiction. I began writing it when I first met these people in 2008, but the bulk of the reporting was done when I returned to them in 2014 and 2015. For months, I lived, ate, slept, worked, and traveled alongside them. We mostly spoke in English, though sometimes in simple Hindi. They spoke in both languages and others among themselves.

I was present for many of the scenes detailed in these pages, but the majority that took place in the distant past were reconstructed based on interviews, photographs, e-mails, text messages, diary entries, and medical and legal documents. I interviewed each couple separately and together, formally and informally, over hundreds of hours.

Even when I was not in India, we spoke constantly. So much that their intimate world in Mumbai often felt more real to me than my life in DC or New York. Despite the vast physical and cultural distance between us, it felt as if we were still in the same room. It was rare that I did not hear from one or several of them every day, often in a flood of messages: recent medical reports; news of a fight at home; photographs of children clowning around before bed.

All the names of the people I wrote about in this book have been changed to protect their privacy. The names I've used were either chosen by them or are analogous in some way to their real names. In India—as in many places—names carry meaning.

In all instances, I have favored the Hindi, Urdu, Arabic, and other foreign-language spellings that the people use themselves. I have also used the English translations of the Quran, *Mahabharata*, and other religious and sacred texts that they keep at home.

This book could not have been written without the generosity of these three couples. In Mumbai, people will discourage you from saying thank you, but I am enormously grateful for how they opened their homes and their lives to me, even when it did not make them look good or wasn't easy. I hope that this book honors their trust in me.

In the end, these are three love stories among millions. I cannot pretend that they represent the whole of India, of Mumbai, or even of the city's contemporary middle class. But, as a well-known Dushyant Kumar poem says, it is when pain grows "as big as a mountain" that walls quake, foundations weaken, and hearts change. I am certain these couples are not alone in their pain, or in their dreaming.

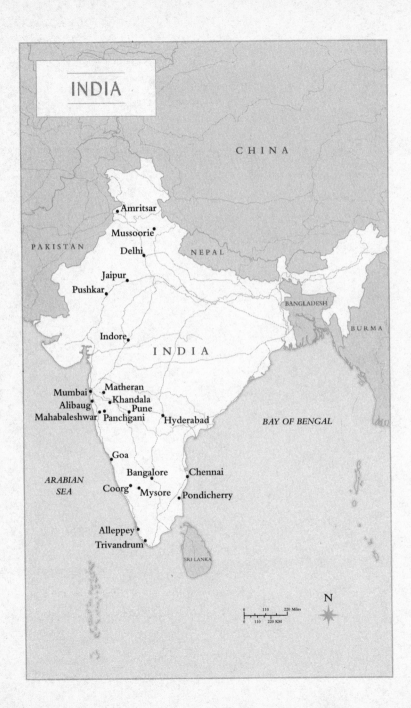

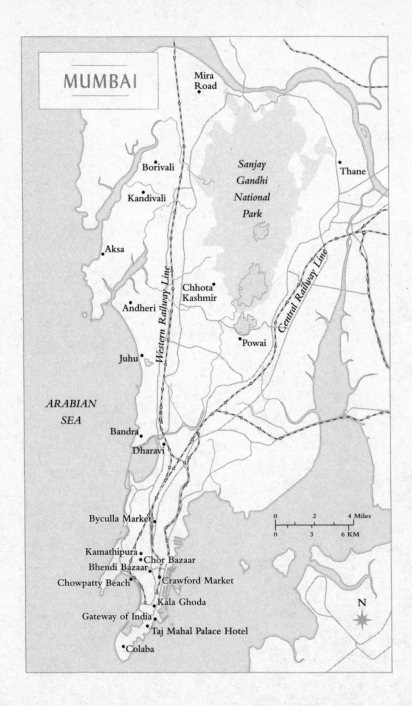

CAST OF CHARACTERS

MAYA AND VEER, *Marwari Hindus*

Maya, a school principal, also called Mayu

Veer, a businessman, nicknamed *Kancha*

Janu, their child

Pallavi, the family maid

Veer's cousin and business partner

Veer's father and brothers, also partners in business, and Veer's
    stepmother

Maya's father, a businessman, and Maya's mother, a homemaker

Ashni, Maya's friend, a vice principal and, later, a shopkeeper

Raj and Anika, Veer's friends

"The other Maya," Veer's former girlfriend

Subal, a businessman and friend of Maya's

SHAHZAD AND SABEENA, *Sunni Muslims*

Shahzad, a chicken seller and, later, a real estate broker

Sabeena, a homemaker

Shahzad's father, a landlord of Byculla Market, and Shahzad's
   mother, a homemaker
Sabeena's father, a sexologist, and Sabeena's mother, a homemaker
Atif, a karate instructor and Shahzad's closest friend
Diana, a woman known around Byculla Market, who works in
   advertising
Farhan, a teacher and, later, a mobile phone technician, and his
   wife, Nadine, a homemaker, who are Shahzad's extended
   family
Mahala and Taheem, Farhan and Nadine's children
Mamoo, a priest
Zora, a salon owner

ASHOK AND PARVATI, *Tamil Brahmin Hindus*

Ashok, a journalist and aspiring novelist
Parvati, a student and engineer
Parvati's father, an engineer, and Parvati's mother, a homemaker
Ashok's father, a jack-of-all-trades Anglophile, and Ashok's
   mother, a homemaker
Nada, works at a British company
Mallika, a filmmaker
Joseph, a student and engineer
"The US boy," works at a tech corporation

PROLOGUE:
MUMBAI, 2014

PUNE: The Indian Institute of Tropical Meteorology (IITM)'s first experimental real-time monsoon forecast for this year predicts delayed monsoon advancement over the country. Scientists said that consequently the first spell of rainfall will be inadequate and scantier than normal. They said a low pressure system over the Arabian Sea is absent . . .

The Times of India, May 21, 2014

Maya and Veer

IN MUMBAI, people say the monsoons make everyone fall in love. But this year the rains are late and the June nights are hot. So are tempers. Maya and Veer fight in the early mornings inside the bedroom of their eleventh-floor apartment, in a colony of concrete apartment buildings in a far-north suburb of the city.

One morning, they fight so loudly it agitates four-year-old Janu, who is playing with his toys in his bedroom down the hall. He pushes the door open to their room to see his father, in dress pants and no shirt, shout and point a finger at Maya, who is seated on their low bed. "Do not raise your voice with my mother," Janu says, in his grown-up way of speaking. "I do not like that. Say you're sorry."

My superhero, thinks Maya. To her, Janu looks every bit the part, even though he is so little, with his dimpled chin and gelled hair combed off to one side, a single lock falling onto his forehead. Maya once thought Veer also looked like a superhero, with his glossy hair, open face, and irresistible smile. She didn't even mind his six toes or lazy eye, which he said were signs of extra specialness and good fortune.

"I'm sorry," says Veer, not looking at Maya, as he gathers Janu up in his arms.

In the days that follow, Veer and Maya hold their tempers in check. On cooler days, it is easier. And on a Sunday morning not long after, when several fragile clouds arrive to mercifully block out the sun, Veer surprises his wife and tells her he won't go to work that Sunday.

Ordinarily, Veer spends Sundays as he does every day: working long hours at the family aluminum foil business. After he leaves, Maya and Janu often board the local train to go to Crossword, a chain bookstore Maya loves for its fiction and coffee shop, and Janu for its toys. The shopkeepers let Janu play on the floor for hours while Maya sits hunched over a book, often by Rumi or Haruki Murakami. They will do anything for the attractive mother with the big, *kohl*-rimmed eyes and petite but curvy figure. *Madame,* they whisper to each other, *looks just like a movie star.* When Janu gets bored of playing, Maya takes him on her lap and tells him fantastical stories.

"Let's go to Crossword, Mayu," Veer says now, using his pet name for her, which he seldom does these days. "I'll come along this time."

If you are a stupid woman, Maya thinks, *you'd say, "Well, at least he's around, baba."* But she knows he only wants to come for Janu.

"Okay," she says, and gathers up her purse and Janu's backpack and checks that she has both her phones. A text from Subal pops up on her screen. She reads it and then quickly puts her phone away.

At the sight of Subal's name her mind often wanders to that first day they spent at Aksa. Aksa Beach is just thirty minutes away by auto rickshaw, but it feels a world apart from the city's pollution and chaos and noise. It is nothing like her frenetic suburb, once a quiet village and now one of the city's most congested areas. But most of Mumbai's suburbs are like this—officially a part of the city, and just as noisy and crowded as the downtown. Within minutes along the drive to Aksa, by contrast, the roads become slow and winding. Along the route are small, quiet rivers, where local people fish and young boys swim. And at the end of the road stands a grove of trees, which opens up onto a magical seaside hotel. Whitewashed and sprawling and encompassed by green, the hotel is called: "The Resort."

The Resort is their place. It is where Subal tried to steal a kiss in

December, when there was a mild breeze. They ate from the breakfast buffet and sat talking for more than an hour beside the pool.
The water was a clear, still blue, and the palm tree fronds hung over
them. Maya found herself drawing lines on his palms. They both
wanted something but did nothing. Then she and Subal had gone
back again in May. May was the "Big Bang," or so they called it—
the day when the energy and tension between them led to a kind of
explosion, everything out in the open at last.

"Come on, Mayu," Veer says, and Maya refocuses on her husband, who is holding open the front door. He stands next to a colorful lettered sign that reads: *"Sukhtara,"* which means "happy star." It
is the name Maya gave their home when they moved in.

To her surprise, their Sunday goes as comfortably as the family
scenes in the Tata phone commercials. A quiet car ride, followed
by lunch at Bombay Blue, a trendy, air-conditioned restaurant in a
central suburb of town, and then to Crossword, where Janu plays as
Maya and Veer talk over iced coffee. Veer reads aloud to Maya the
juvenile messages he received from old school friends that week,
and Maya tells him about a teacher at her school who comes in with
hickeys from her husband. Veer laughs uncertainly at this.

At Crossword their phones are left unanswered. Maya purchases
Sacred Games, an English-language cops-and-robbers novel that is a
kind of love letter to Mumbai. It is a thick book, and it has that perfect piney smell. They buy Janu a soccer ball, which he clutches all
the way home. As they drive, Veer puts on a CD of old Bollywood
love songs, and he and Maya sing along.

But then Janu spots a KFC.

"Drumstick," Janu says, pointing to the red and white sign. "I
want drumstick."

After Crossword, Maya often rewards Janu with fried chicken or
some other meaty treat, because at home the meals are all vegetarian.

Veer doesn't eat meat, or even garlic or onions, nonnegotiable beliefs passed down from his staunchly Hindu family.

"What's a drumstick?" Veer asks.

"I don't know," says Maya, who shushes Janu, and begins singing along again with the song. Veer joins in, though he sings more softly now.

When dark falls, Janu is asleep at the foot of his parents' bed, drumsticks long forgotten. He curls his arms around the legs of his father, who is already snoring. Veer will work longer tomorrow to catch up on the hours he lost not working Sunday.

Maya gazes at the two sleeping figures, one large, one small. She moves Janu, who is shivering in the air-conditioning after the heat of the day, so that his head is on a pillow, and brings a blanket up to his chin. She tucks them both in.

Every night I do this, she thinks. *How long will I?*

As Maya goes into the kitchen to clean up what is left of dinner, she sweats in the cramped room as the ancient ceiling fan circles. Unwashed dishes are piled high in the sink, but she is too tired to do them now. She allows herself a glance at her phone, where a message from Subal is waiting.

Once again she is at Aksa Beach, on the day of the Big Bang, after which Subal had gazed at her from across the hotel pool. As Maya had looked back at him, she'd felt an unfamiliar sense of peace. It is one she has not felt with Veer in a long time. She knows that she and Subal will meet at Aksa again soon.

Maya puts down her phone and plugs it in to charge. She turns off the lights in the kitchen and living room, where no breeze comes in, not now, when a thick heat sits over the city. And not this far from the sea, where the reversal in winds will one day bring the rain. The monsoon is still days away. And then she walks into her bedroom, where, careful not to wake the sleepers, she climbs into the empty space in bed.

Shahzad and Sabeena

IT IS the start of Ramadan, and Shahzad strides toward the mosque in the lightly falling rain. Sudden showers like these keep surprising the city, but the full force of the monsoon has not yet struck. Shahzad's left leg lags behind the other, and he tries to pull it along more quickly. At this downtown mosque, at the southernmost tip of Mumbai, even the men who work in corporate offices answer the call to prayer on time.

At the entrance, Shahzad removes his *chappals* and ducks inside to join the rows of men with heads bowed. They touch their foreheads to the ground, murmuring in prayer. For several minutes, Shahzad dutifully mouths his prayers along with them, touching his forehead, nose, hands, knees, and feet to the ground, playing at being a good Muslim. But then his thoughts begin to wander.

Shahzad thinks of a beautiful woman he once saw on the street, and then another. He thinks about all the beautiful women he can remember: a buxom French woman with whom he sometimes does business, a half-Goan, half-Nigerian woman with siren red lips he used to know, and a platinum-haired woman he has only seen in photos online. He does not think of his wife, Sabeena.

He knows what the Prophet said: "Whenever any one of you comes across some attractive woman, and his heart is inclined toward her, he should go to his wife and have sexual intercourse with her, so that he might keep himself away from evil thoughts." The Prophet does not say what a man should do if he cannot have proper sex with his wife anymore.

For Ramadan, Shahzad has stopped taking the horse pills, the ones the doctor says will make him more like a man. Instead, the pills only make him feel hot inside. Or maybe that is just the swelter of the city. Even now, kneeling on the mosque's cool tiles, made wet by rain, the pills seem to have some power over him. He cannot stop thinking of other women.

The other day, on a very hot morning, Shahzad hugged the French woman and became excited as she hugged him back. Afterward, he went to confess to a local priest, who told him, "Unless you feel like something is coming out . . . the fast is there. It's okay." But Shahzad still feels guilty. He looks around and sees the other men praying with total calm. He forces himself to try harder.

Head to the ground, Shahzad asks God, as he always does, for a son. He thinks of how the conservative *mullahs* sometimes say that those who "have more wealth and more children . . . will not be punished." They don't say what a man should do if he becomes old—old enough to henna his hair to cover the gray—and still a child has not come.

The afternoon wanes, and Shahzad knows he needs to get home. Sabeena will start cooking soon for the breaking of the fast at sundown. For a moment, Shahzad considers stopping at the downtown market to bring home *bhajias*: spicy, crispy fritters wrapped in newspaper; their heat and oil taste so good in the cold rain. It has stopped drizzling, but the sky has gone dark as if it is about to pour. But he worries Sabeena will scold him for squandering money, so he doesn't buy anything at all.

As Shahzad enters his apartment, he can smell the sickness in it. His mother, a gaunt woman with thin lips and carrot-orange hennaed hair, lies in a bed of crumpled sheets in the main room. Cotton balls are stuffed in her ears. Shahzad looks around for his bucktoothed, bright-eyed niece and nephew, who usually greet him at the door. But the house of twelve is quiet.

A moment later, Sabeena arrives, dressed in the black *burqa* she wears outside when she runs errands. Her arms are laden with groceries. "Hi, *maji*," she says, greeting Shahzad's mother in her deep, raspy voice, her round cheeks flushed from the walk. She gives a perfunctory nod to Shahzad. After removing her *burqa*, she moves quickly around the kitchen in her thick *salwar kameez*, chopping vegetables, boiling water, and tossing red chiles, cumin, and coriander into pots. As her scarf falls from her hair, Shahzad stares at her. It has been so long since they made love.

Soon, a spicy-sweet smell fills the apartment. *Where are the children?* Shahzad wonders again. As if hearing him, Shahzad's nephew, eyes ablaze, comes charging out of his bedroom. "AHHHHHHHRRR-RRR," he shouts, waving his arms in the air.

Shahzad's mother cries out and clutches her sheets, and Shahzad's nephew, sensing easy prey, leaps onto her bed. He bounces on it once and rings a bell on the wall above her. *"Masti matkaro,"* she yells, "Stop it." Her sallow face twists into a scowl. He leaps off the bed onto the floor and throws his arms up theatrically. Shahzad laughs, forcing himself not to clap. His niece, who has run into the living room to watch her brother's antics, laughs along with him, her tight braids shaking.

Sabeena watches the scene from the airless kitchen, where the pots have begun to boil. The heat is so oppressive the monsoon must come soon. *Marriage is like a laddoo,* or heavy sweet, she thinks. *If you eat it, you'll cry, and if you don't you'll cry too.* This was true whether or not you had children.

On the porn websites Shahzad sometimes visits surreptitiously, the videos of the heavier Indian women have that tag: *laddoo.* He hides these videos from Sabeena, as many husbands in the country do. And he does not tell the priest about them.

As Sabeena watches him from the kitchen, Shahzad thinks again of the pills he is taking. He considers doubling the dose. The clock turns 7:24 p.m.—time to break the fast and pray—and Shahzad looks up at his wife, but then, embarrassed, looks away.

Ashok and Parvati

THE MORNING the sky opens, Parvati steams flimsy *idlis* for break-fast and curses as they stick in the pan. She wishes she were a better cook. A Post-it note with one of her mother's recipes scrawled on it detaches from the wall. It is sticky and close in their apartment in north-central Mumbai, where many of the buildings are tall—so tall they seem to touch the clouds, almost—but she and Ashok don't live in one of those. It always gets hot before the rain.

As she finishes the *idlis*, peeling them out of the pan one by one, the downpour comes all at once. It gives off a thunderous sound. From the kitchen window, she cannot see the cloud-high buildings through the sheets of water. For many days, the forecasters had prom-ised rain, and the Hindu temples prayed for it, chanting *mantras*. But each day, it had not come.

Parvati does not like the monsoon. To her it means clogged roads, ruined shoes, and that her thick hair goes frizzy and wild. In Trivandrum, down south where she is from, there are two smaller seasons of rain. In Mumbai there is just one big fury. In both cities the sea grows rough when the monsoon arrives.

In the living room, Ashok reads the newspaper on the couch. As Parvati hands him breakfast, he says, "Hey, *Chiboo*," and looks up at her over his nerdish glasses, which have slid to the tip of his nose. "Let's spend our Saturday riding the new metro from one side to the end and back."

He is actually serious about this, she thinks, and shakes her head before disappearing back into the kitchen.

That Saturday, they drive to Khandala instead, two hours south-east of the city. Khandala is in the Western Ghats mountain range, and Parvati hears it will be gorgeous in the rains. With a little thrill, she realizes how much her father will disapprove of this. He will say something like: *You're new to the place, don't take any risks, why did you drive so far?* But he cannot tell her how to behave anymore.

There was a time when Parvati loved the monsoon, when she was little, and she and her sister would play outside in muddy pools after school. They would stay out until their father got home from work or temple, and he would scold them to go inside. She loved it when she was at university too, and she and another student, Joseph, would kiss in the lab as the rains lashed the building outside. After the downpour ended, they always walked their bicycles across a campus that felt cool and clean. Joseph's kisses felt illicit, electric.

"It's responding to my touch, like it wants me to drive," Ashok says, as they get on the highway to Khandala. Parvati rolls her eyes. But she already feels better leaving Mumbai's city limits. Ashok rolls down the window and sighs. "The air is just rarefied," he says.

The road to Khandala winds through the mountains, which are lush and unblemished and fantastically green. It is full of switchbacks and vista points. "Look," says Parvati, pointing. A deep fog is rolling in.

In Khandala, they get out at the base of the Bhaja Caves, ancient rock-cut shelters built by early Buddhists. They walk up the path and pass a waterfall, which cascades down a steep, rocky mountain. Brash schoolchildren scale the rocks to the falls and scream as they dunk in their heads. When Ashok and Parvati reach the top, they take cover under a mounded *stupa*, built long ago for meditation. Protected as they are from the rain, Parvati thinks, just for a moment, that the monsoon feels romantic. She rests an elbow on Ashok's shoulder and does not think of Joseph at all.

On the way back to the car, they get their photo taken, smiling at the base of the path. In Parvati's smile there is just a trace of the six months of difficulty that came before. Months in which Ashok felt afraid of his new wife, who would rant and cry in the night and always blame it on her "past." Months in which she kept a journal for all her dark and wild thoughts, a journal she did not let anyone see. Now, he thinks she has stopped writing in it.

That night, on the drive home, Mumbai's traffic and chaos feel unnerving after the quiet of Khandala. As Parvati guides their car over the wet city streets, the road unexpectedly splinters into five. She slows down and then accelerates through the light, and a police officer flags down their car.

"License, insurance," the officer barks at Ashok, though Parvati is the one driving. Parvati rifles through a pile of papers and hands them through her window. The officer, who is intimidating in his pressed khaki uniform, shakes his head as he walks around to take them. Ashok is not playing his part.

"Baahar aao." The officer's tone is a warning now, and Ashok gets out of the car. After a short conversation, Ashok hands over the bribe, and the officer passes back the license in one swift, practiced movement.

"Why did you give that?" Parvati demands once Ashok gets back into the passenger seat. "You could have told them you are a journalist."

"That doesn't work," he says, and feeling her glare, adds, "Anyway, it doesn't matter."

Parvati says nothing to this. She grips the steering wheel. After a long moment of silence, Ashok bangs his fist on the dashboard. Their trip suddenly feels spoiled. "Fuck," he says, and the statue of Ganesh on their dashboard jumps, the pearls around the Hindu god's neck jangling. "Assholes. Fuck fuck fuck."

"You shouldn't let them affect you like that," says Parvati, primly, not looking at him. As she restarts the car, it begins to rain again. "You shouldn't let them make you say those words and ruin yourself."

Joseph, a good Catholic boy, would never have sullied himself that way.

DEVOTION

Maya and Veer, 1999 to 2009

"It was springtime: her limbs delicate as primrose,
  Radha roamed the forest, searching high and low for Krishna;
  More and more distraught was she in love's feverish delirium . . ."

—*Jayadeva,* The Gita Govinda

Maya first saw him at a wedding. Her friend was marrying his brother in the southern city of Hyderabad, on the banks of the Musi River, which separated the old city from the new. It was the year India and Pakistan fought in Kargil up north. They had been fighting since Partition, but still it was a conflict to be remembered. It was January, and cool, the day before Republic Day, which celebrated India's adoption of its constitution, when the country became truly free. It was held in a hotel alongside a garden. But Maya would not remember most of that. All she would remember of the wedding was that Veer was there.

And that they were both seated on the stage during the *saat phere*, the seven circles of the sacred fire to the chant of *mantras*, and the sweet smell of incense. Around and around the happy couple went, holding hands, walking three times with the bride in front, and the last four with the groom leading. Seven times, because a circle's 360 degrees cannot be divided by seven, and so the marriage was said to be indivisible. Maya, who was sixteen or seventeen and thin and gangly then, could not stop staring at Veer as the priest chanted steadily in Sanskrit, and the bride and groom repeated their vows: *I will be Sama, you will be Rig . . . Let me be the Heaven, you be the Earth.*

Veer, who was older, had spoken a few words to Maya before

the wedding, to ask her the location of a beauty parlor. He said he needed it for his cousin, but she hoped it had been an excuse to approach her.

After the ceremony, as Maya stood in a group of friends across from Veer, she noted that he was handsome, though not in a traditional way. His hair was slicked over to one side, and he had big, full lips set in a smooth, wide face. But it was his eyes—which were large and expressive, and one of which was lazy—that she liked most. He looked intense, poetic, lost in space. He didn't look like any man she knew. He also seemed to know his way around people, which she found impressive.

Something about him made Maya think of the Hindu god Krishna, who was known to be compassionate and charming. Krishna also had a way with women. In his lifetime, it was said he had taken sixteen thousand wives. As Veer spoke, female wedding guests grouped around him in anxious clusters. Several times he made the entire wedding party laugh. Maya desperately wanted to go over and speak with him.

But she wasn't adept at conversation. It was a quality that as a teenager she hadn't developed. And though people said she was pretty, with big, wistful eyes and silky hair that fell far down her back, she was certain that she was ugly. People also told her she had an intense stare and boyish figure. It didn't help that she was smarter than almost every boy in school, which made her feel self-conscious around them. She didn't dare speak more than a few words to Veer after the ceremony.

As the wedding ended and the guests departed, several of the boys asked the girls for their e-mails. Maya gave everyone a wrong e-mail except Veer. She handed it to him on a tiny scrap of paper, just as he was preparing to board a train. "Don't share this with anyone," she said, letting her voice drop low.

"Thanks," said Veer, who gave her an easy smile.

Maya decided then, though she knew it was foolish, that Veer would be the man she'd someday marry.

After several months, Maya received a greeting card in the mail, with a picture of a bear sitting at a writing desk on the front, and the caption: "Thank you just doesn't seem like enough." Tucked inside was a letter.

"It was a very nice time with you. Thank you so much for tolerating us, especially me. Hope I didn't bother you too much," Veer wrote. "I look forward to my next meeting with 'YOU.'"

The capital letters made Maya's heart leap. Below it, he had written, "The secret of happiness is not doing what one likes, but in liking what one does." And a signoff: "With lots of luv and wishes, Veer (*Kancha*)."

Luv.

Kancha. A nickname.

Maya tried not to get excited. She lived in Hyderabad and he lived in Mumbai, which was a full day's train ride or expensive flight away. She had also heard he was seeing someone there. But she kept up the correspondence, hoping that if they built a friendship, someday it might grow into something more.

Three years later, the casual letters between them finally turned into a second meeting and a kiss in Mumbai, which was a sprawling, thrilling place to Maya, nothing at all like home. Hyderabad, an old and crumbling city, was filled with monuments to lost dynasties, while in Mumbai, where Maya was visiting family, every day felt fevered and new. She and Veer met in the city's crowded suburbs for coffee, and then went out to the movies, and finally ended up at a neighbor's home. There, Veer kissed Maya as she stood at a window, like a hero would in a Hindi film. Veer leaned in first, which Maya would always remember.

Afterward, as they took a walk, Veer told her: "I don't want to get into a relationship."

"Okay," said Maya, who was not dissuaded, "but I think you're the one for me."

After Maya flew back home to Hyderabad, she and Veer kept talking, but several seasons passed and they made no plans to meet again. When Veer's birthday approached, Maya decided it was time to do something bold. She had filled out in the intervening years and had begun to line her eyes with *kajal*. At twenty, she now attracted attention from men all the time. She could easily hold her own at a party. And so it was without trepidation that she sent Veer a plane ticket to come visit her in Hyderabad for his birthday. Though the flight was only an hour from Mumbai, it cost 17,000 rupees, which was a few hundred US dollars then. Maya, who was still a student, sold a stack of her treasured books and gold bracelets to cover the cost.

After she booked the plane ticket, she also found herself reserving a hotel room. While she had experimented a little with boys in college, she had never had sex. Almost all the girls she knew were virgins, or said they were; the *kanyadaan*, or giving away of the virgin bride, remained among the most important Hindu wedding rituals. And yet she continued to feel certain that Veer would someday become her husband, and for that reason it would be all right, though she worried that her parents might discover her sneaking out. She knew they'd be shocked if they did. Other girls her age were not so bold.

On Veer's birthday night, they made love in the hotel room as Maya had hoped. But while it was clear she charmed him, she saw that he did not love her. When she said that she wanted to marry him, Veer was kind but firm as he said no. "There is no future in whatever you're saying," he told her. "I'm too much in my past."

Veer's past was another woman, coincidentally also named Maya. It was the woman he had dated when he sent Maya the thank-you card. Everyone said Veer had turned into a *deewana* over the other Maya—had gone mad in love—even though he had met her in person only two or three times.

The other Maya was also Veer's very distant cousin, and so believed to be of his same *gotra*, or lineage. In marriage, a *gotra* was sometimes used to determine whom a person could or could not love. The elders in his family would see marrying this other Maya as taboo, a kind of incest.

When the other Maya broke off their relationship, Veer assumed her family had pressured her into it for this reason. Or because his family's business had taken on too much debt and crashed around that time, and so their new money was sure to vanish soon. Both realities made him a less-than-attractive prospective groom. He was certain the other Maya would never have left him of her own volition. *Because it was a perfect relationship,* he thought.

But even if it was clear to the rest of the world that the other Maya could not be his wife, Veer continued to pretend that it was possible. He kept his cell phone wallpaper unchanged: a photo of her, smiling out at him. She was smiling from his wallpaper even as he made love to Maya on his birthday night.

❦❦❦❦❦

When Veer told Maya of his feelings for the other Maya, at first she was distraught. But then she thought of the old Hindu myth of the god Krishna and his lover Radha, and began to feel better. It was a love story she had read since she was small. Out of all the women Krishna met, it was Radha, the *gopi*, or cow-herding maiden, whom he loved best. But Radha had to suffer for their love. She suffered so much she was known as the personification of *bhakti*—of obsessive, devotional, sacrificial love. And yet she also enchanted Krishna like no other woman could. While they never married, Krishna and Radha's love was considered eternal. Maya thought that she should channel Radha and her sacrifices. *If Veer doesn't love me,* Maya thought, *then he should be with the one he loves.*

Maya called around and found Veer the other Maya's new contact information, which had changed since they'd dated. "Go ahead and talk to her," Maya said, and encouraged him to try to win her back.

But though Veer tried, the other Maya did not want a reunion. She said she wasn't going to hurt her family to be with him. Veer was upset but understood. A common adage went: *Family, where life begins and love never ends.* And a much-repeated *filmi* dialogue: *The value of family is greater than dreams.*

Veer called Maya and thanked her for her help but told her he would not keep trying. He said he had too much respect for the other Maya's devotion to family and would honor that by giving up what they had. *We met perfectly. We left perfectly,* Veer told himself so that it would not hurt so much. *So it is still a perfect relationship.*

Veer continued to call and text Maya often, though he said that they were just friends. Soon, they began talking every day. "I don't think we should be talking," he'd say, but then they would talk for two, four, six hours, until the morning light arrived. When India's telephone companies got the capability for picture messaging, they began sending photos back and forth every day. In each successive photo, they could see the tiny, almost imperceptible changes in the person from the day before. Before long, Veer began calling her "Mayu," and she used his family nickname *"Kancha."*

And then Maya came back to Mumbai several times with her mother, and each time, she snuck out and rendezvoused with Veer in hotel rooms. Each time, they had sex. When apart, they began having phone sex, and Veer knew she was no longer a friend. I miss you, he found himself texting her. I need you.

Soon, Maya allowed herself to believe he had forgotten all about the other Maya. She thought that maybe he could even become a *deewana* over her instead. After many months, Veer said the words Maya had longed to hear for so long. "Let's get married," he told her over the phone, "and see how and where it goes."

Maya tried not to think the words sounded noncommittal.

♥♥♥♥♥

She didn't want her father to find out about the engagement. Not so soon, and not like this. But her brother—who had once drawn a literal dividing line in their bedroom between what was his and hers, playing at the border of India and Pakistan—spilled her secret before she had a chance to.

"Have you gone mad?" her father said, his voice thundering through their big, open home, which was so close to the airport they could hear the planes come in. Her father, a gentle man with professorial glasses, was unexpectedly forceful as he forbade the marriage. He told her to forget all about Veer. "Marry him, and yours will be a life of sorrow," he said.

Maya's father knew Veer's father, because the two men had done business together. They were also both from the same ethnic group: Marwaris, traders, migratory but originally from Rajasthan, and stereotyped for valuing money above all things. He thought Veer's father inhabited the stereotype to the greatest degree. He had heard whisperings about the other Maya, about how Veer could not give her up. In their community, news traveled fast. Maya's father did not trust Veer or his parents. He had heard that women who married into Veer's family were harassed by their in-laws. He swore to prevent the marriage any way he could.

As weeks passed, Maya began to panic. She was convinced that she and Veer would never marry. Not only did her father remain opposed to the union, but Veer made no steps to plan a wedding. She thought that he regretted having asked her. She decided he had not meant it at all. Love marriages were still rare in the city; romance was mostly reserved for the gods and the movies. She had been foolish to believe that Veer was different from other men. But she had believed, and that made it worse.

In a moment of rashness, Maya found a bottle of sleeping pills in the house and swallowed thirty of them, one after the other after the other. Her father came home to find her stumbling down the hall.

At the hospital, they put a thick tube down Maya's throat and pumped her stomach. The tube caused searing pain but saved her life.

Maya took the pills to send a message: *I cannot live without Veer.* She wanted her father to see it, and Veer to see it. And it was true; if she couldn't have him, then she wanted to die. She had begun to feel that life was a constant struggle: with her father, with boys, and with how girls in India were permitted to live. She hadn't been allowed to study what she wanted to, earning a master's degree in analytic chemistry only because it was a field her father found respectable. If she had chosen, she would have studied psychology or journalism. And now her father would also choose her husband. She hoped that swallowing the pills would show him how misguided that effort was.

But after she recovered, Maya was shocked to find her father's stance had not changed. If anything, it had hardened. She should have remembered this about him. When he made up his mind about a subject, it was like he'd completed a Marwari business deal. It was finished, bought and sold. Over. Neither melodrama nor violence could change that.

And Veer still made no steps to plan a wedding. He and Maya continued to talk, but he avoided the subject of marriage. And so, a season later, when Maya's father suggested she at least meet another man, she unhappily agreed to it. There was, in fact, a line of men waiting for her: a fair, well-proportioned Hindu girl, and a supposed virgin, who smiled in photos with her mouth closed. Demureness was always valued in a woman.

Her parents set her up with Anil, a small-time Bollywood filmmaker and aspiring poet with a feminine voice, and a desperate comb-over. They impressed upon Maya that he lived on Mumbai's tony Altamount Road and came from a wealthy family. Equally important was the fact that he was from the same Brahmin subcaste.

Soon a trip was suggested—with Anil, Maya, and both sets of parents—for everyone to get to know one another better. Maya agreed, thinking this might be just the leverage she needed to win over Veer. But when Maya told Veer, he only said, "Go and let's see what happens." Maya thought he sounded upset but couldn't tell for sure.

Anil and Maya set off with their parents for Mysore, a South Indian city of palaces at the base of the lush Chamundi Hills. In spite of the bucolic landscape, Maya found it anything but romantic. She was not at all interested in Anil, with his turtle face and family wealth. Anil found Maya beautiful, but also didn't want to be pressured.

After the trip, Anil and Maya met without their parents at a Café Coffee Day, a Western-style coffee chain frequented by young couples, on a prearranged date to talk next steps. As they sat down, Anil said, "I think this is all bullshit."

"I agree," said Maya.

"I don't believe in arranged marriages."

"Neither do I."

Nor did many young people in Mumbai, and so arranging marriages took a special finesse. Both sets of parents tried to convince Maya and Anil that the other person had come around and asked when they might also give in. As summer neared its end, and Maya's parents kept asking, Maya called Veer to impress upon him that he was about to lose her.

"There is no way they are not going to get me engaged to this guy," she told Veer, with a touch of drama. "The whole society knows. You have to decide what you want to do."

The next day, Veer asked Maya to marry him. This time, she could tell the proposal was different. Something had changed in his voice and demeanor. "Until the eighth of August I wasn't definitely interested in a marriage," Veer said later. "But on the ninth of August I thought: it's okay."

Something had changed because when Veer saw he might lose her, he thought of all of Maya's best qualities. He thought about how she was always supportive. She always told him what she felt. *I have also shown her my life like an open deck of cards,* he thought, and she'd embraced it, not getting hung up on the success or failure of his family business. This seemed like what a man needed in a wife: someone who supported and understood you and always gave you a frank opinion. Veer had also come around after he mentioned the idea of marrying Maya to his father and his father supported it.

But when he asked Maya to marry him, he also told her the other Maya would remain in his life. He said the photo of her might stay on his wallpaper forever.

I should walk out right now, Maya thought. But she didn't, because she was certain he was the one.

And before they married, Maya decided she would visit Choodi Bazaar. There, in the center of a teeming marketplace in Hyderabad, a woman could find bangles in any color and style. There were big shops with glass cases of fancy bangles and little outdoor shops with tarpaulin roofs that sold simpler ones. The shopkeepers always beckoned with cries of *"Choora, choora!"* which could be worn for any occasion but primarily for weddings.

Some were made from the ivory of an elephant tusk or rhino horn and slid on with the help of perfumed oil. Others were twenty-four-karat gold, inlaid with jewels in a glittering red and clasped at the edges with a satisfying click. Most came in red and white, for luck and purity.

Bangles were symbols of a marriage promise, of finality and commitment. If Maya were like her mother—and like most Hindu women—she would wear her red wedding bangles until she died.

✿✿✿✿✿

It was when her parents went away on a short trip that Maya took her chance. She and Veer planned to meet at the airport in New Delhi, and then go on to Jaipur, city of pink palaces, to wed. But as Maya waited for Veer's plane, she worried that he wouldn't be on it. She called her best friend, who would be a witness at the wedding, and asked, her voice tight and fearful: "What if he doesn't come?"

"Then go back home," her friend said, "and no one will ever know."

But Veer did come, and seemed excited, even euphoric, about the wedding. They met up with Maya's friend and her boyfriend and another couple, friends of Veer. These four would be the witnesses at the wedding, in lieu of parents.

Both couples had tried to prevent the marriage at first, saying they didn't think it would work out. Not with how big a *deewana* Veer had been over the other Maya, or how *fanaa*—how destroyed in love—Maya seemed. And not with how controlling Veer's parents were, or how displeased Maya's father was with the union. There was also the glaring problem that Maya and Veer's stars did not match. *Marriage is made in the heavens,* the old adage went. Most Hindus consulted their birth charts before marrying, even the non-believers. Maya's and Veer's stars forecast that their marriage would bring them only trouble.

But then the couples had come around, after seeing that Maya would not yield, and that Veer now called her "Mayu" with affection. They came around after they learned that even Veer's father supported the marriage. In the end, both couples helped organize the entire affair. They planned the wedding for Jaipur, city of epic forts and fanciful palaces, because Veer had been born there and would know how to get around. It was where even Maya's and Veer's parents might have chosen for a wedding, because of their shared Rajasthani roots.

It was August, and excruciatingly hot in the city, as they ran from one temple for the ceremony to another for the *pooja*, fearing at any moment that they'd be found out. Maya wore a hot pink *sari*, a deep red–colored shawl, and cheap plastic red bangles, which Veer's friend had gifted her. She had not bought the bangles at Choodi Bazaar, because there had not been time. Veer wore a majestic white, gold, and red *sherwani* and a tall turban that didn't fit quite right. They both wore garlands of pink and white carnations. They married in the style of Arya Samaj, the equivalent of a court wedding, for couples that married across caste or religion, or without parental approval. Arya Samaj ceremonies were simple and inexpensive but still included all the essential Vedic marriage rituals and blessings.

There were some minor mishaps during the ceremony, which worried both sets of friends. Marriages were supposed to take place before sunset, but by the time Veer and Maya married, the sun had already gone down. It also began to rain very hard, as if to signal bad luck. When Maya and Veer walked around the sacred fire, they accidentally did it eight times instead of seven. The *pandit* said not to worry, that the last time was "just to finish." *What is this?* thought Veer's friend. *No one does eight times instead of seven.*

But in a photo from the day, Maya and Veer do not seem worried. Maya smiles in her hot pink *sari*, her hands and feet dyed deep red with henna, and she leans comfortably into Veer. Veer, who is still in his tall turban, stands with his arm draped around his new wife.

As they left the temple, Veer received a call from his older brother. Maya's father had called Veer's family and told them he was searching for the couple.

"We've already done it," Veer told his brother, his voice calm. "Let's not talk much now," he continued. "Just give it two days. After two days you can call me, and if you feel at ease then it's good. If you say anything right now, you will be shouting and regret it later." Though Veer's family had initially approved of the marriage, he knew Maya's father's anger could stir up trouble.

Veer hung up and switched off his phone, as did Maya. They spent several more days in Jaipur, switching hotels every night. Maya worried her father might show up at any moment, though she did not know what he would do if he came. At the minimum, he would take her back home to Hyderabad and never allow her to see Veer again. To be extra safe, they stayed one night at the house of a Jaipur mafia don, the father of one of Veer's old school friends. *No one is going to catch us here,* Veer thought.

For Maya, their week on the run was the most terrifying and romantic of her life. She found herself even more besotted than before. Veer felt only at peace. He thought he had made the right decision. *I am marrying a good friend,* he thought. In the end, he hoped the marriage would bring two respected, middle-class Marwari families together. Marriage was, as it had always been, a kind of transaction. But their families would only come together if Maya's father forgave her.

When Maya and Veer flew to Mumbai, Veer's father and stepmother were waiting at the airport to receive them. They were thrilled for the new couple. Their son was thirty, so it was past time he settled down with a young, supposed virgin, only twenty-three, and from his same background.

Soon after, they hosted a grand wedding reception in a banquet hall, inviting some five hundred people, including Maya's parents.

It was unusual for the groom to bear all the costs of a reception, but Maya's family wasn't going to do it. Maya's mother attended the party, along with Maya's brother, uncle, and other family members. But her father did not show up. "These people will mistreat you," he warned his daughter over the phone. His view had not changed.

And it didn't change even after Veer's father took Maya home to Hyderabad after the reception, to try to mend what was broken. In their living room, Maya found her father crying, with her grandfather seated beside him.

Maya's grandfather had always been intimidating, both in height and demeanor. He was a government man, and he'd worked for the railroads. His posture was ramrod straight. He was also a man of strict principles, which could be good or bad for his grandchildren, depending on whose side he was on. This time he stood by Maya. He thought that if she had found a good man she loved, she should be allowed to marry him. He was only upset that it had been done in a way that could end her relationship with her father.

"You should have told me," her grandfather said, sadly. "I would have gotten you married."

Maya began to cry along with her father. "But this is what I've done," she said, looking from one man to the other. "Now I'm responsible for my life. You have to trust me."

Her father said he couldn't, because he knew what lay ahead.

Veer's father sat watching the scene coolly, and, when everyone was finished crying, took Maya back home to Mumbai.

༒༒༒༒༒

As was customary for a new bride, home was now Veer's parents' house, which was in a crowded suburb on the northern outskirts of the city.

Maya had always pictured Mumbai as the city of love. Mumbai, which until not long ago was called Bombay, and before that

Bom Bahia, Boa-Vida, Mambe, Mumbadevi, Heptanesia, and many other names that captured the city's glamour. A city ruled by the Portuguese, and then given to the British as part of a marriage treaty, before it wrested itself independent with the rest of the country. A city renamed Mumbai, because a political party wanted to rid the city of its British history, though many locals still used the sexier *Bombay*. Even Mumbai's nicknames were seductive: the City of Seven Islands, City of Dreams, and City of Gold. It was the home of Bollywood and all the most *filmi* love stories. It was the gateway to all of India. If there was anywhere to be in love, it was in Mumbai.

Veer, who had lived in Mumbai all his adult life, saw it differently. To him, Mumbai was first and foremost a trading city, a city of transaction. A big and bursting city of eighteen million, it was India's financial hub and the source of much of the country's wealth. Bollywood didn't mean big romance; it meant big money. Mumbai was every good Marwari businessman's dream. It was called "the Gateway to India" because so much trade flowed through the city's port. And Mumbai was just one big island now, with the center of the city at its tip.

There was also a monument called the Gateway of India at the southernmost end of the city. It was a basalt arch structure, and it stood proudly between the Taj Mahal Palace Hotel and the shore of the Arabian Sea. The arch had been built to commemorate the visit of the British royal couple King George V and Queen Mary, who were not supposed to marry but fell in love and did. Just before the monsoons started, kite birds always circled the Gateway of India monument, filling the space between the water and arch with the beating of wings. They often landed at the arch's base, where the muddy water met the land. Or they perched on the trash gathered there in ugly clumps or on the residue of those who used the sea as their toilet.

All of downtown Mumbai was like this: dazzling from one view, horrifying from another. Downtown, the city fell easily along the curve of the shifting sea. In the daytime, the melting heat created a foggy haze that gave the illusion of a dreamscape.

At night, along Marine Drive, which followed the shape of the coastline, the road's streetlamps lined up to look just like a string of pearls. Farther inland, the Victorian and Indo-Saracenic buildings maintained a crumbling dignity and beauty. They sat beside open green cricket *maidans* and blocks filled with Irani cafés, tourist stalls, corner shops, and beer bars. Between it all were the hawkers of the city's favored street foods: deep-fried *vada pav*, buttery *pav bhaji*, and spicy-sweet *pani puri*, with mango *lassis* and *masala* Cokes to wash it down.

Mumbai was dazzling despite the clear signs of the city's rapid deterioration, the unrelenting honk of taxicabs, and the smell of human waste. Even with the sting of polluted air and the memories of the violence that came before. There was no privacy, and no space. But the lack of space offered reassurance that everyone was in this city together: majority Hindu and minority Muslim, wealthy and famished, native and migrant, hopeful young men and bent old women, all brushing up against one another. Touching was a way to speak when more than a hundred languages were spoken. Or it could be a way to hurt children, women, or neighbors. Nothing was simply good in this city. Beauty and brutality were intertwined. But it was a city that was Maya and Veer's now, together.

The suburb where Veer's parents lived was crowded and noisy, and almost twenty stops north on the Western Railway line from the center of the city. It was nowhere near Mumbai's Marine Drive, where lovers went to walk hand in hand. And it looked nothing like the downtown with its wide and airy streets. Instead, like most of the city, its roads were clogged with cars, motorbikes, and rickshaws that darted across the street like cockroaches at dusk.

Farther into the suburb, past the shops selling fabric by the yard, liquor by the peg, and flowers by the garland, it was mostly new construction. These buildings were low and painted in unimaginative hues of brown and tan and gray. They were often covered in *paan*, the favored *betel* leaf and tobacco combination that when spit looked just like blood. The tallest structures in the suburb were the glittering new malls, plastered with advertisements in garish colors and signs that promised objects few could afford. The shorter structures were the *chawls*, or tenements. Even smaller were the shanties, made of bamboo, tarps, and corrugated metal, which lined many of the suburb's lanes. Downtown Mumbai was overpopulated, but the suburbs seemed on the verge of collapse.

But Maya didn't see any of this, not at first. She saw only that she had made it to Mumbai, City of Dreams, with the man she married.

❦❦❦❦❦

Veer's parents' home was a joint family arrangement. Though Maya had finished college and earned a master's degree, it was assumed that she would not work, except to help cook for the household of seven. She often started preparing food at sunrise along with the other women, kneading the *roti* and adding spices to that morning's meal.

She was also expected to wear *saris*, a change from her school-going Western dress. She didn't know how to tie one, which was always difficult for girls the first and even tenth times. She didn't own many clothes, traditional or Western, but she was always careful with her appearance. On a visit with Veer to see his grandmother, she chose a plain but smart-looking *sari* and thought the visit went well. That night, Maya remembers his parents bursting noisily into the house after work. They would not speak to her, and after a little while the other members of the family began treating her coldly.

What is happening? Maya thought. In her childhood home, people talked about issues and moved on. Here, it seemed that problems festered.

The next day, Maya overheard Veer's parents say that his grandmother scolded them about the *sari* she had worn. They agreed that Maya went out "wearing clothing not fit for a new bride." They said that it "spoiled our name" for Veer's new wife to dress in plain clothing. Panicked, Maya went into her bedroom and dialed Veer at work.

"I'm new to their ways. If there's a problem, have them talk to me about it," she said. "I'm willing to compromise."

"Mayu, it's a family. These things keep happening," he said, which Maya didn't find helpful at all.

"Talk to them. Please."

But when Veer came home he didn't.

Veer didn't like to confront his father, an imposing man with a thick belly, dense mustache, and lazy eye just like his son's; some said he resembled a traditional Bollywood villain. Veer and his father had always been close, and they had become closer still after the death of Veer's mother from cancer a decade and a half ago. The stepmother who replaced her was a tall, cruel woman with a hard face and quick tongue. Veer and his brothers seemed only to tolerate her. Some said she had turned Veer's father into a harsher man. Still, Veer always listened to his father.

Maya bought better-quality *saris* after that and worked harder on her cooking. When Veer was at work, she tried not to call him, even if his parents shouted at her, as they had increasingly begun to do. It helped that Veer sent her loving messages when he was away.

Hi jaana, he'd write. *My life.*

I think I am already missing you a lot & so lil out of place as well.

Mayu . . . I miss you *yaar* . . . yu dint send me even one mms.

When Veer finally came home from work at the end of the day, Maya tried not to complain. She could tell how exhausted he was. She noticed his fraying dress pants, sweat-stained shirt, and belt that often missed a loop. And when he smiled and crawled into bed beside her, Maya felt their joint family home was not as bad as it seemed.

But she sometimes grew restless in the afternoons, when Veer and his father and brothers were at work, and the other women in the house took their daily naps. In these hours, Maya would flop down on her stomach in her bedroom and open the laptop Veer had given her to use. She would have liked to surf the Internet— maybe even look at porn, which more women in the country were watching. But the laptop was primitive, and it took forever to boot up or load a page, so videos were mostly out of the question. When she was able to get into her e-mail, she sometimes sent messages to school friends or waited for a message from her father, who had not spoken to her since her marriage.

But her father didn't e-mail or call. She received one unexpected note, from a college boyfriend, who wrote: "I sent a gold watch to your friend's address for you. I am still waiting." For a moment, she wondered where that relationship would have gone. *No,* she thought. *He is nothing like Veer.*

It was not long after Maya began using the laptop that her father-in-law called her into his bedroom. Grim-faced, he stood flanked by Veer and his older son.

"Put your laptop and your phone on the bed," he said, and Maya obeyed. "Now what?" she asked.

"In our house," Veer's father said, "we don't bring up daughters-in-law to use gadgets or to be technologically advanced."

Veer's father had heard rumors that Maya was miserable in the joint family home. He had heard she wanted to leave and take Veer with her. And so now he thought he would have to cut off her ability to communicate with the outside world.

"Is that what you called me here for?" said Maya, growing pet-
ulant with her in-laws for the first time. It was true she had told a
friend, one of the witnesses at their wedding, that she was unhappy
with her living situation. But she had never said she was going to
leave the house or break up the family.

"See, is this how your wife talks?" said Veer's father, turning to
Veer, who didn't know what to say.

"You're just standing there," Maya said to her husband, accus-
ingly, "while they're treating me like dirt."

Veer looked at her but didn't say anything. He had always felt
that it was better not to speak up during conflict. *It is better to keep
a horse's view,* he thought. If he was doing the right thing, and not
speaking ill of anyone, that was all that mattered.

He also knew that everyone would have their own spin on it. "If
we re-create it after five years," he would later say, "everyone will
be putting their own *masala* on it. What is the pull or push on these
people? I don't want to know. I don't want to be involved." But Veer
was involved. After Maya handed over the phone and laptop, life
in the joint family home only grew worse. In January, a month in
which many Mumbaikars take vacation, Maya told Veer she needed
to get away. She said she would go mad if she didn't.

Veer's father tried to prevent them from going. He said that Maya
was sick and couldn't travel. For once, Veer stood up to him. He
argued that the trip would be their honeymoon, which every new
couple deserved.

That month they flew to Mussoorie, a hill station at the foothills
of the Himalayas, once used by the British as a getaway. In Mussoorie, the temperatures were cool and the clouds sat low over the
mountains. Maya and Veer visited temples and shrines. Their days
were filled with happy wandering. Before they left, they had their
picture taken beneath a waterfall. The water was so white and the

exposure so bright that it looked like a backdrop of snow. They both wore small, hopeful smiles.

But after they returned to Mumbai, Maya saw that nothing had changed. She realized that Veer would continue to be away for long hours at work, and that while he was gone his parents would verbally abuse her. Like many women in the country, she saw that she would never be allowed to work. She made plans to visit her father and make amends, but Veer's parents told her she could not go. Considering a future she could not bear, Maya picked up the inhaler she was prescribed for her asthma and swallowed all the medication inside.

This time, Maya intended more than a message. She was hospitalized for three days, during which time Veer hardly left her side.

On the third day, Maya woke up in the hospital room to find her mother and father standing over her. "Who has been taking care of you?" her father asked.

"Veer," she said. He had been good to her.

After she felt well enough, Maya's father brought her home to Veer's parents' house. He laid her on her bed and went out in the hall to talk to Veer's father, who told him he believed his daughter's hospitalization had been a stunt.

"No," Maya's father said. "Maya is very sick. She needs to be taken care of. She has lost seven kilograms. I will take care of her, and then send her back to you."

From the bedroom, Maya heard Veer's father start shouting. After marriage, a girl belonged to her husband's parents, not her own. Unless she was pregnant, it would not be acceptable for her to go back to her childhood home in Hyderabad. But as Veer's father became more and more worked up, he said that he wanted Maya out of his house. "Take your daughter," he shouted, as Maya remembers. "You have not given her any values. She does not respect anyone. Take her wherever you want to take her."

Maya's father dropped to the ground at this show of fury and began kissing the man's feet. He begged to be able to take his daughter back home with his permission, not his anger. Maya, who was still groggy from medication, dragged herself out of her bed. She could not reconcile the father she knew with this fawning display.

"Don't kiss his feet for me," she told him as she came into the living room. "Get up. You don't deserve that."

To Veer's father, she said, as coldly as she could: "What you give to me, I'll give back to you."

Maya's father left the joint family home, perhaps knowing he could only do more harm by staying. The next day, he called Maya to tell her that he and her mother had decided to go back to Hyderabad and leave her with Veer's parents. "We don't want to break your house," he said, his voice weary. "But can I see you and Veer before we go?"

Veer felt caught in the middle. On one side were his parents and on the other were Maya and her parents, he thought, *and everyone has their own cycle and mood*. He knew people didn't change, especially Indian elders; instead, they only kept pushing. Though he saw that his parents were torturing his wife, he also believed that drama toward daughters-in-law was part of the Indian lifestyle. Even these days, when Indian women were becoming more assertive, many of the TV soaps were still of the *saas-bahu* genre, in which the controlling and cruel mother-in-law treated the daughter-in-law like dirt. This dynamic existed even in the old songs and the folktales. Most girls just dealt with it. *But Maya, when pinched, blows up*, he thought. When handed drama, she became insolent and angry. Veer knew his parents would hold on to these first impressions of his wife for a lifetime. And now Maya was forcing him to get involved, which he did not want to do.

"Are you coming?" Maya asked.

"I'll ask my father and come down," Veer said, but several minutes passed before he appeared. When he did, he took her hand and said, "Mayu, let's go back home."

"No," she said, her voice firm. "I have to meet my father."

"Don't do this," he said. "You will create a scene."

"I need to meet my father," she repeated.

Veer's cell phone rang, and she could hear his father shouting as he picked it up. "You can't control your woman," his father said, his voice like a threat. At the same time, Veer's stepmother came out and ordered them back inside.

"Who are you to stop me?" said Maya.

In Maya's memory, Veer's father came out next, and the four of them began pushing and shoving on the street. Maya wrenched her arm free to put a hand up for a passing rickshaw, which screeched to a halt before them. As she and Veer climbed in, his father tried to get in with them. Maya turned to her father-in-law and addressed him icily. "There is a policeman there," she said, pointing to a uniformed man down the road. "And if you don't get out, I will file a complaint against you."

"So this is the culture you were brought up in," Veer's father said, and let the rickshaw go.

In the rickshaw, Veer turned to Maya and asked, "What have you done? You've blown everything."

Maya began to cry. "What do you mean?"

"I don't know if we can be together anymore," Veer said.

"Why are you saying this?" Maya was sobbing now. But she knew. To Veer, like many Indian men, family was everything.

Inside the house, Veer's father called Maya's grandfather in Hyderabad. Over the phone, he rained abuses on her grandfather for how she was raised. And while Maya and Veer's rickshaw steered through the trafficked streets to meet her father, whom they found crying inside a café, her grandfather's blood pressure shot up and he had a stroke while still clinging to the receiver.

♥♥♥♥♥

The week after the incident, Veer sent his wife an e-mail from work that began: "Dear Maya." He almost never addressed her as Maya, not since he had started calling her "Mayu." In the e-mail, he wrote that his parents were "broken from the inside," and that an episode like this could not happen again. He said they must think in the present and plan for the future. He ended the e-mail with "love always," but his sign-off didn't seem convincing.

The drama in the household was not over, because every morning, Maya woke up thinking of the long years ahead. Years of his parents berating and belittling her, and Veer keeping silent. One day, she walked out of the joint family apartment and took a bus to Pune, a three-hour ride from Mumbai, and Veer had to come and take her back home. In the middle of the night, she woke up screaming, and was put on antipsychotics and antidepressants. She went to the doctor, feeling unable to breathe, and Veer's father followed her inside the office to prove she was making it up. The doctor, a sweet, white-haired man with a large nose and wide smile, told Veer's father, "Leave now, you're only making it worse."

In the end, Maya and Veer moved out of the joint family home. At first, they moved to a temporary apartment, and then another, and finally to the new apartment they'd call home. More couples in the city were choosing to live apart from their parents and in-laws, despite how the conservative politicians and older generations railed against it, blaming the creeping influence of the West. But couples often did not move far away. Maya and Veer moved only a suburb over from Veer's parents. When at last they moved out, Veer's father and stepmother seemed glad to see Maya go.

Maya's mother came to visit soon after the move and sat her

daughter down for a talk. With her square cheeks and thinning hair and rolls of fat, she was what many dutiful Indian mothers grew into—and what Maya didn't want to become.

"You have to take things in stride, and don't get so mad," her mother told her. *"Thoda compromise karo."*

Maya had heard the phrase many times before. She knew that Indian women were conditioned to compromise. But she didn't think there was such thing as "a little compromise." Even small compromises chipped away at what a person held dear, until much had been taken from her.

In moving to the new apartment, though, Maya had gotten what she wanted. Veer saw that his parents and Maya could not live under the same roof, even as he was haunted by something his father had said years before, just after his mother died of cancer. "We men must stay together," Veer's father had told his three sons. "But watch out, because there will be people who will try to break us up." And yet, in the first few months, in the time of settling and nesting, their new home felt as auspicious as if they had followed *vastu shastra* in its design. The two-bedroom, two-bath apartment was roomy and airy in a city without space. It came with an AC unit that was a decade or two old but made them feel removed from the city's blur of heat. They bought an LG TV and TV unit, tall Godrej dressers, and two low beds. They inherited deep leather couches and wooden tables from Veer's family home. And they made plans to buy a washing machine, and someday hire a maid, which would decrease Maya's daily workload. Water came on for just an hour in the morning and evening, but it was their water. Best of all, there were two tin-roof porches that overlooked the city and wavy hills beyond. The apartment signaled their arrival to Mumbai's middle class, which had been growing steadily, along with India's economy. Foreign investors were flocking in. *India is on fire, India is the next superpower, India will overtake China*—this was what all the papers were saying. Veer thought there was no better time to be a Marwari.

Maya decorated the apartment to make it feel like theirs. Over the dining room table she hung a painting of Krishna and Radha, showing the lovers seated side by side on a swing. Lord Krishna, blue-skinned and handsome, was painted in a turban and golden harem pants, while the milkmaid Radha wore a long braid and flowers in her hair. The swing itself was garlanded, and the lovers were positioned facing each other, their knees touching and foreheads close. Krishna gazed in rapture at Radha as she looked out into the distance. To Maya, it portrayed companionship and comfort—what she thought it must be like when you were with someone for a long time. When he moved, you moved with him.

On the living room shelf, Maya placed a framed photo from their honeymoon in Mussoorie. By the front door she hung a sign that read *"Sukhtara"* or "happy star"—a name for their new home.

Over time, Maya also placed teddy bears she'd kept from ex-boyfriends in different corners of the house. Button-nosed and glassy-eyed, the bears were reminders of bad endings and of men less perfect than Veer. Veer didn't buy Maya stuffed animals because he said he didn't see any life in them. Once, before Maya had learned this, she bought him a teddy bear that was pink and fluffy. Now it was kept in the apartment's second bedroom, which they hoped would someday be the bedroom of their first child.

They didn't have a timeline for when Maya might get pregnant, but they prepared for a baby anyway. Maya wanted a baby in part because of how often Veer was away. He worked harder than ever now at the family business, and they both agreed Maya would go to work only after they started a family. Veer wanted a baby because that's what came next. He had suffered from epilepsy since childhood and had some attacks as an adult, which worried him, so he thought it would be better to have a baby sooner than to wait. He also thought that having a baby would make Maya feel less alone.

In the second bedroom, they placed a tall dresser for clothes, a wooden cabinet that could be used for children's books or toys, and a low single bed with two mattresses for comfort. But they did not buy toys or blankets in pink or blue, because it was bad luck to prepare for a baby before the child was born. Even in big cities with good hospitals, many children did not survive.

A few months later, over Diwali, festival of lights, Maya found out she was pregnant after she missed her period. She was twenty-four now, which was considered old for a first pregnancy; the average age for first-time mothers in the country was nineteen. But women in cities were waiting longer to have children, and Maya was glad she did not live in a village. When she called Veer at work to tell him, she said she was worried because she'd recently taken antibiotics. "What if it harmed the baby?" she said.

"Calm down, Maya," he said. "We'll go to the doctor."

The doctors told Maya the pregnancy would be a difficult one. Not because of the antibiotics, but because Maya had ovarian cysts and other gynecological problems. They ordered her on strict bed rest until the baby was born: no going out, no exercise, and no strain. Maya was scared, but Veer kept saying there was nothing to worry about, that she was "perfect" and nothing would go wrong.

A month or so into pregnancy, Maya began to bleed. She and Veer had just gotten home from a wedding ceremony, and she called the doctor in a panic. "What color is the blood?" the doctor asked. "Bright red or dark red?" "Bright red," said Maya. "Nothing to worry about," the doctor told her. "Some people just bleed throughout their pregnancies."

The next day, she began to bleed again, and this time a local doctor gave her a painful injection, after which Veer brought her home to rest. "I'm going to the office," he said, turning his attention back to a problem at work. "You call me if you need anything."

Half an hour later, Maya began to hemorrhage again. Maya's doctor told her to go to a hospital downtown, at the very tip of the city, because all the beds in the nearby hospital were full. It was an hour-and-a-half drive south from their apartment in traffic. On the way Veer insisted they stop at his parents' house to pick up his stepmother, so another woman would be with them. Maya remembers his stepmother dawdling as she bled in the car.

In the days that followed, the doctors did sonogram after sonogram to try to identify the problem. On the third night, they told Maya they would do a CT scan in the morning and told her to go to sleep.

But Maya couldn't sleep, and when she got up to use the bathroom that night, she felt something drop out of her. It was small, fleshy, and reddish purple in color, a tangled mass that she caught in her hand. She tried not to think about what it was. She kept it, and later the doctor came and swiftly took the mass away.

In the morning, she prepared for her CT scan. Veer came in and held her hand. "Am I going to do the CT now?" she asked, looking up at him.

"No, we're going for a D and C. Not a CT," he said, his voice quiet.

A *D and C*. Maya knew what that meant. A dilation and curettage was a procedure that would dilate her cervix and scrape her uterus of tissue.

"You already miscarried, Mayu."

"I won't do the D and C," Maya said, and began to cry. "I'm not going to let go of whatever is left inside me."

"You have to. It'll be toxic."

To do the procedure, the doctors had to hold Maya down while she screamed and cried. After it was over, Veer told her there was nothing to worry about. "You're very young, we can try again," he said.

Veer was upset but told himself not to go overboard with his emotions. *Emotions don't help us much,* he thought. He remembered back to something he had once read, that if a child was not competent to survive in the world, it wouldn't join it. This was better than the child being born unable to cope. Veer held on to this thought as comfort.

♥♥♥♥♥

Outside the gates of Maya and Veer's apartment colony, past the security guard who often dozed, there was a long, potholed lane that led to the main road, filled with people on foot and bicycles, in rickshaws and cars. It was bordered by a dozen shops and *chawls.*

Maya frequented the shops for necessities. There was a ladies' tailor, a *chai-wallah,* milkman, eggman, and shoe cobbler who sold glittery Kolhapuri sandals. The corner stores stocked sugary biscuits, cheap water bottles, and plastic bags of salty *channa* to cater to the nearby *chawls.*

The *chawls* were several-story structures that charged little in rent, and the walls between neighbors were often thin and temporary. Inside, the kitchen sometimes served as the dining room or bedroom or all three, which led to ongoing mini-dramas. Out front, there were clothes on the line, children playing naked in the dirt, and men passed out from cheap liquor early in the day. The women who lived there came to Maya's apartment to ask for money, because she was kind, and their husbands had drunk it all away.

And there were dogs in the lane, dozens of them, which Veer had to navigate around carefully on his way home from work. Many had been struck by cars or rickshaws. They had been hit as puppies, before they knew better, or when they were older and didn't have time to run. Some had three legs, or walked with a limp, or dragged a lame limb behind.

Mostly, the dogs did not want for food. The people who lived in the *chawls* and the shopkeepers all threw their trash into the lane. When not foraging, the dogs spent their days playing atop parked cars, lazing in the street in the sun, or rolling in the dust to keep cool.

From the time they moved in, Maya was afraid of the bigger dogs, which she feared would attack her. She had seen wild dog attacks in Hyderabad as a child. But she liked the puppies, which kept being born in the squalid lane every season. She sometimes saw one learning to stand on uneven legs or yelping as it figured out how to play.

One day, Maya was walking to catch a rickshaw when she saw a dead puppy in the lane. It had been raining for weeks in Mumbai— cold, heavy rains—and its body was swollen and bloated from the wet. Maya wanted to bury the puppy, but she couldn't bring herself to touch it. She called several city offices and many animal NGOs, but no one called her back. Day after day, she passed the small, distended body, which the shoppers in the lane seemed not to notice.

Finally, she begged the manager of the housing society to get someone to bury it. He agreed and asked a trash collector to take it away. The next time Maya walked down the lane, the dead puppy was gone, and there was nothing in the space where it had been.

✾✾✾✾✾

Since losing the baby, it had been mostly peaceful between Maya and Veer. At night, they tried to eat dinner together or watch a movie or talk on the tin-roof porch before bed. But as Ganesh Chaturthi, the Hindu festival for the god Ganesh, approached, they found themselves fighting. They planned to bring home Ganesh in the form of a statue, hire a local priest, and invite their extended family over. After Maya had organized the party for weeks, however, Veer's father said he was taking over the arrangements. Veer told Maya it was easier to give in. She and his parents had developed an uneasy but polite rapport since they'd moved out, and he didn't want to jeopardize it. Maya disagreed, and spent the night on the couch to make her point. In the morning, her eyes had dark circles under them as if she'd slept in her *kajal*.

On the morning of the party, Veer checked his text messages, which were holiday-themed greetings (Wishing you happiness as big as Ganeshji's appetite, and life as long as his trunk!), while Maya went from room to room in agitation. She didn't have to worry about food, which her father-in-law had ordered, including Veer's favorite *chole bhature*. *Do you know how much indigestion that gives you?* she thought. But she had won control of the house, and wanted the day to be flawless. She purchased small idols of Ganesh to give as party favors to the guests. She painted the linoleum floor in henna with curlicue designs. And she hung garlands of fresh marigolds over the door. The statue of Lord Ganesh, with his long trunk and healthy stomach, presided over the dining room from inside a golden throne.

Maya loved the story of Ganesh's origins: how his mother, the goddess Parvati, asked him to stand guard while she took a shower, but then Parvati's consort Shiva, god of destruction, came for a visit and chopped off Ganesh's head. To remedy his mistake, Shiva replaced Ganesh's head with the head of an elephant. She and Veer also loved what Ganesh stood for: remover of obstacles, god of new ventures and beginnings. And they thought of Ganesh not so much as a god but as a famous, real-life man who later inspired many myths— *Beautiful stories to keep man close to religion,* Veer thought. Hinduism, after all, was not really a religion but a way of life, driven by the idea of *dharma*. Of one's duty to the universe. Duty to yourself, your ancestors, and your children. Duty to your fellow human beings and animals. And duty to society, to living a life of morals and faith. Fulfilling your *dharma* was more important than the worship of any god. Still, sometimes Maya and Veer asked Ganesh for help, just in case.

As the guests arrived, Maya greeted them warmly. She glided around the room in her bejeweled *sari*, gold jewelry, and thickest *kajal*, making sure everyone felt at home. She made small talk and laughed gaily at the festival jokes. She poured tea for the men, who gathered in the living room to talk business. A few of them snuck outside to smoke a cigarette, where they made lewd comments about Maya's good looks. She shepherded the children into the second bedroom, where she gave them sweets to eat. Maya avoided only the female guests, who gathered in her bedroom to gossip about her, inspecting her belongings and looking for dust or dirt.

Late in the afternoon came the *pooja*, and all the guests gathered to watch Maya and Veer recite a prayer before the local priest. The priest, who was dressed in a *dhoti* and kept a long *sikha*—the rest of his hair shorn close—had a pinkie finger that dangled as he spoke. People whispered that it made him more holy. As the priest led the prayer, Maya and Veer offered Ganesh *laddoos*, incense, and coconuts to appease him, and Maya looked at Veer with lowered eyes. Whenever she caught sight of the pinkie, she tried not to laugh.

Later, after the last guests had left clutching their small Ganesh idols, Maya sat down in her bedroom and sighed, and Veer went out on the porch to smoke.

Changing into a T-shirt and jeans, Maya began to take down the decorations. She used nail polish remover to remove the henna from the floor, though most of it wouldn't come off. She threw the remaining *chole bhature* in the trash.

But Ganesh would stay on his throne for another ten days. After that, Maya and Veer would join the many in the city who took their idols to the water to immerse them.

Every year, thousands in Mumbai flocked to the Arabian Sea for the Ganesh immersions. The lines to see the largest Ganesh idols sometimes stretched kilometers long. Idols sat on floats, trucks, and thrones made with wheels. Some idols stood fifty feet tall, towering over the crowds. Others were as small as a child's hand. In each iteration, Lord Ganesh looked regal and strong, with the ample stomach of a well-fed man and the crowned head of a mighty elephant. In five of his six hands he held a trident, ax, conch shell, *laddoo*, and lotus blossom; his sixth hand was upraised in beneficence. Garlands hung around his neck, and his trunk was covered in jewels. As people walked the Ganesh, or Ganpati, idols to the water, they sang loudly, voices straining, *"Ganpati bappa morya!"* along to the steady beat of drums. When they reached the sea, men waded, shirtless, into the murky, waste-filled water, carrying the life-size statues above their heads. Women trailed behind them, letting their *saris* get wet, and the children ran into the water splashing. As Ganesh crashed into the ocean, the crowd let out a guttural yell.

The Arabian Sea was full of Ganesh idols from years past. For days after the festival, the statues would bob above the surface, until at last they sank into the muck. Over weeks, months, even years, the idols disintegrated slowly in the water.

Before Maya and Veer immersed him, they both privately asked Ganesh, remover of obstacles, for the same thing. They asked him for another child.

❧❧❧❧❧

In the weeks after Ganesh Chaturthi, Veer got up early, as always, to read the papers, and Maya to make him tea. If she was slow to get up, he would call out to her in a singsong voice, both inhabiting and lampooning the role of a traditional Indian husband, until he heard the crackle of the gas stove turning on. Veer always read the *Times of India* first, which contained exciting headlines about local rapes (the numbers increasing yearly, though perhaps more women were reporting), the latest controversy with Pakistan (over land, over water, and over cricket), and India's exponential growth (inching up on China, soon to surpass it, or so the papers said). He ended on page 3, which covered Bollywood celebrities and glitterati, who lived a world apart from middle-class families like theirs and from the poor. Unlike them, Bollywood celebrities could do what they wanted: actresses could wear skimpy skirts and have affairs, and a famous actor got away with a drunk driving hit-and-run. Veer liked to stay informed about both politics and entertainment, which he thought helped a man get ahead.

After the holiday, he also reread Osho, the spiritual teacher and mystic whose controversial writings he had always appreciated. Though deceased, Osho had followers all over the world, people who liked that he challenged politicians and organized religion, that he embraced free sex and living and thinking, and that his beliefs had evolved over time. Veer loved Osho's writings on how to live.

Osho argued that the route to happiness was to worry about oneself, which aligned with Veer's sense of the world. Osho also said people felt good or bad based on their unconscious. He said no one was responsible for anger or joy but you. And he said that if you did not realize this, you would live your life like a slave.

Veer also liked that Osho had been a wealthy man. Osho collected a hundred Rolls-Royces in his lifetime and never apologized for owning them. He was rumored to never wear the same clothes twice. *Every man deserves to find wealth,* Veer thought. *And every man deserves to be at peace.*

Veer saw himself as a bit of a philosopher, though nowhere near Osho's level of understanding. He liked to wax poetic while having a cigarette on their tin-roof porch, where Maya often joined him. It was a nightly tradition he called *"dam,"* which was Urdu for "life breath" or "moment." He smoked fake Marlboros imported from

Pakistan, which were said to be mixed with cow dung. He joked that it made the cigarettes more holy.

On the porch, smoking, the city at his feet, Veer came up with new names for Mumbai. To him, the *City of Dreams* moniker wasn't quite right. Mumbai was more like a slap or a punch in the gut. It overwhelmed people, shoved them down—or at least knocked them off their balance. Dreams were squashed in the city, rebuilt, and squashed again. Mumbai was the *Maximum City*, like one author had written, but Veer also found the name too positive. "The city of everything," he said. *Yes, that was better,* and Maya agreed. A great maw of a place that could swallow you up but that could also make you into a star. A city in the aggregate: of both good and bad and everything in between. Satisfied, he tossed his cigarette butt off the porch and went inside, the ash scattering in the night breeze.

Veer also liked to find metaphors to describe their relationship. When he and Maya reminisced about their early days, when they had constantly messaged between Hyderabad and Mumbai, running up phone bills they couldn't afford, he said: "That was when things were *biryani*."

Like *biryani* rice. Wild, with a lot of spices. A dish you only have once in a while. Maya nodded, and joked back, "And now, now it is all white rice."

"It's still *biryani*," he countered. "But only sometimes."

"And who wants to eat *biryani* every day? No one," she said.

As Veer's family business grew, and he began to travel more, he tried out his philosophizing in other countries. He bragged to Maya that in Africa he kept a client up talking until six in the morning, a client who told Veer he was like a "great prophet."

In China, Veer said, he persuaded a woman selling handbags on the black market to sell him an imitation Louis Vuitton for one-hundredth of her quoted price. He told Maya he convinced her using a philosophical explanation of the market.

Maya found these stories amusing, as well as the way her husband carried himself in their apartment building. Instead of saying *"na-maste,"* he greeted neighbors in the lobby with *"Allah Hafiz,"* which made people think that he was Muslim.

"What are you even saying?" Maya, laughing, would ask Veer after the elevator doors closed, leaving a perplexed neighbor behind. Veer would only grin at this.

Sometimes, while Veer was at work, Maya took little trips into the city by train, so that she wouldn't get bored at home. When she did, she tried to arrive early to the station so that she could board the women's compartment, where men could not go. If she arrived late, she'd have to get on the general train car, which wasn't considered safe for women. It was said that a disabled girl had recently been gang-raped on a Mumbai train, while the other men in the car sat doing nothing.

That kind of assault might be rare in the city, but Maya knew harassment was not. Some men grabbed between a woman's legs on a crowded train car so that it wasn't clear to whom the hands belonged. Others groped or grazed a woman's chest and then disappeared into the crowd. And still other men—many of them—liked to make a *"chh chh"* sound of appraisal at a woman's backside and, when the woman turned around, greet her with a leering face.

All of it was lumped together as "Eve teasing," a term many women in the city didn't like. Its very name suggested that women were temptresses and that the harassment was the woman's fault. The right-wing politicians said women wouldn't have a problem if they didn't go out on their own. But Maya knew she'd go mad if she didn't.

ʊʊʊʊʊ

For years, Veer had worked in the family aluminum foil business with his father and brothers. But now he also became business partners with his cousin, a hard-drinking, hardworking mountain of a man with a proclivity for wild business schemes. He was the kind of new Mumbai man who believed *karma* was dead and that you made your own destiny.

Together, they decided to open a pharmaceutical business in Africa, which had lost trust in Chinese drugs because they were so often fake. Africa wanted better-regulated pills now. They thought they could easily sell antimalarials, blood tonics, and anti-acidity drugs to African buyers, which the family business could help package.

His cousin's other business was sex toys, which Veer was not actively involved in, though it operated out of the same office. Within India, his cousin sold toys with the label *massager* to avoid attracting government notice. The sale of sex toys was suspect, if not illegal; the Indian Penal Code barred the sale of any object that was "lascivious" or that "appeals to the prurient interest." Dildos, lotions, and gels were sold in open-air markets and online anyway. The most popular product Veer's cousin sold was a gel that delayed ejaculation. This was not surprising to them, because it was found that half of all men in the country struggled with premature ejaculation due to anxiety or inexperience. Veer's cousin saw the demand and produced more.

Since the launch of the new businesses, Veer was home less and less. He worked six days a week, and then he began working seven. When Maya called him now, she often got no answer. He spent long hours at his family office, a cramped two-room space that he, his father, and two brothers rented inside a residential building not far from home. The office was nothing extravagant: two dusty rooms, a few desktop computers, and documents stacked to the ceiling. When the business had crashed years ago, they'd learned the importance of being frugal. In the corner of the office was the only decoration: a sepia-toned photo of Veer's mother, taken when she was very young.

Veer was also often out of the city, on visits to his aluminum foil factories, which were scattered across rural Maharashtra. He most regularly visited a factory several hours north of Mumbai that smelled like *daaru*, or bad moonshine, combined with gum and wet tar. It had big boilers that stank as they burned. The malarial mosquitoes that swarmed outside were as big as a child's hand. But the tribal men who worked there were used to them and did not mind.

Outside the factory, warthogs ran through the grass. Flamboyant pink and blue butterflies gathered and fluorescent bugs glittered in the night. Veer didn't notice any of this. When he was at the factory, he worked nonstop. Sometimes, he stayed for ten days straight, sleeping on the dirt-stained floor. During his long absences, Maya grew anxious and upset.

And over time, as the pharmaceutical business grew, Veer also spent more time at his cousin's office, which seemed to smell of new money with its recessed lighting and blasting AC. Their business in Africa was already booming thanks to the antimalarials, which were intended to cure, not prevent (three doses of shots plus a pill). Antimalarials were desperately needed in African countries where nearly the entire population was at risk. Soon, Veer and his cousin began traveling to the continent for weeks at a time. On these trips they met local businessmen in hotel bars and drank too much as they closed deal after deal. The trips invigorated Veer and made him want to work harder.

If Veer ever felt lazy, he thought of his grandfather. For the last seven months of his grandfather's life, when he had been very sick, Veer was his primary caretaker. In long afternoons at the hospital, his grandfather had sung Hindi ballads to Veer, which he never did with anyone else. Veer had sung him back the old songs he knew.

In the last weeks of his life, Veer's grandfather also stressed to Veer the importance of hard work. Historically, the business of their family's subcaste was moneylending to kings, but his grandfather had diversified into pharmaceuticals and become rich. It allowed him to pay for the weddings of all five sons, plus nearly a dozen other people. Veer felt ashamed that few remembered his generosity now. *This much is true, if you do something good, no one will remember,* he thought.

After his grandfather died, Veer vowed to honor him by making just as much money and giving as much away. To do this, he knew he would have to work night and day.

But Veer often promised Maya he'd be home in time for dinner. For hours, she'd cook his favorite dishes and then sit alone at the kitchen table, watching them grow cold. She'd call him a dozen times to ask where he was and, caught up in something at work, Veer wouldn't answer the phone. When, exhausted and stressed, he finally arrived, he would eat the cold meal and pass out within minutes, not even asking about her day.

And though Veer watched his cousin sell sex toys with beguiling names, he also told Maya he was no longer much interested in sex. Maya would joke, a little bitterly, that it was illegal in India not to have sex with your spouse; the Hindu Marriage Act of 1955 mentioned the "conjugal rights" of a spouse several times. She wondered what happened to the man with whom she had steamy phone sex from Hyderabad to Mumbai.

In the mornings, Maya began to make Veer's tea and put out his work clothes in silence. As she handed him his *tiffin* for lunch, he would nod at her, talking into multiple cell phones at once, like many businessmen in the city did. He talked in loud, exaggerated tones of Hinglish. And then, *tiffin* in hand, he'd walk out the door.

At home alone all day, Maya read books she'd bought by authors she liked, including V. S. Naipaul and Chimamanda Adichie. On her laptop, she listened to *ghazals*, Indian classical music and old Hindi film songs. She read the newspaper and cleaned the house. After she exhausted all these activities, she cooked dinner and tried to show her love for Veer in other ways, some of them traditional. On Karwa

Chauth, the holiday on the fourth day after the full moon, when a wife was supposed to fast for her husband to live a long life, Maya fasted from sunrise to moonrise. She wasn't very religious or superstitious, but she liked the idea of practicing sacrifice. During her period, she followed the old rules that said she was unclean, because she knew the women in Veer's family followed them. She also slept in a different bed, did not cook or enter the kitchen, and did not touch Veer at all.

But Maya's attempts were lost on him. He barely noticed her efforts, or commented on them. There wasn't time to devote to both a wife and work. He chose work over Maya every time.

It was after nearly three years of marriage that Maya remembered what her father had warned her about marrying another Marwari. Marwaris were money-driven. Marwaris cared about nothing but their work. A joke: *What happens if you give a Marwari a corner in soccer? Oh, he'll set up a shop in it.* Especially a Marwari in Mumbai, where shops were sometimes constructed wholesale overnight. She and her father had slowly repaired their relationship, and they talked more often now, but she didn't want to admit that he'd been right. She didn't want to tell him that Veer was as absent a husband as he'd predicted or that she had begun to question her marriage.

It was true that Veer cared mostly about money and work, but he always said it was for a larger purpose. He insisted that making money was their best chance for a life of *azadi*, or freedom. Making money meant that he could relax one day not far off. He imagined retiring at fifty-five and moving to a seaside town, where he would live in a small shack. He would sell beer, whiskey, and coconut water on the first floor to keep busy and live on the floor above. And he'd take royalties from his pharmaceutical sales in Africa to supplement retirement.

Veer's businesses, though booming, had not yet turned much of a profit. He assured Maya that soon his businesses would become more lucrative, and then he'd spend more time at home. Maya did not believe him.

One night that winter, to test him, she walked out of their house, as she had once left his parents' home, and Veer had to drive around the city to find her. When he picked her up in the central suburb of Bandra, he pretended as if nothing had happened.

"Thoda compromise karo," Maya's mother had told her just after their move. *Make a little compromise. Be patient.* This was necessary in a marriage, she said. Maya did not believe her either.

Soon after Maya walked out, a honeybee hive formed on their tin-roof porch. Veer told Maya it was a sign of good luck. He said bees foretold one of two events: a visitor or a big windfall of money. He insisted not a single bee be harmed.

Left unchecked, the bees formed a giant, amorphous nest, from which a dull hum could be heard through the window. Dozens of bees circled the nest. Some died and fell in clumps on the porch. Others clung tight to the hive. While Veer waited for a big windfall of money, Maya desperately hoped for a visitor. She thought a visitor—in the form of a baby—might help solve the problems between them. A baby would mean she was no longer alone.

PRODUCE A CHILD,
AND GOD SMILES

Shahzad and Sabeena, 1983 to 1998

Shahzad and Sabeena met in a drafty room on a bitter-cold day in December. It was a good year for India, the year the country won the Cricket World Cup. It was the year the so-called bandit queen, a Robin Hood–like figure, surrendered on her terms from a life of crime, laying down her rifle before a portrait of the goddess Durga. It was just after the Golden Age of Indian cinema had ended, and Bollywood had become fixated on new stories, big money, and assured commercial success. *Coolie*, starring the dark and brooding Amitabh Bachchan, was the year's runaway hit. When Bachchan punctured his intestines filming a fight scene, the entire country prayed for his recovery. The high drama and romance of the silver screen regularly spilled into daily life.

By the time Shahzad and Sabeena met, Bachchan had recovered. Sabeena wore a deep purple dress, the color of a blooming iris flower, and a cloud-colored *dupatta* wrapped around her face. When Shahzad looked at her, she did not look back; shyness was expected from a prospective bride. Several women pulled down Sabeena's scarf, so that he could see her better. He could tell how beautiful she was—like a movie star—just as his family had told him. Both families stood, watching and waiting for his answer. Still, he worried and wondered what to do. He did not feel ready to get married, though everything in his life, and in Sabeena's, had led up to this moment.

Shahzad had been born the year *Mughal-e-Azam* came out, a film so popular it ran in theaters for seventy-five weeks—what everyone called a "diamond jubilee"—and then it ran for seventy-five weeks more. His father named him after the main character, who was a *shahzad*, or prince, and whom Shahzad would not grow up to resemble. Instead, he was born a frail baby and grew into a scrawny boy with a nervous demeanor, bright eyes, big teeth, and a prominent nose; the wrong features stood out from his face.

In the film, the prince falls in love with a magnetic court dancer against the wishes of his father, an all-powerful Muslim Mughal king. Their forbidden love affair sets off an epic battle between father and son. As Shahzad got older, people would joke: "Is your life story the same as the movie?" Shahzad always answered them seriously. "Yes, my father and I are divided," he'd say. "But not like this."

They were not divided over a woman, and they were not royalty. They certainly were not Mughals, the Muslim emperors who'd once ruled India, before the British routed them and the Hindu kings. Today, Muslims like them were in the minority, just 12 percent or so of the country, and they held little power. Shahzad and his father's war was not an epic one, complete with thousands of troops, horses, and camels. Still, Shahzad felt that his father had waged some kind of battle against him since birth, one he did not quite understand.

During childhood, Shahzad often fell sick. When his mother asked his father for money for a doctor, his father would shout, eyes flaring, until she did not ask him anymore. Instead, Shahzad's mother found resourceful ways to care for her young son. When Shahzad was four and came down with a heavy fever, his mother took him, crying, to the *dargah* across the street, placed him on the cool white marble, and demanded of the saint buried there: "You are going to cure him. You pray to Allah that he's cured very soon." Before long, Shahzad stopped crying and his fever subsided.

But Shahzad did not remember much of that. The first time he remembered realizing that his father did not care for him was when he contracted mumps at age sixteen. First his throat began to hurt. Then, his Adam's apple, bulging, seemed to grow larger and larger. Next his testes, still an unknown body part, also swelled. The viral infection grew more serious, and it had everyone concerned except Shahzad's father.

It was Shahzad's uncle who ultimately took Shahzad to the doctor. People whispered that Shahzad must have caught mumps somewhere, but the real reason he contracted the infection was because he wasn't being looked after properly. Even the neighbors knew Shahzad's father, with his hard face, unkempt hair, and sad, distant eyes, was friendly enough outside the house but cruel to his family. They knew he was especially punishing to Shahzad, who was born frail and weak, the opposite of his namesake warrior prince.

The apartment Shahzad grew up in—and lived in still—was dingy and overcrowded. But the building was sturdy and British-built, with giant archways filled with flowering plants. Their downtown neighborhood was also populated mostly by other Muslims, which Shahzad's family preferred, and was not far from Victoria Terminus, the old, cathedral-like train station named after an old British queen. Most important, they were just a cricket pitch's distance from Crawford Market, where Shahzad's mother could buy anything she needed to make their meals that day. If only she could get the money. Shahzad's father would always shout before handing a few rupees over.

Crawford Market, one of the most famous bazaars in the city, and Shahzad's favorite place, was a holdover from colonial times. It was housed inside a grand Norman and Flemish-style structure, with pointy roofs, vaulted entryways, and a big clock tower. Since the British had left, its skylights had grown dusty, and many of its windows had popped out of their frames. But inside the wonders of the sprawling wholesale fruit and vegetable market remained unchanged. The moment Shahzad's mother entered the market, she was barraged by vendors loudly hawking their fruits and vegetables, as well as poultry, mutton, beef, candy, and cakes. Though this was before the economic liberalization of the early 1990s—when the Indian government opened up the country to foreign goods and markets—even then Crawford Market had green peas, leafy spinach, ridged okra, and Alphonsos, the juiciest type of mango.

In the back alleys of the market, there were illicit wares for sale, including exotic songbirds, trafficked illegally from across the continent. It was said that the birds traveled hundreds of miles stuffed inside water bottles, their beautiful feathers crushed, with tiny holes poked through for air. After their long journey, they were released, wings spreading, into a wire-frame cage. Shahzad was a sensitive boy and hated knowing that was how they came to the market. But he loved walking past the birds on his way home from school, and would often stop to listen to their calls. He also loved to watch the monkeys that hung off the arriving mango trucks.

It wasn't that Shahzad's father didn't have the money to give his wife for Crawford Market. He came from great wealth; he simply didn't want to share it. At least not with his family, who lived as though they were barely middle class, though he would give a few rupees to any beggar, street boy, or madman he saw on the road. His wealth was the reason Shahzad's mother had married him. She was a poor girl from a village who had won this moneyed man with her beauty.

But it was not long into marriage before Shahzad's mother understood her mistake. She understood when her husband began getting nosebleeds and then fell over, shaking, and went unconscious. They would wake him by putting leather near his face—an old belief held that "shoe smell" revived epileptics. It was then that Shahzad's mother began to see her husband for what he was: brain-damaged.

Later, when Shahzad's father became obsessed with foreign cars (buying a boxy Hillman and Austin and a sleek Opel) and started talking to them, when he took to wearing *pyjama* pants with a winter coat to go to work, and when he viciously mocked his youngest son, Shahzad—in these moments she knew there was something very wrong with her husband. Maybe his unkindness was not born out of cruelty but of a failure of the synapses in his brain to fire as they should.

Life improved for the family when Shahzad's father was asked to run part of Byculla Market. His domain, a three-thousand-square-foot plot of land, was crowded with vendors, and his job was to collect rent and keep it clean. Every day, he collected a single rupee from every cross-legged fisherwoman, blood-spattered butcher, *tomato-wallah*, and hawker of chiles and *channa*. Next, he swept the entire area, a Sisyphean but necessary task—the rough dirt of the market mixing with rotten food, fish bones, urine, and spit. He also cleaned up after the market's many animals: fat cats on the hunt for unattended fish, goats grazing freely before slaughter, rats nosing for scraps, a chicken running headless through the passageways. Byculla Market wasn't as big as Crawford Market, but still it was daunting to clean, and sometimes just as noisy. The market was loudest when the butchers brought in the chickens for slaughter, holding them five at a time, heads toward the earth. The birds would squawk, bodies writhing, as they were carried to their death. Blood would run through the dirt, crows would circle, and Shahzad's father would furiously sweep.

"*Chee,*" Shahzad's mother would say when his father came home just before midnight. "So much smell is there. And dirt. Keep your clothes outside."

"Nobody is there to do this but me," Shahzad's father would

tell her mournfully, because at night he did not have the energy to shout. "I am alone."

Most nights, he did not even speak to his wife and children. He just disappeared to talk to his cars.

Shahzad didn't enjoy being at home as a child, nor did his brother or sister. He didn't enjoy school much either, where he was often singled out as the only Muslim in class. The other students would beat him, taunting him in the singsong way of bratty schoolchildren: "You're a Muslim, you're a Pakistani." Shahzad could have been Pakistani, if his family had chosen to immigrate to Pakistan after Partition. When the British, bowing to demands for freedom, had hastily divided India into two countries in 1947, they had created in Pakistan a new Muslim nation-state. They had also, in abruptly withdrawing from India after two hundred years of rule, left terrifying sectarian violence in their wake. Even now, schoolchildren learned that Partition had been a kind of apocalypse. Babies were carved out of bellies. Neighbors stabbed one another in the night. Hundreds of thousands died, and countless women were raped. Millions of uprooted people also fled the rioting: Muslims moving one way to start new lives in Pakistan, while Hindus walked another—the biggest mass migration in history. The violence made it seem impossible that any Muslims would choose to stay. But Shahzad's family had stayed, because his grandfather had businesses and property in Mumbai, which was then called Bombay. And so, instead of dealing with the problems facing the brand-new nation of Pakistan, Shahzad and his family had to face living as Muslims in Hindu-majority India. After Shahzad complained to the teacher, the beatings had stopped, but he did not make many friends.

Instead, as he grew up, he spent time with his birds, pigeons he bought from Crawford Market. He kept the birds on his verandah and grew to love them as if they were family. He tossed them so much seed that they soon became fat, until he got in trouble for making the verandah dirty, and wasn't allowed to keep pigeons anymore.

Shahzad made one friend in those years: an Arab girl, the youngest of four sisters, who had the sweetest face he'd ever seen. After school and his tuitions in the Quran, they would play *carrom* together, using their strikers to push their *carrom* men toward the pockets, and giggling whenever one of them succeeded.

But over time the games grew less frequent and the Arab girl became distant. Shahzad realized she had fallen for his bigger, stronger cousin instead. She had a direct view of his cousin's room from her apartment, across a courtyard, and Shahzad was certain this was how they fell in love. He had seen it happen in the movies. He thought he'd like to court a woman this way someday. But he also worried that girls might always prefer bigger, stronger men than him—a boy given the name of a prince but who had grown up to be gangly and uncertain.

❦❦❦❦❦

Not far away, in Bhendi Bazaar, Sabeena, the second child of four sisters, and the liveliest and most beautiful among them, was given a nickname. Her father christened her Madhubala, after the actress who played the court dancer in *Mughal-e-Azam*—the woman whose dancing sent father and son to war. Like Madhubala, Sabeena had apple cheeks, strong, straight nose, and Cupid's bow lips. She had the same eyes that danced below dramatic brows. She even had the same raspy voice and effervescent personality, in a house that desperately needed it. Sabeena lived with her grandfather, who was a tyrant, her mother and other sisters, whom she found dull, her brother, who had anger issues, and her father, whom she loved but who was strict with her. Outside of the movies, the actress Madhubala was barely seen out on the town. She never went to the big Bollywood parties or award shows, because her father did not allow it. It was the same for Sabeena, whose father rarely let her and her sisters out of their small apartment.

But Sabeena knew her father loved her and wanted to protect her. She knew that many Muslim girls were kept inside. He told her as much, warning that if fathers gave their daughters freedom, they could take a wrong step. And if they didn't take a wrong step, a boy would for them. Sabeena mostly didn't mind. She and her father would make *masti* at home, telling their own private jokes that the rest of the family members—who Sabeena and her father agreed were all "half-nut" or brainless as cows—would never get.

Still, sometimes Sabeena longed to go outside. Her grandfather, who could not walk, would go to the bathroom in his bed without warning and shout: "You all are not looking after me." She did not find much joy in talking to her mother or sisters either. And her father was often away at work, especially in the evenings. Without him their cramped apartment seemed a sad and shabby place.

But through the windows of the apartment, which was in the heart of Bhendi Bazaar downtown, Sabeena could see all the activity and life of the outdoors. She could see the rows of shops selling gold jewelry, dusty old antiques, and colorful rows of cotton *kurtas* and fancier *salwar kameez*. Bhendi Bazaar sprawled over sixteen acres and was populated mostly by other Muslims. She could hear the call to prayer from the local *masjid*, the honk of cars, buses, and scooters, and the persistent call of the *chai-wallah*. It was only after she began going to school that she understood that more worlds existed beyond the bazaar. In geography class she learned about far-away countries, including Sudan, which she dreamed of visiting to see how African Muslims lived. When her father also began taking his daughters to the movies once a year, Sabeena began dreaming of Kashmir. Kashmir, though marred by violence since Partition, remained a majestic region of craggy mountain ranges and tranquil lakes. It appeared in almost every Bollywood film. When Sabeena asked her father about Kashmir, he told her, "Madhubala, anywhere you want to go, you can go in a marriage."

All through her primary and secondary education, before she reached a marriageable age, Sabeena went directly home after school. She obediently completed her homework and Quran tuitions, wore her head covering, and did her five-times-a-day *namaaz*. And she spoke to few people outside of family. Her father, who was a doctor of skin diseases, often entertained his daughter by sharing his medical knowledge, telling her about the body and heart and brain. He was an intelligent man with bright eyes and big, owlish glasses, and he spoke with the confidence of a professor. Sabeena did not know then that he was a sexologist, or that when he came home late it was because he worked in the nearby red-light area, which was called Kamathipura. In Kamathipura, he gave injections and tablets to protect the men who had sex with prostitutes from getting *gupt rog*, which meant the "secret illness"—STDs. Sabeena's father could not tell these things to a young girl.

About sex, he told his daughter that childbirth was painful. He warned her that when a woman got married, she freed herself of her family, but when she had a child, she became like a slave again. "Because through you he has had a child," he said. He had seen this happen with couples in his practice. Sabeena knew her father wanted to prepare her for marriage, but she could not help feeling anxious. She knew she'd be married off eventually, matched with someone from her community. She found most of her immediate community *bakwaas*, rubbish: full of Muslim butchers who spent the whole day in the shop, leaving work with blood on their hands, and fighting with their wives in the night. But she told herself that her father would find her a better man.

Sabeena's beauty was known throughout Bhendi Bazaar, and in the surrounding Sunni Muslim communities, and so she received dozens of marriage proposals. The first came when she was just ten,

from a man in Pune, and later from all over Mumbai, for the girl
who looked like the actress Madhubala. Child marriage had been
outlawed in the country some forty years ago, but Islamic personal
law—which had its basis in the Quran, decisions of the Prophet, and
prior legal precedent—sometimes allowed for child marriage with
the consent of a parent. Still, Sabeena's father would wait until she
was older. Whenever he told her about a proposal, Sabeena would
laugh her long, throaty laugh, and her eyes would crinkle at the
edges. With marriage a prospect for the faraway future, the proposals
only delighted her.

But when at age twenty her father sat her down in their apartment to show her a photo of Shahzad, she knew this time it was different. Though she had not been sent to college, her education was
now considered complete. This boy, Shahzad, was a Sunni Muslim
like they were, and from another Muslim market area downtown,
just a kilometer or so south. His family also went to *dargahs* and followed the same practices in prayers and fasting. They took seriously
the edicts issued from Saudi Arabia but weren't hard-liners either.
And, like her family, his family followed the Hanafi school of law,
meaning, among other things, they read the *hadith* to know how to
live a good life. Though Sunnis and Shias mostly lived in harmony
in the city, the same branch of Islam was preferred in marriage.

But there was one major difference: Shahzad came from a wealthy
family. Sabeena looked at the photo again. She noticed Shahzad's fat
mustache, which he had worked hard to grow, but otherwise found
little to remark on. Not that it mattered. Her father had trained her
to like what she saw. After she looked at the photo and realized this
man could become her husband, she began to cry. She wasn't ready
to leave her father or childhood home behind.

After this Sabeena's father went to visit Shahzad at his shop, which
was a cold storage business for chicken. Shahzad had set up the shop
inside Byculla Market while still in college. He had not wanted to

be in such close proximity to his father, who passed through his shop three or four times an hour, asking anxiously, "How are things going on?" But the market was close to a church and a mosque, and with both Catholic and Muslim customers, who shared some of the same meat-eating habits, Shahzad's business soon began thriving.

Sabeena's father asked Shahzad what he had studied at university (*English-language school, BComm*), and ensured Shahzad wasn't a butcher or involved in the mutton business (*No, no*). Did he chew *paan* and roam around? (*Nothing like that.*) What marks, then, did Shahzad get in his secondary education? (*Good enough.*) Sabeena's father nodded. All satisfactory answers. Most important, he was the son of a landlord of Byculla Market.

ᔆᔆᔆᔆᔆ

Weeks later, Shahzad stood in Sabeena's lane beside his mother, sister, and, begrudgingly, his father, to meet the girl his mother had chosen. His mother had first noticed Sabeena's movie-star looks at a wedding, learned she was the daughter of a doctor, and set up a meeting.

Shahzad saw Bhendi Bazaar with different eyes than Sabeena. To him, it seemed filled with cheap jewelry sellers, broken antiques, and cut-rate women's clothing shops. His shoes were getting dirty. The walls of her building were stained with *paan*. Inside, laundry was hung at random. *These people are not poor, but they do not have much money either,* thought Shahzad. To him, it did not seem a suitable place to meet a bride.

When they reached Sabeena's apartment, Shahzad was ushered into a small side room, so he would not see the rest of the flat. A window was open, and Shahzad felt cold. *Why would they leave the window open in December?* he thought, and wished he were at home. For more than an hour, Sabeena's father peppered Shahzad with many of the same questions he had already asked at the shop. "What are you doing now?" "Where have you studied?" "Which college did you go to?" "How is cold storage?" As he spoke, Shahzad felt the room grow colder. He tried not to shiver.

And then the door opened and Sabeena walked in, eyes cast down, in a deep purple dress, and on her head a cloud-colored *dupatta*. She was accompanied by several women from her family. She did not look at Shahzad, but he could see her well enough. He observed with pleasure her resemblance to Madhubala: her look-at-me nose, inviting mouth, and round cheeks. The women accompanying Sabeena pulled back her head covering. Still, she did not look up. *I have no choice,* Sabeena thought to herself, *so why should I look?* But Shahzad saw what he thought was the trace of a smile. *So she's got energy,* he thought. *He is from a rich family,* Sabeena told herself, as she tried to hide her expression. *So even if I have to leave my family, my future is secure.* If she kept thinking this, maybe she would not cry.

Shahzad wanted to say yes. He thought of the Arab girl who had chosen a stronger man over him. He thought of the boys who teased him at school, holding him down until he couldn't breathe. And he thought of his father, who made him think he didn't know anything, and that he'd never find a woman. Now, he faced a lovely woman who was willing to be his. He knew he should give her an answer. But he needed time to think.

At home, Shahzad's mother and sister worked on Shahzad. "What are you thinking?" they asked. "Tell us."

"Stop," Shahzad said. "I'll let you know."

But they wouldn't let up. "Other girls are not so educated." "Look at how badly other girls live." "Other girls have a habit of eating tobacco to enjoy." "She is looking better than them." "Her father is an important doctor." "She is the best you'll find."

Two days later, Sabeena's family called for an answer.

"Yes," he said. "Okay."

"Pakaa?" Sabeena's father asked him. "You're sure?"

Shahzad nodded into the phone. He was twenty-three, and Sabeena just a little younger, twenty-one. When his mother put sweets in his mouth to celebrate, he dutifully swallowed them all.

There were also sweets at the engagement ceremony, along with gold bangles, dresses, and *saris* for Sabeena, and dress slacks, shirts, and wristwatches for Shahzad. After gifts, the couple exchanged rings. Throughout the ceremony, they did not speak to or look at each other. Sabeena wore a shy, almost sad expression. *Shyness is the ornament of a girl,* a common expression went. A garland was placed around Shahzad's neck, and rose petals were scattered over Sabeena's hair. *Sharbat,* a cold drink made with flower petals and fruits, was served. People neither Shahzad nor Sabeena knew signed the engagement book, wishing them health and happiness. To Sabeena, the day felt like a dream.

It was very cool in the city. Later that year, the prime minister, Indira Gandhi, would be assassinated by her own bodyguards. She flexed her power in too many ways: cracking down on civil liberties, imprisoning opponents, even allowing her son to carry out a program of forced sterilizations to help control overpopulation. And so people would say that she had gotten her due.

After her assassination, there would be riots and mass killings up north. But that was months off, and the unrest would take place primarily in a state far away, against a community not their own. The political machinations of the country were of little importance compared to finding the right match for a son or daughter. Or so many parents in the country believed. In this engagement hall, with the right boy and girl brought together, all was right with the world.

All is right, Shahzad thought, as the ceremony wound down. *I made the right choice.* He was sure everyone in his community would tell him, "Oh, how beautiful your wife is." He looked over at her now, sitting shyly in an ornate wooden chair, and felt happy. She wore a thickly embroidered pink and white *sari* and garlands of pink roses and white carnations around her neck. She was weighed down by gold: an ornate *jhumar* ornament on her forehead, a heavy necklace and earrings, and a thick stud in her nose. Her hands were darkly hennaed.

During the ceremony Sabeena, who had stolen a glance at her husband, decided she had also made the right choice. To her, he resembled Amitabh Bachchan, the handsome, brooding actor from *Coolie*. He looked like a man with a lot of emotion locked inside him, a man with whom Sabeena would not be bored.

But after the ceremony Sabeena's best friend pulled her aside. "I saw Shahzad's mother scolding someone," she whispered. "She was hyper and shouting. Your mother-in-law is very tough. You're gone."

"What?" Sabeena whispered back. She had heard stories of dangerous mothers-in-law, the kind who threw plates against the wall if the food wasn't made right. These were the mothers-in-law of the *saas-bahu* TV soaps, which girls across India watched in terror. Suddenly, her life ahead with Shahzad seemed uncertain. Her friend disappeared into the crowd, but her words echoed in Sabeena's ears: *You're gone.*

‏♥♥♥♥♥♥

They married in January, on a day that happened to be the diamond jubilee of a local religious leader, and so the whole road to the wedding hall was lit up with lights. "What kind of wedding is this?" the guests asked in wonder.

Again, Sabeena felt lost in a dream. As was tradition, she had not seen Shahzad for three years. Her family brought her into the wedding hall with her face covered by a veil of the finest fabric. She wore a thick red Benares *sari* and flower petals strewn over her hair. The photographer asked her to sit on a pink throne to pose for photos. Sabeena had been to many weddings but still had not anticipated this level of pageantry.

In their community, the father of the groom had to give his son permission to marry before the ceremony, but Shahzad's father was nowhere to be found. Shahzad knew where his father must be: at home, with his cars, having forgotten all about the wedding. And so he rushed home on his scooter, cursing his father as he navigated through the crush of traffic. He was going to be late to his own wedding. When Shahzad made it home and found his father in the garage as expected, his phone was already ringing. "Come soon, Shahzad. The priest is waiting for you for the ceremony to begin."

Shahzad arrived just in time, with his father in tow, and his permission. The hall was filled with a throng of guests—some three thousand people from the community. Sabeena's father began delivering the gifts: a bed, cupboard, fridge, TV, and gold. Every item was carried through the hall for the guests to see. The dowry was not so extensive as at a Hindu wedding but still enough to impress. Shahzad stood smiling in an expensive dark blue suit brought from Dubai by his brother, who had moved there for work. As the gifts paraded by, Shahzad felt he was living up to his princely name at last.

And as the ceremony began, Shahzad felt another swell of confidence, because his best friend, Atif, sat beside him. Like Shahzad, Atif was built thin like a reed, and had an equally long mustache. But he was taller and more muscular, and ahead of Shahzad's wedding day, Atif had worked to make his friend strong. He'd taught him weight lifting and karate and taken Shahzad to the gym, where with each punch he made him repeat in Japanese: *"Ichi. Ni. San. Shi!"* They'd done knuckle push-ups until Shahzad worried the skin on his middle finger would fall off. Now, as Shahzad sat on his own throne-like chair, with Atif beside him, he thought it didn't matter that his father had forgotten the day.

"Do you accept Sabeena as your wife?" the priest asked, breaking through Shahzad's thoughts. "Yes," Shahzad said, three times, as was required. Afterward, Shahzad's family gave Sabeena's side five thousand rupees, a generous amount, and she and Shahzad were both asked to sign the marriage contract. They recited the Quran, which guided the Muslim wedding ceremony.

As the wedding ended, a very sad song by Mohammed Rafi was played, and Sabeena began to cry. For the first time that day, she thought again about leaving home and her father, about her difficult mother-in-law and the great unknown that lay ahead. As her sister came over to comfort her, Sabeena wiped her tears with the edge of her *dupatta*, and her father enveloped her in a hug.

As Sabeena cried, Shahzad began to have second thoughts of his own. Perhaps the diamond jubilee lights were not a beautiful addition to the wedding. *What if they were a bad omen instead?* He worried that there could be a *nazar*, or curse, on their marriage. Superstition guided Shahzad's perception of the world, as it did for many of his community's religious leaders. Before the wedding, a local priest had advised Shahzad's mother that Sabeena change her name in order for the marriage to succeed, saying the two *S* sounds were not a good combination. The priest said that with a different name, the connection between them would be stronger. But that felt wrong to Sabeena, who told Shahzad's mother in a rare show of obstinacy: "My father gave me this name. You call me this." Shahzad agreed, and her name had not been changed.

As the clock ticked past midnight after the wedding, Shahzad nervously looked for other signs of bad luck. When Sabeena went to her apartment and said good-bye to her mother, everything went smoothly. There was no trouble when Shahzad took her to his family home, showed her the elaborate British-built exterior, and brought her upstairs to their small but private room. But when his family set up a wedding game—a bucket of water with a ring dropped inside for the new couple to find—it was Sabeena who located it. Shahzad searched and searched, but his hands grasped at water.

Shahzad's anxiety continued to rise as the end of the festivities approached, because Atif had not taught him one thing. His best friend had not taught him about sex, because Atif was also unmarried, and sex before marriage was *haram*. Shahzad knew he had to perform on the first night, but he had no idea what that entailed.

Shahzad pulled aside a family friend. "How do you fuck a woman?" he whispered, hoping the desperation wouldn't come through in his voice. "Back side or front side?"

"Are you feeling sleepy and all? Wake up!" his friend told him, laughing, and sprayed soda in his face. "Of course the front side, *pagal*."

Later, Shahzad would learn that anal sex was also *haram* in his community, along with oral sex, sex during menstruation, and sex during fasting times. Now, he only worried about doing it wrong, Sabeena laughing at him, and other people overhearing his struggle. In his community, women often came and pressed their ears to the door on a couple's wedding night. It was almost 3 a.m., and Shahzad prayed the women would be too tired to listen in.

But it was Shahzad who was exhausted as he climbed into bed beside Sabeena. His eyes had never felt so heavy as they said their nightly prayer. Sabeena was also tired, glad to be able to take off her thick *sari* and heavy jewelry.

Front side, front side, Shahzad told himself.

Within minutes, they were both asleep.

♥♥♥♥♥

Sabeena knew that Shahzad would try to initiate sex soon, and that she would have to comply, despite her fear. She would have to continue complying for years and years, any time he wished. It was what a good Indian wife did. Even the Indian Penal Code said sex between a man and his wife was never rape. But maybe Shahzad would not be a demanding husband that way. For the last day or so, they had simply relaxed in the apartment, which, like most middle-class apartments in the city, was modest and utilitarian. Still, it was far nicer than hers. From morning until night, they had listened to Mohammed Rafi songs on the record player, surrounded by all their new things. They had lain in the double bed for hours in their tiny room that faced out onto the street. Outside, Sabeena could hear the rumble of train tracks and the call of a pair of pigeons that liked to land on their windowsill. Nearby was a bright green *dargah* devoted to a saint who could levitate. And there was new construction for a Haj House nearby, a place where pilgrims could stay en route to Mecca. Sabeena hoped she and Shahzad would one day take the trip, which had long been government subsidized. Beyond the Haj House and the *dargah* was Crawford Market, where she knew Shahzad liked to go. It was all very romantic to Sabeena, and not the worst place to make love. Still, Shahzad did not make a move.

On the third day after the wedding, Shahzad worked up his nerve. *Front side, front side,* he told himself again. It was not as complicated as he thought. As he moved, Sabeena told Shahzad he was hurting her a little. But she also said it felt good. Afterward, they had to go wash. Their community was very strict on the requirement of ablutions after sex. As Sabeena got up, she was alarmed to find that there was no adjoining bathroom. She would have to walk outside to take a shower, and everyone in the family would know. But Shahzad's family was discreet and did not comment.

After that, they continued to spend their days relaxing, talking, and listening to records, because Shahzad had taken a month off from work. Over and over again they played Mohammed Rafi's song "Janam Janam Ka Saath Hai," which was about living many lifetimes together. People said his voice was magic, and that no one sang a love song the way he did.

As Mohammed Rafi's music played, Shahzad told Sabeena about his childhood and his father's mistreatment. Sabeena told him his father sounded like a small man, who only wanted others to feel small. She also told Shahzad about her own father, how he was strict but good to her, and how her grandfather had been even stricter and not so kind.

Shahzad understood that Sabeena's father meant well. But he thought that keeping her indoors was akin to putting his daughter in a *kundu*, in a faraway village, isolated from the world. In a *kundu*, people didn't go out and gain knowledge, and the knowledge didn't come in. More people were moving to cities, but Shahzad knew the majority of the country still lived in rural areas, where TV had not yet arrived. In Mumbai, Shahzad had watched television and gone to movies all the time as a child, favoring the English-language spy pictures that starred Sean Connery and Roger Moore. His mom would give him the single rupee for admission, and they'd get *mawa* cake afterward. He couldn't imagine a life without movies. For him—for most children and adults he knew—movies were everything. He thought that people who grew up walled in, away from films and news and the world, didn't know how to think for themselves. He promised himself he would try to change that in Sabeena. Sabeena told herself she'd try to free Shahzad from the hurt of his father.

In the big Hindi movies, which were often set in Kashmir, the heroes and heroines stood atop mountains as snowflakes fell onto their tongues. Or they floated across gentle lakes in boats made just for two. In the movies it was as if the fighting in Kashmir did not exist. Sabeena remembered what her father said about Kashmir: *Madhubala, anywhere you want to go, you can go in a marriage.* Those words echoed now in her mind. Sabeena imagined the trips Shahzad took her on would be as idyllic.

But after Ramadan ended and their honeymoon approached, Shahzad's mother interrupted that dream. She told them she was coming with them on their trip. Sabeena cried at the thought of it.

How could she think she should come on our honeymoon? Shahzad re-assured his new wife. His mother was confused because she was from a small village and had a backward mindset. "Just don't answer her when she asks," he said. In the end Shahzad's mother stayed home.

They set off first for Matheran, a tiny hill station in the West-ern Ghats mountain range, whose name meant "a forest on the forehead." The train took four hours or so, and when they arrived Shahzad woke to find Sabeena asleep on his shoulder, a sea foam–colored scarf wrapped around her hair. A voice boomed over the loudspeaker, and he heard the sound of a dog's bark. As they roamed around Matheran, they took photos of each other beside a river, under a gazebo, and atop a mountain, though it was not snowing that time of year.

After Matheran they visited two more hill stations: Panch-gani, where Shahzad rode like a hero astride a white horse, and Mahabaleshwar, where they went boating like the couples in the movies. In Mahabaleshwar, they stayed in a hotel called Anarkali, which meant "pomegranate blossom," and was the name of the court dancer in *Mughal-e-Azam*. In the hotel, as they made love, their life felt just like a film.

But on the train ride back to Mumbai, Sabeena asked Shahzad an uncomfortable question. Perhaps she had started to notice small details that suggested Shahzad wasn't a serious man: how spit gath-ered at the sides of his mouth when he talked or ate, how his smile was goofy, or how he kept his shirt unbuttoned too low. Or she was just curious. "My father told me that if a woman sits next to a man, a man should get a current, should get excited," she said. "Why isn't that happening to you?"

Shahzad didn't understand. He couldn't be excited all the time. They didn't talk on the ride much after that. And as their train pulled into Bombay Central, a tooth in Shahzad's mouth began to ache. When they got on the bus from the station, the pain continued to increase. By the time he got home, Shahzad had a toothache that made it hard to speak or think.

The next day, he went to the doctor, who removed the tooth, but Shahzad couldn't shake the bad feeling. It was like the *nazar* had followed them silently on the honeymoon and reappeared when they got close to home.

※※※※※

The photos of their first anniversary celebration, which Sabeena placed neatly inside their wedding album, show a blissful day at home. Shahzad chose a casual red-checked shirt for the party, which he buttoned to his chest, and American-style blue jeans. Sabeena wore an iridescent pink and white *sari,* her red wedding bangles, and white flowers tied in her hair. Both have the glow of youth. They look thin—so thin it seems that they could live on fatty *laddoos* and still remain this beautiful. In one photo, Shahzad's father even lets them feed him a slice of cake. In another, Shahzad and Sabeena are laughing at something, and Sabeena's veil is falling off, and tiny wisps of hair frame her face. In the last photo in the album, they pose side by side, and Shahzad's arm is wrapped around his wife. There is a mirror behind them, and the camera catches it, so that the space between them is obscured by a flash of light.

They both knew what came next, after a year of marriage. For almost any Indian couple, a year meant it was time for children. Shahzad dreamed of having four, five, even six children, whom he imagined waiting for him at the door every night when he came home. They would all be smiling and plump and healthy. They would be mostly boys, and they would clutch at Sabeena's long *salwar kameez.* Despite her father's warnings that giving birth was difficult, Sabeena also wanted children.

As they tried for a child, Shahzad took Sabeena out of the house as often as he could. He wanted to get her out of the *kundu* mind-set before a child tied her down. He took Sabeena out on his scooter. They drove past the old art deco movie theaters to the Oberoi, a luxury hotel so high it seemed to tower over the city. They sat at the seaside talking for hours, looking down at the concrete tetrapods that broke the ocean's force. As Shahzad drove her home, he felt proud of his new scooter and the freedom it gave him. But he was not a good driver, and Sabeena swore she'd never go out on it again.

After that, when Sabeena went home to her parents' house for visits, Shahzad always picked her up in a taxi. As the taxi idled outside, Shahzad would shout her brother's name up to her apartment window, because it wasn't proper to call out for a lady. Shahzad's voice always rose uncertainly through the hubbub of butchers, jewelry sellers, and street vendors. Sabeena's brother would yell back, and after a little while Sabeena would come down, her head covered. And then they'd take a cab somewhere, usually to the sea.

Shahzad also liked to take out Sabeena's sisters, most of whom were younger and impressionable. Whenever the sisters learned Shahzad was coming, they got ready by four p.m., though he wasn't arriving until five, and shouted with excitement: "*Bhaijan* is coming! *Bhaijan* is coming!" They rushed to do their hair and makeup. After Shahzad picked them up in a taxi, they would drive to Apollo Bunder. There, they'd gaze up at the Gateway of India and, behind it, the Taj Mahal Hotel. Or he took them to Chowpatty Beach, where they sat and watched the waves for hours, ate *bhelpuri* and *pav bhaji*, and felt the ocean's breeze.

Shahzad had first learned about Chowpatty from Atif. As teenagers, he and Atif and two other friends, one a millionaire's son with a flashy car, drove to Chowpatty every Sunday. They'd park and make *masti* and talk until the sun went down. Or, if it was during the Hindu festival of Navratri, they'd drive from Chowpatty to the grounds of Walkeshwar, where they would watch Hindu women—

women they could never marry—do the *garba*, twirling in their colorful flared skirts.

Since he had gotten married, Shahzad had seen less of Atif. He had attended Atif's engagement to a good Muslim girl from the community. But after that Atif had been elusive. He had become a well-known karate instructor and had little time for anyone, even his oldest friend.

But one day Atif reappeared to tell Shahzad about a problem. He had fallen in love with one of his karate students, a Gujarati girl. More problematically: a Jain, a religion that seemed to Shahzad far removed from Islam, because of how it emphasized renunciation. Atif wasn't married yet and said he was going to break his engagement and marry the Jain girl instead. "But how can it be?" Shahzad asked him nervously. "She is a Hindu. Even worse, a Jain." Atif just looked back at him. Atif always did what he wanted.

After that, Shahzad did not hear from Atif until months later, when he saw him in a restaurant with ladies' *surma* rimmed around his eyes. The Prophet had said wearing *surma* could be auspicious, but on Atif it looked like a disguise. *"Oye,"* said Shahzad, laughing. "You are looking very different." Atif grabbed Shahzad by the shirt and brought him into a corner. "I ran away with that Gujarati girl and got married," Atif said. "And the girl's father is now looking for me." He told Shahzad that the girl's father had even given a local inspector ten thousand rupees to arrest Atif on a false case, to maybe even "encounter" him, which meant when you shot a person dead and made it look like an accident. Police in Mumbai used encounters to pick off members of the city's underworld, but Shahzad knew parents sometimes resorted to desperate methods when their children married across religions. He was terrified for his friend. Atif said he was going to hide out at his aunt's place for as long as he had to and, before Shahzad could say more, disappeared. After this, Shahzad did not hear from Atif for a long time.

Shahzad could have used Atif around, because after that day, life went very differently at home. Or he could have used his brother, but his brother was many kilometers away. And so none of the men Shahzad trusted were nearby when life for Sabeena and him began to unravel.

It started with Shahzad's mother. After their first year of marriage, she began pestering Sabeena daily. The laundry was done too late in the day. Or Sabeena hadn't spent enough time tending to her needs. Mostly, she was on her daughter-in-law about her cooking: the food had been oversalted, it was too well-done, or Sabeena had bought the wrong meat or vegetables. "You don't know how to cook," Shahzad's mother would shout, or, "You need to learn everything." If Sabeena dropped a utensil, Shahzad's mother would demand, "Why did you throw that away?" Or, the more stinging insult, "Your mother and father have not taught you how to behave."

Sabeena, always the most outspoken among her friends and sisters, forced herself not to talk back. It had been a peaceful first year, but now her best friend's warning had come true. Sabeena told herself that most mothers-in-law were like this. It was a kind of national tradition. She was an outsider coming into their family—a threat—and over time Shahzad's mother had become jealous. *She has grown afraid that her son will go into his wife's hand,* Sabeena thought. If that happened, Shahzad would only listen to Sabeena, not his mother.

Sabeena tried not to let his mother's cruelty get to her. It helped that she could tell Shahzad about it. The incidents mostly occurred while he was at work. When he got home from the shop, he'd listen patiently as Sabeena recounted what his mother had done that day. It made Shahzad tense to listen to these stories, but he forced himself to tell her calmly, "*Chod de.* Let it go." And Sabeena would, knowing there was no other choice.

As Shahzad's mother grew stricter, Sabeena felt something shift within her. Nothing had prepared her for this level of criticism. The freedom she felt on her honeymoon already seemed far away. Even Shahzad realized that she was becoming a prisoner again—just inside a different jail. They both felt grateful that Shahzad's father was not also cruel to her. He had become so enamored with his cars and the market that he hardly spoke to anyone in the family.

As time went on, Sabeena decided she needed to accept that what had lived in her as a girl had died, and that marriage was all a matter of adjustment. She had to adjust for her husband and his parents. And she had to adjust for herself—to accept that maybe she would not get to be happy. Shahzad also had to adjust for her, taking time after a long workday to listen to her complaints. She saw this as similar to when a person clapped. *You clap with both hands, not one,* she thought. Both have to clap together to make a sound. If not, there will be only silence.

Sabeena was also distracted by the effort of trying, unsuccessfully, for a baby. More than a year passed, and no baby came. Shahzad felt strong and virile; he had no problem getting erections. He could not understand why a baby did not arrive. Soon, people in his community began to talk. Shahzad watched many of his extended family members become pregnant. Some had three children, then four, five.

Sabeena began to worry. There was a common story of a man who went to the Prophet and asked about marrying a woman of good lineage, high honor, and immense beauty. The only problem was that the woman could not reproduce. *No,* came the answer. *Do not marry her.* Because to have more children was to increase the size of the *ummah,* and the size of the Islamic nation was what mattered most. It was not so different from Hindu ideas about reproduction. Both religions stressed how essential it was to continue the family line.

Shahzad had seen movies where people couldn't have children. It was always the girl's fault. Even if it wasn't, the girl was blamed for it. But Shahzad began to worry that if Sabeena wasn't the problem, then something must be wrong with him. Men who were sterile in his community were viewed as weak—not real men. "No, no," said Shahzad's mother, when he told her this. "Always check the girl first."

And so he and Sabeena went to the doctor, a kindly man who took Sabeena inside a small room and ran a battery of tests. As part of her pelvic exam, he put a finger inside her. When Sabeena came out of the room, she looked like she was about to cry. "Why did he put his finger inside me like this?" she asked Shahzad. It seemed a clear violation of the Quran's rule that no man touch a woman except her husband. "No, no, he's a doctor, it's okay," Shahzad assured her. "We have to see if you can become pregnant."

When the doctor came out, he said, "She's perfect." He looked at Shahzad. "Now I have to see you."

Shahzad went to the clinic later, in secret, to drop off his semen sample. He hoped no one had seen him go. He waited anxiously for the results. After what felt like hours, the lab technician reappeared.

"Kuch bhi nahi," the technician said. "Nothing is there."

Shahzad rejoiced. *Nothing is wrong with me after all.* It was just taking Sabeena time to conceive. There was no problem. No reason for worry or shame. A son or a daughter would eventually arrive.

Later, a doctor clarified the results. The technician had meant *no sperm* was there. There was nothing in the semen. *Shunya.* Zero. The doctor told Shahzad he suffered from azoospermia, a medical condition in which a man has a low or even zero sperm count.

He took down Shahzad's entire medical history. The list of ailments was long: prolonged periods of unexplained weakness in childhood, an ear infection that had permanently thrown off his balance, and a more recent keloid scar from an aluminum locket he wore around his neck that contained verses of the Quran. And, at age sixteen, the mumps. When Shahzad mentioned mumps, the doctor paused.

The mumps were worrying, the doctor said. The viral illness could stop sperm production temporarily, or in rare cases, forever.

"The mumps likely affected your testes," the doctor told Shahzad. "But there are many people like this. Your erections will be all right. It's just that you can't produce." He told Shahzad he was almost sterile.

Shahzad turned what the doctor said over and over again in his mind. He felt like he was cursed. He thought back to his wedding day, to the lights that had lit up the road.

Finally, he worked up the courage to tell Sabeena. His voice was unsteady and he hung his head. Sabeena listened, her bright eyes focused on his face. *"O,"* she said gently, when he was finished, using the term of endearment she had taken to calling him. "It's God's will. It's okay."

"But our generation should go ahead," Shahzad said.

"If God doesn't want to give children to us, then he doesn't."

Sabeena remembered what her father had told her—that childbirth was painful, and that afterward men gained control of their wives. But he had also said something else: "With children, Madhubala, your life will be happy always." She wondered what their life would be like now, without them.

She also thought of her cousins, the ones with housework piling up and children to attend to. It seemed like a lot of work with a mother-in-law also on your back. And it seemed impossible to both run a house well and take care of children the way you should. She told herself it was better this way.

"It's God's will," she told Shahzad again, and Shahzad couldn't decide if this made him feel better or worse.

A saying came into his mind then, about how a man and a horse never get old, not if they are virile and strong. He was determined not to feel old yet. He was only twenty-nine, and Sabeena not yet twenty-seven. He wanted to hold on to the man who had stood like a prince in a fancy suit from Dubai, receiving expensive gifts beside his lovely wife.

Shahzad was stuck on a single word the doctor had said: "almost." He had not said "sterile" but "almost sterile." That meant there were options. Pills. Powders. Tests. The doctor had even mentioned an operation.

Without taking time to consider, Shahzad told the doctor he wanted them all.

❦❦❦❦❦

When Shahzad went in for the operation, it was a private affair. It had been a quiet year for his family, and for the city, except for the *fatwa* against Salman Rushdie. Though the *fatwa* was issued in Iran, Rushdie's *The Satanic Verses* had also angered Muslims in Mumbai with its portrayal of the Prophet Muhammad. It had angered people in Shahzad's own community, who marched past his house shouting slogans and starting fights in the street with police. The same people who would talk if they knew the real reason for Shahzad's operation. And so he went to a private hospital, where he wouldn't risk running into anyone he knew. His brother flew in from Dubai over the holidays to keep him company, but Sabeena stayed at home, so as not to arouse suspicion. When it was over, neighbors were told Shahzad was treated for a bump near his groin.

Before he left for the operation, Shahzad sat Sabeena down and told her, "If I get the operation, everything will be good. We will have a child."

"That's okay, *O*," she said. "Let's just see."

Shahzad was nervous, but the doctor, a well-known physician at a hospital downtown, laid out the problem and procedure plainly. He explained that the mumps may have caused a varicocele, a network of swollen veins that caused blood to pool, which could affect sperm production. He told Shahzad the surgery would manipulate the veins to allow blood to flow more freely. But he could make no promises of a miracle cure. Shahzad nodded, though he hardly heard the last part. He was certain he'd be healed after the operation.

It was all over in half an hour, but Shahzad stayed in the hospital for several days. He was in intense pain, for which he was given painkillers. The doctor told him that the veins had been put right.

After Shahzad's pain waned, the doctor reminded him that repairing a varicocele could mean better sperm production—or it could do nothing at all. Shahzad's family grew upset. Rumors swirled that the hospital had not given them a report they asked for. Someone suggested the lost report was to save Shahzad the embarrassment of learning the operation hadn't worked. Shahzad only wanted to go home.

The doctor released him with tablets to help increase sperm production. In the months that followed, Shahzad took them, though they made him feel sleepy, giddy, and a little nauseous. *Arey, this is to make me strong, but it's making me feel weak,* he thought. But then he had sex with Sabeena and saw that he could last a long time.

When Shahzad went in for a checkup, the doctor clapped and crowed at his patient's erection. But while Shahzad's sex life was better than ever, he had taken the pills for many months now and still Sabeena wasn't pregnant.

"It's okay, O," she told him again, but he didn't agree.

One night, as Shahzad walked through an area of town he didn't usually venture, he was startled to see Sabeena's father sitting on the side of the road. They were in the red-light district. He had known Sabeena's father was a doctor who treated skin diseases; now he understood what that meant. Shahzad greeted him, and they exchanged pleasantries. He wanted to ask the man's advice. *Perhaps he could help me,* he thought. *Now is my chance.* But he didn't want word getting back to Sabeena, and after a short conversation, he continued walking.

After this encounter, Shahzad decided to go to a sexologist, one with no connection to his family. He knew sexologists treated all kinds of problems: *gupt rog*, impotence, even homosexuality, which was then considered a disease. But Shahzad had no trouble having sex, and the sexologist turned him away. "If you don't have a problem, I can't do anything for you," he said. "But, Doctor," Shahzad persisted, "why is my sperm count not coming?" "Mumps," the sexologist said, like the other doctors had. "Your testes were very damaged." Shahzad grew angry and could not help but think of his father, who had not taken him to the doctor when he should.

For the next five years, Shahzad spent money going to every doctor, trying every pill, and asking about each new technology that hit the market. He did this especially when a neighbor would prod him about why he did not have children and help spread the religion. "Every time you produce a child, God smiles," they'd say, piously. Or they'd goad him to take a second wife, because his first wife was assumed to be barren. Shahzad could not tell them that Sabeena was not the problem. Once, Shahzad's mother needled him that "Even a gay got a child," because the wife of a gay man in their neighborhood had gotten pregnant. In Shahzad's community, being gay was *haram*; in the Quran, it was said that men who preferred men were "transgressing beyond bounds." Legally, it was a crime punishable by a life sentence. If even a gay man got his wife pregnant, Shahzad knew there was something very wrong with him.

After reading about a new medical advance in the paper, Shahzad went to see a famous fertility specialist, who yanked so hard on a nerve Shahzad thought he'd pass out. She told him that he needed another operation. Before the surgery, they had to conduct more tests, for which Shahzad spent an extravagant twenty thousand rupees.

It was then that Sabeena decided Shahzad's obsession had gone far enough. He was spending so much time and money, and only growing more anxious. But when she confronted him about it, he would not listen. So she took him to visit their family doctor, whom Shahzad had seen for years, to ask whether all these specialty appointments, pills, and operations made sense. The doctor, a thoughtful man, peered at them gravely over his glasses when Shahzad mentioned another operation.

"It's a waste of time," he said, his voice stern. "Don't do it. And stop what you're doing now." Shahzad hung his head. "I'm sorry, but there is nothing that can be done for you."

៚៚៚៚៚

Water was scarce that year in Mumbai, as it often was after a season of low rainfall. And it was especially scarce for Shahzad's large joint family, where he, Sabeena, his parents, uncle, aunt, and a handful of other family members shared a single water tank. Before long, Sabeena began arguing with Shahzad's aunt over the lack of water, saying the woman had used it all up, or closed the knob so Sabeena couldn't access it to cook or wash or clean. Sabeena told Shahzad she barely had enough water to use each day. After several tense weeks, Shahzad decided to speak to his uncle.

This uncle had always been Shahzad's favorite. Throughout childhood, whenever Shahzad's uncle saw Shahzad's father mistreating him, he would ask his brother, "What are you doing? Why are you doing this?" This was the uncle who took Shahzad to the doctor when he had the mumps. He had always been friendly and had a casual manner, and Shahzad thought he would know how to solve the women's problem. But Shahzad also knew his uncle had been stressed recently—smoking more than a pack of cigarettes a day. He would have to approach the matter with care.

"Uncle," said Shahzad, speaking with a little more force than he'd meant to. "Why is your wife making the knob slow? We are not getting enough water."

His uncle did not respond as Shahzad had hoped. Instead, he shouted a *gaali* at his nephew, a word Shahzad had never heard in the house. Before Shahzad could stop himself, he shouted a *gaali* back. His uncle grew angry in a way Shahzad had never seen. He took out a stick they kept at home to kill mice and shouted, "I'll beat you."

Shahzad retreated in surprise. It was Ramadan, a time of fasting and reflection, and that night there would be prayers. It was no time to fight. He vowed to talk to his uncle again more calmly tomorrow.

But the next day, an ambulance came and took his uncle away. After that, he did not return.

The family was told that he died of a heart attack, perhaps due to stress, and immediately they turned on Shahzad.

"It's because of you he died," Shahzad's mother told him. "It's because you shouted at him that way." The rest of the joint family agreed. Most of them would not speak to Shahzad or made snide comments as he passed them in the house. The only elder who did not criticize Shahzad was his father, who seemed not to notice his brother was gone.

Shahzad was frantic. He had killed his favorite uncle and his protector, all over some drops of water.

"It's not your fault, O," Sabeena told him, gently. "They are wrong." She wanted to stand up for Shahzad against his family. She had often wanted to in the years she lived with his parents. But she knew from watching the other women in the family that this would make the problem worse.

At the funeral, the first Shahzad had ever attended, he watched as they covered his uncle's face—which was turned to face the *qibla*, in the direction of Mecca—and lowered his body into the grave. Dried mud was collected in an earthen pot to scatter on top of the coffin. Flowers were placed beside the body. Everyone prayed the Quran. As Shahzad collected his share of dirt to throw into the grave, he felt ill. *It's all because of me,* he thought.

Later, the family learned that Shahzad's uncle had been under other pressures. For weeks, there had been troubles with his property. The day before his death—and the day Shahzad approached him—his uncle's friend and business partner had stolen his land out from under him by putting a license in his name. If anything had killed his uncle, it was this.

Despite this new knowledge, and no matter how many times Sabeena assured him otherwise, Shahzad still heard his mother's words: *It's because of you he died.*

In the days after the funeral, Shahzad felt as if there was still dirt underneath his fingernails. No matter how often or forcefully he washed his hands, they never seemed to come clean.

Sabeena did her best to comfort Shahzad, but she was soon distracted by trouble of her own. For weeks, her father had been acting anxious and jittery. He said he was worried about the marriage prospects of his other daughters. Not long after he began acting strangely, he went to the hospital for a hernia operation.

It was a complicated surgery, but Sabeena's father told his family it would be simple. He had problems with his heart, and so the operation was a risk, but he did not tell them this either. He had also arranged to have it done at a cheap hospital, which they did not know. Such hospitals were terrifying places, with instruments unsterilized, malpractice common, and reports of a thriving black-market organ trade.

Sabeena was sleeping when a woman from the hospital came to their house late at night and told them that the operation had gone wrong. "He's very serious, come soon," she said, and Shahzad and Sabeena hurried to get dressed in the dark.

By the time they reached the hospital, Sabeena's father was dead. His heart had given out in the surgery.

Sabeena knew immediately that her life would be divided into two parts: the time before and the time after her father's death. She was twenty-seven, and perhaps she had already been an adult for years. But she saw she had not experienced true suffering until now.

She did not understand why her father had not confided in her. She thought that perhaps it was because of lack of money. But when she got to her family home, crying as she climbed up the stairs past the *paan* spit and the hanging laundry, through the drafty room and into their messy front hall, she opened her father's cupboard and found seventy-five thousand rupees—a large sum—inside.

Not long after Sabeena's father died, Shahzad went away to Dubai. He said he needed to be with his brother because of the continued shaming of his family over his uncle's death, which Sabeena understood. But with Shahzad gone, she felt she could not talk to anyone—not her mother or sisters, who acted like sheep, or her brother, who was angrier than ever. The only person she wanted to talk to was her father. If he were here, though, she knew what he'd say. He would tell her to pray hard to Allah.

♥♥♥♥♥

After Shahzad returned from Dubai, the 1992 riots took place, as if death begot more death, and on a larger scale.

It started when he was in his shop at Byculla Market, listening to the radio, and heard news of a faraway mosque being burned to the ground. Right-wing Hindu groups had organized a rally, which devolved into a riot, which gave way to the demolition of the Babri Masjid, one of the largest mosques in the northern state of Uttar Pradesh. The Hindu groups had been rallying to reclaim the birthplace of the god Ram, and the place where a Hindu temple supposedly once stood, before a Mughal emperor built a mosque in its place. The rally was organized, in large part, by the RSS, a volunteer Hindu nationalist group whose agenda was to push for a Hindu nation. A group that said India experienced a "golden age" until it was ruined by the Muslim Mughal kings. Men the RSS had sent to rally at the mosque shouted "Death to the Muslims!" as they destroyed it with pickaxes and hammers. Now, the Babri Masjid was rubble.

As Shahzad listened to the radio, he thought the demolition didn't sound like a rally that spontaneously transformed into a riot. To him, the destruction sounded preplanned. He wanted to keep listening to the news, but all the Muslims in the market were closing early. There was talk of violence in Mumbai, though they were many miles from the Babri Masjid. Maybe it had started already. Shahzad closed his shop and went to find his father, uncle, and cousin. They were all ready to leave. The buses and taxis seemed to have stopped running, and so they rushed home on foot instead. In the streets, they saw tires burning.

As the men approached their mostly Muslim neighborhood, Shahzad heard what they all feared—that Muslims were coming out to kill Hindus in retaliation. And the Hindus would retaliate after that. This was how trouble often started in the country: all was calm among ordinary men until more powerful people lit a match. And then the violence spread like a market fire. But as Shahzad and his family passed their local tailor, who was Hindu, the man called out to them, his voice kind: "Come inside and sit until things are safe." He had been their tailor for a long time, starting with Shahzad's grandfather, followed by Shahzad's father, and now Shahzad, always making the men special *kurta pyjamas* at Eid and Ramadan time. They were a block from home, but they hurried inside the tailor's shop, which was attached to his home.

Huddled in the tailor's apartment, they heard that angry Muslims were burning more tires now and not letting any remaining public transport move. The police had come out, but it was rumored that they were protecting only Hindus.

When they finally ran the last block home, Shahzad used the landline to call Sabeena, who was out visiting her mother and sisters.

At least she is in a Muslim locality, Shahzad thought. *So maybe she is safe.* But Shahzad was also in a Muslim locality, and now there was a Hindu man outside throwing rocks at his window, trying to break the glass.

There was a Hindu inspector who lived in the next building who Shahzad knew liked Muslims and Muslim culture. He played *qawwalis*—Sufi devotional music—almost every day. And so Shahzad called the inspector, who confronted the man slinging rocks. In Shahzad's memory, the inspector held up his gun and said, "If you do that in my area, I will shoot you dead."

The man left, but the violence continued to rage. Muslims, furious over the demolition of the mosque, set public buses on fire, and Hindus damaged more mosques in the city. In the central neighborhood of Bandra, some people simply vanished, taken from their beds in the night. Men were torched alive, while women were stripped and gang-raped. Shops and homes were burned. On the trains Hindu men caught Muslim men whose beards gave them away and threw them onto the tracks. Muslim men stoned Hindus, shouting *"Allah-hu-Akbar!"* as they hit their targets. Police were also killed. When whole Muslim areas were set on fire, the police radioed, "Let it burn."

After four days, the violence waned, and Sabeena called Shahzad to beg him to bring them some milk. Her family had not eaten in days. Shahzad, who was growing more anxious the longer he stayed inside, and the longer he was away from Sabeena, was grateful to have a job to do.

Outside, the streets were eerily quiet, as empty as he'd ever seen them. His destination was the Regal Theater downtown, which was three and a half kilometers away. Here, a store might be open. As he walked, he saw small fires in the road, but no one gave him any trouble. As he approached the theater, a bearded man called out, *"Chali jao,* they are killing Muslims still." Shahzad nodded curtly and walked on. *"Wapis jao, chalo,"* the man shouted, his voice persistent. "It's started again, they are killing Muslims. They are even putting poison in the milk and giving it."

Shahzad stopped, startled. He stared at the open shop by the theater, turned around, and went back home.

As Shahzad told his family what he'd heard, they whispered that it was all a big plan, this killing of Muslims. They said that it didn't make sense that Sharad Pawar, the defense minister, hadn't immediately sent the army to help the police, and that many more Muslims were being killed because of the delay. Rumors began circulating that Prime Minister Narasimha Rao had been part of the planning of the mosque's demolition, and that the RSS had gotten permission to stage their attack. The fact that the police had done nothing to stop the violence was only more evidence.

For eight days, Shahzad did not see Sabeena. Curfew had been imposed on the city, and Shahzad's family had very little to eat, just a stock of dry *chapatis*. Finally, the army came from New Delhi and declared that whoever continued to riot would be shot. Bit by bit, after the last fits of rage were expended, peace was restored to the city.

The violence stopped, but Shahzad did not know how he or anyone else in Mumbai could forget what had taken place. Not all neighbors were like the tailor. Stories circulated about a neighbor who had murdered another, a shop owner who stoned a family he once fed, and a policeman who shot a man he'd been charged to protect.

In the end, some nine hundred people were dead: the majority of them Muslims, but also many Hindus, and fifty who were not declared either way. Thousands more were injured. One of Shahzad's doctors watched a man die by sword and went mad afterward. Shahzad's brother-in-law witnessed a murder he would not talk about. In January, Shahzad realized that the Catholics had not celebrated Christmas.

When Sabeena returned, she seemed different, as if she were holding a secret inside her. Finally, she told Shahzad what happened in Bhendi Bazaar. She said that police had broken soda bottles and told Muslims to kneel and walk on their knees on the broken glass until they bled.

In the days to come, though, the city achieved a kind of equilibrium. The newspapers reported that the police were encouraging Muslims and Hindus to sit together in public spaces. But Shahzad and Sabeena could not so easily forget. They would be polite to the Hindus they knew, as they always had, but the riots had given them cause to be more cautious, and more pious. They had always been good Muslims, reading the Quran and performing their daily *namaaz*. Now, they both attached a deeper feeling to their faith.

Shahzad thought back to his childhood, when he had learned from the local Catholic kids in plaid uniforms that they went to church just once a week. *Once a week only.* He'd marveled at the thought. Now, he felt that his five-times-a-day prayers weren't enough.

Sabeena read the Quran every night. During Friday prayers, while Shahzad was at the mosque, she fingered her *tazbih* necklace, like the Catholics did with their rosaries, repeating *"Subhan Allah, Subhan Allah,"* "Glory be to God," thirty-three times, once for each bead. As Sabeena prayed, she remembered that her father had told her that the goal of any Muslim was to pray twenty-four hours a day, but that since she had other duties, she should just pray as much as she was able. After the attacks, she decided to move as close to that ideal as she could.

ళళళళళళ

Not long after, there were bomb blasts in Mumbai, thirteen in a row. It was said to be retaliation for the demolition of the Babri

Mosque and for all the Muslims who had been killed and raped and burned in the riots. And for all the pain and injustice Muslims had suffered over the years. India blamed Pakistan for the blasts, which Pakistan denied. This time, some 250 people were killed, and many more injured, most of whom were Hindus. The TV images were horrifying: severed limbs, contorted bodies, blood running in the road like a stream. While they didn't condone the bombings, Shahzad and Sabeena were not surprised. This was a wound that had been deepening since Partition, maybe even from before. And like many Muslims, they felt that if Muslims did not retaliate, they would all be killed. Just one in ten people were Muslim, while eight in ten were Hindu; they could not stop the Hindus if they tried. First, their jobs would be taken away, then their rights, and finally their bodies, by Hindus who felt they could do what they wanted to the minorities of the country, as they had been emboldened to do since Partition.

Once the blasts were over and life resumed normalcy, Shahzad fixated again on the lack of a baby. He continued to frequent priests and quacks and to hemorrhage money, attempting to change the unchangeable outcome with tests, powders, and pills. As he spent and spent, Sabeena recalled something else that the family doctor had told them: "You will spend *lakhs*"—hundreds of thousands of rupees—"and nothing at all will happen."

And yet Shahzad showed no signs of stopping. In fact, Sabeena thought it was as if her husband had become *bimar*, as if he was not well, suffering from some disease without a cure. The word *bimari* meant a physical illness, but Sabeena used it to describe Shahzad's mental unrest, which had begun to seem almost physical. Her husband had always had a nervous demeanor, but now he seemed anxious all the time—as if he was anticipating a disaster she could not see. People in the community spoke of him in a certain way, always with the same subtext: *There's Shahzad, the mad one, the silly one, the one whose pants are too big and who sweats through his clothes*. It was as if they were speaking of his father.

Sabeena did not care what other people said. But she was growing more worried about her husband. Once, just being with her had made him happy. Now it seemed like nothing she did could calm him down. He had also become obsessive about washing his hands, often staying in the bathroom so long people had to bang on the door to get in.

And he had started seeing an alternative doctor, a *hakim*, who practiced extreme methods. Once, he told Shahzad to go buy sweet *paan* from a corner shop, tie the tobacco's *betel* leaf around his penis, and start a fire on the leaf to produce heat there. After this, the *hakim* promised him, "You'll get a child very soon. In two, three months." Shahzad followed his instruction, though it stung and burned. Months passed after the *betel* leaf experiment and still a child did not come. Shahzad stopped seeing the *hakim*, and moved on to an *unani* healer for his homemade powders and oils. Sabeena feared what expensive, harebrained scheme was next.

And then it came: adoption.

Shahzad got the idea after tracking down his childhood friend Atif, who had come out of hiding and gone back to karate after his wife's father had given up and accepted the marriage. When Shahzad told his friend of his sterility problem, Atif's answer was simple: "Just adopt." Shahzad did not think adoption would go over well with his father. But Atif had a bold, persuasive way of speaking, and Shahzad convinced himself it would be easy.

He asked his other friends about adoption. He had a Christian friend whose wife couldn't get pregnant and chose to adopt. His friend told him it cost an exorbitant three *lakhs* but that the child's parents never came back to bother them, which Shahzad worried would happen. "Is it *pakaa* that no one will bother you?" Shahzad asked. *"Pakaa,"* his friend said.

Shahzad broached the subject of adoption with his mother, who seemed open to the idea, at least at first. But then his father, who rarely spoke to the rest of the family, let alone involved himself in their lives, reemerged with a firm opinion.

No, came the answer, through Shahzad's mother. *Not in my home. No outsiders allowed.* The one time Shahzad had brought a friend home for lunch, his father demanded the friend leave and sulked for days afterward at the imposition.

But Shahzad thought a child might be different. A child could never be an outsider, at least in his mind. When Shahzad brought up the subject with Sabeena, he was surprised to find his wife agreed with his father. "An adopted child is an outsider," she said.

"But how can this be?" Shahzad asked.

"You can adopt as a Muslim, but you cannot give him your name," said Sabeena. She was sure on this point, which she had learned from her father. It was an old rule, interpreted from the Quran, which said that an adopted child was not equivalent to a biological one and should not take an adopted father's name. "In the eyes of God it's not your child," Sabeena said.

Over the coming decade, fewer priests in their community would enforce this rule on naming and adoption. And fewer people in their community would follow it. But in 1998, even in cities, priests were still being taught the most conservative interpretation of the Quran.

And Sabeena showed Shahzad the passage, incontrovertible evidence, there in verses 4 and 5, sura 33. "Nor has He made your adopted sons your sons. Such is [only] your [manner of] speech by your mouths," the passage read. "Call them by [the names of] their fathers: that is juster in the sight of Allah."

Shahzad wanted to be a good Muslim. But he couldn't believe what he read. He couldn't believe that God would prevent a couple from adopting a child in need. Even the Prophet Muhammad had adopted a son. And Atif, the Muslim he respected most, had been the one to suggest it. Shahzad wondered, in some back part of his brain, if Sabeena and the Quran both were wrong. If that were the case, he knew, he'd do whatever it took to get a child.

A SUITABLE MATCH

Ashok and Parvati, 2009 to 2013

> *"What can I do for you? I smiled.*
> *A smile is such a detached thing . . .*
> *I want your photo . . .*
> *Sure. Just arrange my limbs and tell*
> *Me when . . ."*
>
> —Kamala Das, "The Testing of the Sirens"

Parvati was on the overnight train home when Joseph first spoke to her. She was a shy-seeming student with nerdish glasses, a heart-shaped face, and thick hair that had a habit of becoming unruly. She also didn't socialize much at her university, so when Joseph approached her, she was surprised.

"Hi," he said, smiling, as friendly as if they knew each other well. Parvati barely recognized him from school. She appraised his brushy mustache, dark complexion, and glasses that were thicker than hers. She told herself she didn't find him attractive. She did not know then that he was a Christian; if she had, she might have been even more dismissive. While there were many Christian boys down south—almost more than anywhere else in the country—they were still in the minority, and not meant for Hindu Brahmin girls like her.

She and Joseph talked about their break, and then he retired to his train car. But the next morning he was back. "Let's take an auto together when we get back to school," he said, his voice earnest, and Parvati found herself nodding yes.

Over her break at home in Trivandrum, a green and leafy city at the southernmost tip of the country, Parvati did not think of Joseph.

Home was a sprawling compound filled with all kinds of trees—jackfruit, plantain, teak, mango, and coconut. Her mother used the coconuts to make curries. Home was shuttlecock and roller-skating with her older sister, who was her closest friend. Home was visits with her father, a devout Hindu Brahmin, to quiet, clean temples surrounded by even more trees.

But after they returned to graduate school in Chennai, a city on the coast of the Bay of Bengal, about five hours by train from Trivandrum, Parvati agreed to meet Joseph for coffee. Somehow he seemed more decent than the other boys at school. Or maybe it was that closemouthed smile he wore, suggesting he knew something she didn't. They planned to meet in the university canteen, where the South Indian filter coffee was rich and thick.

Parvati had a difficult time talking to the other students at IIT Chennai, one of nearly two dozen institutes of technology for the best and brightest in the country. It wasn't because she was unintelligent, or haughty, or shy. It was because of what she lost at the end of college, which she could not forget.

The first loss was her best friend, who was short and bubbly with buckteeth and big, shining eyes—Parvati's physical opposite. During their senior year, her friend had grown jealous of Parvati's relationship with a Jacobite Christian boy at school. On the last day of college, she had called Parvati a "cheat" in front of everyone, accusing her of betraying their friendship for a boy. "I know you're not the kind of girl who would marry a Christian guy," she said. They hadn't spoken since.

The second loss involved the boy. When the Jacobite Christian told Parvati he wanted to marry her, Parvati had said no. She had always known she couldn't marry him. She was a Hindu and a Brahmin, and Hindu Brahmins didn't marry Christians—at least not Hindu Brahmins from Trivandrum, a small and conservative city. Her parents might disown her if she did. Still, she thought they'd remain friends. But after she turned down his marriage proposal, he had also stopped speaking to her.

At coffee now with Joseph in the university canteen, the conversation turned to religion. Parvati's parents had always told her: "It's a privilege to be a Brahmin, because it's top class." Brahmins were first. Brahmins were pure. Brahmins were the most educated and intelligent. It was said that this idea came from the Vedas, because in the ancient Hindu scriptures the Brahmins were the priestly class. But the Vedas could be twisted all kinds of ways to suit all kinds of purposes. Parvati had repeated that Brahmins were superior, or something like it, and now Joseph challenged her: "It's not good to have this kind of opinion," he said. "You should not judge someone based on this, just because he's not a Brahmin."

Parvati's thoughts flashed to her father, who was a devoted Brahmin. Every week he met with other members of the community to chant the *Vishnu sahasranamam*—all one thousand names of Lord Vishnu—which took a half hour to complete. It was considered one of the most holy and powerful *stotras*. The ancient warrior Bhishma, from the *Mahabharata*, the epic story that taught man how to live, had said this chant could transcend sorrow. It was said it could unlock the universe. Though it was a chant available to any Hindu, the temple priests were mostly Brahmins, and some believed this made the caste superior.

But what Joseph said now made sense. It was a flaw, for example, that Brahmins thought so highly of themselves. She remembered how in college an outside professor had once come in to grade papers and failed every student in the class. Parvati's father, tall and imposing, had marched into the principal's office to complain. When he came home, he told Parvati the papers were graded unfairly because the professor was "scheduled caste." Parvati knew what *scheduled caste* meant—that, according to the constitution, there were officially disadvantaged groups, including the *dalits*, or "untouchables," and the *adivasis*, India's tribal people. That many government jobs and seats in schools were reserved for them. She understood in a vague way that these people had been neglected, exploited, or worse. She also knew that many Brahmins disliked the idea of such reservations, because they believed the scheduled castes were stealing their jobs. Her father was no different.

"That's why he did this, for revenge," he told Parvati. Parvati held a different point of view. Even if the professor had failed the students as some kind of reprisal, her father had not considered the man's motivation. She thought that to mistreat lower castes over time, and, when they responded in anger, point fingers, was not the right approach at all.

Parvati realized that she had always found Brahmins lacking. Maybe she even had when it came to boys. She had chosen the Jacobite Christian boy over many Hindu Brahmin suitors, because no one else had seemed as mature or intelligent. She told Joseph she'd think about what he said.

The next time they met for coffee, Parvati told Joseph, "What you said about Brahmins is right."

Parvati still didn't know Joseph well, but she saw that he had the power to change her views. He spoke persuasively but was not pushy, always using reason to make his points. And in every conversation, he came across as more perceptive and knowledgeable than the other boys at school. She wanted to spend more time with him. But he was leaving soon for a nine-month research project in Germany to study the applications of inorganic chemistry, which impressed her.

The day before Joseph flew out, they had coffee one last time in the canteen. Parvati told him about her college relationship with the Jacobite Christian boy, who had believed that he could marry her. And Joseph told Parvati about a prior relationship with a Hindu Brahmin girl. He said her parents had initially agreed to

a marriage with Joseph but later changed their minds. He said that
he still loved her.

᭟᭟᭟᭟᭟

Ever since coming to Mumbai, Ashok had been thinking about
girls. He was twenty-eight and had never kissed a girl, but now he
lived in Mumbai, the most permissive of cities. Mumbai, home of
Bollywood romance, dance-bar girls, and lovers' points along the
sea. He had never been to a dance bar, but he'd heard of the girls
who used to twirl in *saris* for piles of rupees until dance bars were
banned in the city, and many of the girls went into prostitution instead. Still, there was talk of the bars reopening. And sex scenes in
films were now getting past the censors—scenes that made it clear
what transpired. This would never have happened when he was a
boy. He sometimes walked past the lovers' points along the ocean,
where couples sat and French-kissed on the rocks, and didn't seem
to care who saw them. To Ashok, Mumbai seemed like a place
where he could be young and loose and free.

Ashok's background wasn't his problem with girls. He came from
a good middle-class family and had received a good education. He
also didn't think it was about his appearance. He was tall (medium
height, depending on who measured), lanky (some would say pencil
thin), and had pale skin (*theek hai*, maybe it was almost wheatish,
but pale sounded better). He had big cheeks and soft brown eyes and
round glasses that worked their way down his nose. He wore his
jet-black hair slicked over to one side and collared shirts that were
often wrinkled. People said he looked younger than he was.

And, though he was a Tamil Brahmin, born a Hindu Brahmin
and (partly) bred in the state of Tamil Nadu, he spoke with an unusual, almost British accent, one that girls seemed to like. It was an
accent acquired from his father, who had the same odd way of speaking, and whose own father had been a postmaster in British India.

The British had only left India sixty years ago, and evidence of their influence remained everywhere—in the schools and infrastructure, the common law and penal code, their liquor and language. It was fashionable to speak with a bit of a British affectation. The accent had always helped Ashok get jobs. But though it also attracted girls, a conversation was where it always ended.

Ashok had been exposed to all kinds of girls, thanks to his father's itinerant lifestyle and career choices, which mostly involved teaching English or selling English-language tapes. The first girl Ashok had a crush on, another Brahmin, was in a Protestant school down south in Tenkasi. Ashok used to stare at her during class until she complained and the principal reprimanded him and several other boys. Then there were the girls in Trivandrum, the highly literate town of coconut trees where his father brought them next. In Trivandrum, some of the girls were bold, sitting alongside the boys in campus protests for local politicians. Others came from small towns and were quiet in class, their goal only stable jobs in the government. But Ashok paid little attention to any of these girls, because this was around the time he discovered books. He would often cut class just to sit and read alone in the university library, which smelled romantically of withered books and damp plaster.

Mostly, Ashok remembered the *firangi* girls, who came later, also in Trivandrum, and whom his father would recruit off of beach resorts to do voice-overs for documentaries. Afterward, these foreigners—Brits, Jews, and many Americans, a second wave after the initial Peace Corps arrivals—would come to Ashok's house for authentic Indian food. Ashok's mother would cook up *sambar* and *rasam*, made with sweet-and-sour tamarind, along with cabbage, spinach, beans, and *papadums*. The *firangis* loved the *papadums* best, which were crunchy and smelled pungently of mustard seeds and *daniya*. After they finished eating, Ashok's father would play Tamil and classical Carnatic music and expound at length on Indian history, literature, and music. Sometimes, these *firangi* girls would stay for weeks after they finished their voice-overs, preening for his father. *Firangi*, depending on which local language you used, could mean either "foreigner" or "a double-edged sword."

From a young age, Ashok saw that his father was handsome and brilliant and a true polymath. For long hours, he would tutor his sons on a variety of subjects, but most often on English idioms, using flash cards. An Anglophile, like many of his generation, and his own father's generation (even Gandhi and Nehru, fathers of the nation, had been English-schooled), Ashok's father told his son that English was the path to success. Though Ashok did not grow up with the British, he could see for himself that this was true. He saw it in the call centers and tech jobs and multinationals popping up across the country, all of which required English. But though Ashok sometimes impressed the *firangi* girls with his English idioms—*A penny for your thoughts? I don't want to beat around the bush here*—he was never able to kiss any of them.

In the big cities there had also been girls, but Ashok had been too absorbed in his work to try courting them. He had been focused on becoming a man with a steady paycheck—a man unlike his father. Ashok secured his first job in Bangalore at a business process outsourcing firm, which were proliferating across India, and then as an English-language journalist and editor. This second gig paid less but lasted longer. Eventually, he moved to a publication in Mumbai, where he found a decent job and a decent apartment in a more-than-decent suburb of the city. On the side, he worked on a novel that he dreamed would be a bestseller one day. Still, he couldn't get a girlfriend. It should have been easy in Mumbai, where the girls were assertive and provocative and oozed sex appeal. They were nothing like the girls down south. But somehow they didn't seem interested in Ashok.

Finally, a friend set him up on a date with a small-framed Gujarati girl. To his surprise, it went well, and for the second date he brought her flowers. They were yellow marigolds, because his friend had told him not to buy red, and definitely not red roses. Red was a sign you were in love. When he presented the girl with the flowers, he could tell she was surprised but pleased. But he was also anxious, hoping she wouldn't expect the date to lead to something more. Like many boys of his age and background, he had no idea what that would be.

On the first date, the Gujarati girl told him about her family—how her brother beat her, and how she didn't have a father to intervene. On the second date, over coffee by the sea, they talked more and then went back to Ashok's apartment. There, she asked Ashok if he would dance with her and taught him salsa. It was the first time Ashok ever held a girl. When they stopped dancing, he knew he was supposed to kiss her. But if he kissed her, he reasoned, he might have to marry her—especially if his family found out. And if he married her, he'd have to be with her forever. Ashok sat her down on the couch.

"See, I might not be the right guy for you," he said. The words came out in a rush. "I am from a traditional family, a Tam Brahm family, and I see myself not settling down in Bombay. I might be in Chennai. I'm not really up for dating now. I'm having second thoughts . . . And I'm new to the whole thing."

The Gujarati girl began to cry.

After she was gone, Ashok's mind ran. *Who would give a bunch of flowers to a girl, take salsa lessons from her, and then that very same night break up with her?*

I'm freaked out.

I should call my father.

ভভভভভ

Not long after Joseph left for Germany, Parvati walked into a hostel on campus and found a cluster of people sitting in strained silence.

After a minute, someone spoke. "You know this guy?" *Joseph*. "His friend passed away."

Which friend?

It was the Brahmin girl, the girl he had wanted to marry. The girl he still loved.

After the girl's parents rejected Joseph's proposal, they started showing her to other boys. She had been keeping Joseph updated about the progress—what boys were coming, and how she felt about the arranged marriage—but then she stopped speaking to Joseph altogether. Joseph assumed she had fallen in love with one of the suitors, and that was why she didn't call or answer the phone. But she had been in the ICU, sick with a heart disease he never knew she had.

When Parvati called Joseph, he was crying.

"It's okay, we're all there to support you," Parvati said, unsure what else to say.

For a week or two afterward, Parvati didn't talk to Joseph, thinking she should give him space. But then they spoke again and started e-mailing and Gchatting. As they did, Parvati found her sympathy turned into affection. Soon, they were talking all the time. Later, Parvati worked up the nerve to ask him for a photo of the Brahmin girl and saw that she was not the kind of girl you noticed in a crowd. But she had very long, beautiful hair.

Over the nine months Joseph was in Germany, he and Parvati spoke often. Sometimes, he told Parvati what he learned from living in a Western country. "Don't stare when people are hugging or kissing. It's a natural thing," he told her. "It is not common in India, but in the West people do it." A common joke: *In India it's okay to piss in public but not to kiss.* Or, from a *firangi*'s Internet list about annoying things in India: #1: *Why do you keep staring at me?*

Still, Gandhi, father of the nation, founder of the *swadeshi* movement to boycott foreign goods, might have been unhappy to see how Westernized India had become. The influence wasn't limited to the British. Now, there were American chains like KFC and McDonald's, girls pairing Italian jeans with traditional *kurtas*, and creamy peanut butter and flavored potato chips edging out *masala channa* on the shelves. The middle class and rich were going West to study and to marry. Bollywood songs had the overlay of hip-hop. Though both Hindi and English were the official languages, it was English that in many ways had taken precedence; most educated, moneyed people in cities were at least bilingual. And, despite the complaints of right-wing parties, couples were celebrating Valentine's Day. Local politicians warned that couples would soon hug and kiss on the street, just as they did in Joseph's Germany.

Sometimes, Joseph told Parvati about how well his experiments were progressing abroad, and Parvati would feel dejected. She was not doing well at IIT Chennai, where the engineering classes seemed deliberately complex and confusing and where she was one of the only girls. The campus, a six-hundred-acre forested area filled with banyan trees and crisscrossed by wide promenades, was a lonely place without friends. Though about eight thousand students attended the school, the grounds sometimes seemed more populated by animals, including antelopes, deer, rabbits, and snakes. Some days, Parvati encountered only a wily troop of monkeys on her way to class.

As the semester progressed, Parvati found herself sleeping all the time. She had never taken great care with her appearance or worn makeup; she was pretty and didn't need to. But she now took even less time and care. She went to class in wrinkled *kurtas*, often in a dull saffron color. She stopped trying to tame her thick hair and let it go frizzy and didn't bother to clean the smudged lenses of her glasses. She kept thinking that if she had chosen her master's degree on her own, she would have never chosen engineering. She would have chosen art.

In college, Parvati had made a number of elaborate line drawings of Hindu gods and goddesses, which the teachers and other students all admired. Once, she had spent seven hours sketching a dancer of Kathakali, a style of dance known for its intricate costumes and exaggerated facial expressions, and people told her it was a masterpiece. But when Parvati's father had discovered the line drawings, he told his daughter they were a silly hobby and to throw them all away. "Why are you wasting your time?" he asked. Even Parvati's sister, who usually took Parvati's side, agreed. "Oh, so this is the big thing you've been up to?" she said.

Engineer, doctor, lawyer—these were the acceptable occupations for the wealthy and the middle class. They were stable and paid good salaries. They kept you out of poverty, which about a third of the country was still in. Indian aunties could often be heard muttering to an aspiring young artist in the family: *"Arts? Arts lekar kya karoge?"* "Whatever will you do with the arts?" Parvati's father, a prominent engineer, had always expected his daughter would follow his path. But Parvati kept drawing.

Now, Parvati told Joseph how much she wanted to quit IIT Chennai and study art instead. It didn't help that her sister had just gotten married. Her sister, who had always been her best friend, but would now have her own family. "Just hang on," Joseph told her. He was coming back to Chennai soon.

When Joseph returned from Germany, he looked different from how Parvati remembered him. He had shaved off his mustache. His clothes were more Western. And he possessed a new, *firangi* style of confidence. Many of his views had changed. He also returned laden with gifts for the other students in his hostel. For Parvati, he brought a Japanese fan with a Michelangelo painting printed on it. Michelangelo, who had been both an artist and an engineer.

❧❧❧❧❧

Ever since he could remember, Ashok had assumed he'd have an arranged marriage. It remained the most common form of marriage in the country. Studies varied widely but found between 60 and 90 percent of unions in India were arranged. Ashok told himself that even the British did it for centuries. An arranged marriage offered a set path and security. There might be more love marriages now, but people said these were behind the rise in divorces. To him, a love marriage seemed inherently uncertain and bound to come with expectations he'd never meet. His father had other ideas.

"I thought YOU might find a girl on your OWN," his father told him, in his oddly punctuated English, where the emphasis was always on the wrong word. "And spare ME the trouble." Ashok's father and mother's marriage had been a love marriage. They'd married despite the disapproval of her family. They reasoned that if they had had a love marriage back then, surely Ashok could find a girl in today's Mumbai.

But as the years passed and Ashok approached thirty, he still hadn't found a girl. He had gone on few dates since the disastrous date with the Gujarati girl, the yellow marigolds left behind wilting in his apartment. And so his father and mother intervened. They put up a profile for Ashok on BharatMatrimony.com, which boasted of having "millions of brides." They hawked him under the section on the site for Tamil Brahmins, called "Iyer grooms." *Iyer* came from a word meaning "respectable" or "noble." *Better.* Being labeled a Tam Brahm and Iyer implied that you were educated and conservative. It meant that you were pious and pure. In marriage, Ashok's father reminded him, it was essential to claim the privileged caste.

This was the way it had always been, or had always seemed to be. Brahmins first, others below, and *dalits* so low as not to be included in the hierarchy. Caste divisions were said to have originated in ancient India's four main specialized professions, with priests at the top, then warriors, traders, and lowly laborers below. These divisions were only further encouraged and solidified under colonial rule, with the British urging Brahmins like Ashok's family to see themselves as superior.

Ashok found the assumptions associated with Brahmins misleading. He was not that conservative; he had eaten meat and drunk alcohol before. At times, he felt like a pseudo-intellectual, talking with confidence about subjects he did not understand. This was what many Indian journalists did, that and adding their own *masala* to stories. None of that went into the profile.

Instead, Ashok's parents checked the box for "upper middle class," though "middle class" would have better described them, with all the money Ashok's father had lost over the years. "Lower class" wasn't an option. They did not provide a number for Ashok's salary, which was nowhere near that of a doctor, engineer, or lawyer, and would hurt his chances. And then they screened girls using their own parameters: she should be Tam Brahm, at least three years younger, beautiful, vegetarian, a nondrinker and nonsmoker. They preferred that she be educated yet conservative, a tricky balance to strike. And, of course, her horoscope must match his own.

"She's YOUNG, she's not bad-looking, she has a JOB, but making slightly less than what my SON is making," said Ashok's father, scrolling down a girl's profile on the matrimony site. "THAT will mean Ashok has the upper HAND."

For a man who had lived abroad, had many foreign friends, and spoke like a Brit, Ashok's father still went about the arranged marriage business with the gusto of any desperate Indian father. It was as if he had forgotten he wanted Ashok to find a girl on his own.

After a year had passed and they still hadn't found a match, Ashok's father began to worry. "Ashok," he said, "let's find a girl who is maybe NOT from a small town, who won't MIND marrying someone older."

What he meant was it was time to widen the search.

But Ashok was surprised to find that he was picky. At first, a lot of girls reached out to his profile, and he said no for the slightest of reasons. If a girl weighed more than him—which was easy, since he had not even the hint of muscle—he said no. Or if she was wearing glasses, no, even though he also wore specs. Big nose: no, no, no. He knew he was being shallow. They'd reach out, and he would reply: "You know, I'm focusing on my work of fiction, I might not be ready for marriage right now."

"Ashok, just say YES to the girl we throw up in FRONT of you," his father said, accusing him of setting a bad example for his unmarried cousins. But Ashok couldn't just say yes to any girl.

In Mumbai, Ashok tried hard to find a wife on his own. After the Gujarati girl, he went to a speed-dating event hosted by the Bombay Expats club and bought an expensive blue collared shirt for the occasion. The girls were foreign, fascinating, and beautiful—everything the girls on BharatMatrimony.com weren't. But he found himself telling them all the same boring spiel: "I want to be a writer. I work as a journalist. I stay in Bandra." Next.

None of the foreign girls followed up with him.

On the matrimony site, Ashok began to try harder. He found a few girls he liked, Indian girls who seemed worldly and cosmopolitan. He blamed that preference on his father, who had always made it seem like India was too small for them. As a child, Ashok had watched Remington Steele, Agatha Christie, and Sherlock Holmes on television. At his father's urging, he had read Shakespeare and Shaw, and then moved on to the Americans: Roth, Hemingway, and Bellow. Bellow, who once wrote: "All a man has to do to get a woman is to say he's a writer. It's an aphrodisiac." When he was younger, getting a beautiful wife had looked easy.

One girl Ashok liked on the site was a Tam Brahm professor in South Africa. He liked that she spoke and wrote well, and in English. But it turned out she wasn't interested in Ashok and didn't care that he was writing a novel. Over e-mail, she wrote that men raised in India were domineering and did not want women to work. She said they placed demands on their wives to be home with their children or relatives. While Indian men wanted Westernized girl-friends, in the end they wanted traditional Indian wives. Ashok tried to tell her he wasn't that kind of man. He wanted a girl who worked and spoke her mind. But she soon stopped responding, and he saw she'd only talked to him to please her parents.

Ashok also realized he wanted the other trappings of the char-acters on American TV shows, such as girls who wore lipstick or high heels. Indian girls did not often wear lipstick or heels. He felt duped by the mismatch of what he had expected and what was possible.

New profiles were put up on Bharat Matrimony all the time.

"My daughter is a confident, independent girl . . ." "My sister is very talented she is so sweet also . . ." "Am a jovial, helpful and humourous person with traditional views in life . . ."

For each profile, there was a pile of data to review. Each applicant had answered more than a dozen questions, which might have been insulting if every Indian boy and girl hadn't been asked the same questions since birth. *Willing to marry from other communities or only the Brahmin Iyer community? Body type slim or heavy? Complexion very fair, fair, wheatish, wheatish brown, or dark? Physical status normal or physically challenged? Monthly income? Veg or non-veg? Joint or nuclear family? Star and moon sign? Have Dosham?* And it went on.

Ashok was glad he didn't have to check the box for "Have Dosham." A person with *mangal dosha* had a bad astrological combi-nation, with the planet Mars in an inauspicious spot. A person with *mangal dosha* was such bad luck it was believed they could cause the early death of a spouse. And if Ashok had *mangal dosha*, it would be almost impossible to find him a spouse.

At the end of every profile, there was also a section to "express yourself," in which people talked about how "well-settled" their siblings were, how "homely" their daughter was, or how "humble" they'd be as a bride. *"Origin of 'humble,'"* his father might say, quizzing him and his brothers on note cards, from the *Oxford Dictionary of English*: *Middle English: from Old French, from Latin* humilis *"low, lowly," from* humus *"ground."*

Ashok felt turned off by the whole exercise.

"I need a break, *Appa*. For at least a month."

Ashok had quit his job at the magazine without having a new one, which he hadn't told his father. He couldn't; his father would be apoplectic. Ashok had left to work on his novel, which he never had enough time to focus on, and because the effort of constantly looking at girls was rattling him.

"Can we stop this for a year?" Ashok asked.

"No," his father said. He could have a break, but a short one. "After a little while, we are back AGAIN on the HUNT."

On the hunt, a metaphor for a man's quest for a woman, his father might say as he flipped over the card.

Ashok hung up the phone.

❦❦❦❦❦❦

It was the beginning of the third year of her four-year master's program at IIT Chennai, and Parvati planned to drop out. She told this to Joseph as they sat at the university's Café Coffee Day, drinking the expensive, bitter coffee that wasn't as good as the canteen's.

"I'm glad your work is coming to an end. You've done all your experiments," said Parvati. "But I am hopeless. I am at the same place I was. I might just quit."

Joseph listened to her and then said, in his careful way, "No, I see us graduating together." It was a simple statement, and Parvati laughed when he said it. But after he did, Parvati knew they would.

And after this, Joseph began helping Parvati with her lab work. He went through her presentations with her point by point. Classes soon began to seem easier. Parvati started sleeping less and wearing better *kurtas*. She even looked forward to the lab, because Joseph was always there. They would work separately, and then he'd ping her online, saying, "Wanna come for coffee?" "Wanna come for tea?" They'd do this throughout the day: lab, coffee, lab, tea. And then they'd study together in the lab until late. Sometimes, Parvati's parents would call at night and ask where she was, and she'd lie and say she was in her hostel getting ready for bed. She had never really lied to her parents before.

Soon, Parvati and Joseph also began taking long walks across campus, meandering under the banyan trees with their aerial roots and wide leaves glossy from rain. On their walks, they talked about books, and Joseph urged her to read more widely. At first, they both read the same biographies of historical figures, but after a little while, Parvati moved on to fiction. She picked up Arundhati Roy's *The God of Small Things*, which was said to be banned at home in Kerala, because it featured an affair between an upper-class Christian woman and a caste-less "untouchable" man. In it, Roy wrote of the unspoken "love laws" that dictated "who should be loved, and how." Laws that demanded that differences in caste, class, or religion keep two lovers apart. After reading it, Parvati began to wonder why Indian society banned people from loving who they chose because of how they were born.

Parvati also found Kamala Das, a fierce confessional writer who wrote plainly and without guilt. Kamala Das was a Hindu turned Muslim, a rarity in the country, and she was from Kerala, Parvati's home state. Parvati started with her autobiography, which chronicled the tumult of Das's inner life, the trials of her marriage, and her sexual and literary awakening. Das wrote fearlessly about taboo subjects and Hindu gods. In one poem, she recounted the famous story of the time Lord Krishna lay down on the riverbank with his lover, the milkmaid Radha. In Kamala Das's telling, Radha "felt dead," and when Krishna asked if she minded his kisses, Radha thought, "No, not at all . . . What is / It to the corpse if the maggots nip?"

It seemed Kamala Das was not afraid to write anything. She didn't care what her parents or husband thought, or that her writing was called "histrionics."

Reading her, Parvati felt for the first time that she could think as she liked about men, family, love, sex, and religion. If famous women—even Kamala Das, even Radha—had thought that way, why couldn't she?

You don't have to just live the way your parents have told you, Parvati thought, and was surprised at her own defiance.

Parvati had rebelled some as a teenager. Her grandmother, a staunch Hindu Brahmin who led her life governed by strict param-eters, had always maintained that women on their periods were un-touchable. The old Hindu rule was rooted in science, supposedly—a woman's foul smell, the toxins in her blood, the simple fact that blood turned from red to black. Women on their periods could not enter the kitchen or go near the *pooja* stand. In Parvati's house, they also couldn't sit on the cloth seats in their living room; Parvati's grandmother always made this very clear. In the old suppression of women, women sometimes led the suppressing. But when Parvati and her sister had their periods, they sometimes wouldn't tell their grandmother and sit brazenly in all those places anyway. Or they would tell her, and wait for her fury to come, and then run away, giggling.

This, though—this was not the same. This had bigger conse-quences. Now, Parvati and Joseph were taking walks so often that other students at their university began to talk. One girl told Par-vati, "People think that you are seeing each other."

Unsettled, Parvati said to Joseph, "I don't want this. I don't want people to think this."

"Is this a reason to not hang out anymore?" he said, and she could tell he was upset. "Are you really going to care?"

As always, he was right, and Parvati began ignoring the comments and whispers.

Several weeks later, Joseph suggested they venture off campus. They took a rickshaw with a group of friends to a showroom to go shopping. Parvati and Joseph both ended up near the cash counter. She looked at Joseph, and he looked back at her, and they held each other's gaze for a long time. Parvati was wearing a maroon-colored *kurta* and a white *dupatta*—details she would always remember, as if it were a still from a film. It seemed like Joseph wanted to tell her something. But then he lowered his eyes and they all piled in a rickshaw and headed back to school.

They did not talk much about religion, because they didn't want to fight. But one day, on the pretense of running an errand, Joseph got Parvati on the bus, only to tell her he was taking her to San Thome Basilica. She knew he expected her to get off or say she needed her parents' or sister's permission. San Thome Basilica was not close. But she surprised him. "Let's go," she said, and felt a little thrill in her chest.

When they arrived, morning mass had just ended. Parvati stared up at the walls and paintings in wonder. She had never been in a church before. "This is one of the most important churches, because Saint Thomas is buried here," Joseph told her. "There are only three churches in the world where a church is built over a saint. For Christians, this is a very huge thing."

He did not mention that San Thome Basilica was also built over the place where Hindus said a temple to Shiva once stood. Portuguese Catholics had apparently demolished it. But many holy places had changed hands like this, from Christians to Hindus, or Hindus to Muslims, and back again. And there had never been the same animosity between Christians and Hindus as Hindus and Muslims had.

After that day at St. Tom's, they ventured beyond campus all over the city. Joseph had always been up for adventures, and now Parvati was too. Chennai was a sprawling city, known for its long stretches of white sandy beaches, packed Carnatic music halls, and ancient temples with fantastic backstories. At one Chennai temple, a man's vision was healed miraculously. Another temple brought a man's daughter back from the dead, or so it was said. At a third, it was common knowledge that Lord Shiva had once appeared. Soon, Joseph and Parvati were taking day trips outside the city, including to Kanchipuram, famous for its silk *saris* and old Hindu temples. On these trips, Joseph sometimes talked of how much he admired Hindu chants or Carnatic music, especially songs that featured the *mridangam*, a double-headed drum. But they did not talk more seriously about Hinduism or Parvati's beliefs. She was certain they'd stop talking if they did.

Sometimes, though, they discussed with admiration the marriages they'd heard about between Hindus and Christians, or Hindus and Muslims, which were taking place more often in the city, despite the consequences. After one such engagement in Mumbai, the parents held a mock funeral for their daughter. The girl married the boy anyway. These people often had simple ceremonies, as if making the point that they did not need the pageantry and only wanted to make their love official. Their weddings were not at all like the lavish, many-thousand-guest weddings common among Hindu couples, which seemed designed to conceal any problems between the boy and girl with pomp and circumstance.

On the one-year anniversary of the Brahmin girl's death, Joseph told Parvati, "I don't want to be alone tonight." And so they stayed up late in the lab, until everyone else had gone home. In the lab, Joseph began to cry, and Parvati hugged him. He smelled powerfully of his Axe cologne, a smell Parvati would always remember. She leaned in and gave him a kiss on the cheek; she would not kiss him on the mouth. *A kiss just for comfort,* she thought. *The first kiss I am saving for my husband.*

After that, they began to text more regularly, starting as soon as they woke up and ending just before bed. Joseph had always gotten up early, and Parvati got up late, but soon they began waking up at the same time. The texts themselves were often just a simple Good morning, or Good night, but it was how they measured their days. One night, Parvati forgot to text Joseph and fell asleep. The next morning, Joseph was furious, a side of him Parvati had not seen before.

"You have to promise to text me every night before you go to bed," he said.

Parvati promised, though part of her wanted to refuse. It felt as if he were trying to control her. But Parvati also thought she understood. They had not named their relationship, and so they were becoming very anxious with each other.

Soon, though, they began texting about how they felt, putting voice to what those long walks and e-mails and conversations over coffee and in the lab added up to.

Did you think that you would have ever fallen in love with me? Parvati texted Joseph, half joking, half hoping to provoke a real answer.

If your parents did not have any problem with this, he wrote back cautiously, I would have seriously considered you as my partner.

Parvati called him. She wanted him to say the three words, though she knew she shouldn't. She longed to hear them, savor them.

In the Hindi film *Dil To Pagal Hai,* which came out when Parvati was a child, when she first started watching Bollywood films, a line of dialogue went: "Have you ever . . . even for a day . . . even for a moment . . . loved me?"

"Yes, I think I love you," Joseph said, finally, into the phone. In the movies, lovers often overcame the objections of their parents. Parvati knew real life wasn't the same way.

"I love you too," said Parvati, though she knew this was the path to trouble.

ღღღღღ

Ashok got a new job and a promotion. He was relieved but mourned the long expanse of days he'd had to concentrate on his novel, which followed a dysfunctional married couple, who—the husband too ambitious, the wife too shallow—face a string of bad luck. It had a complex narrative, with interlocking story lines; he did not know where all the ideas in it had come from. Now, he could only work on it on weekends and at night.

Sometimes, people in the newsroom made good fodder for the book. He based a female character on a buxom journalist he knew. She was a lot like the American girls he saw on TV, but he was also certain he could not have pulled off her sex appeal without the real woman in mind.

The job and the promotion also meant it was time for marriage, which he knew, though he tried to push away the thought. He had a job and a steady income. There was no excuse left. *I'm ready for it. I'm game,* he told himself, like a *mantra*, as if saying it would make it true.

Ashok's father responded to his son's renewed interest with excitement, inundating him with girls' profiles, all of them Hindu, Tamil Brahmin, and Iyer. There was never a Christian or a Muslim in the mix, because, as his father explained again, distinctions of caste and religion were essential in marriage. Ashok might like to think this was changing in the country, but his father told him he was wrong.

Sometimes, Ashok wondered why he was so shy with girls. He wondered why, when others chose to go out, he stayed at home with his books. Perhaps it was in his nature. He had been shy and bookish from the start. But he also wondered if it had a little to do with the episodes that came before.

The first time was in Chennai, when he was about eight or nine years old. His dad had run a company that produced English-language tapes and employed many local men. A *chai-wallah* there used to dote on Ashok, taking him out of the office to buy him little treats. On one of these excursions, he tried to touch Ashok in places he shouldn't. He took Ashok out a second time, and again he did it. After the second time, Ashok told his father. His father shouted at the man, who was never seen in the company building again.

It happened again in Trivandrum, when Ashok was almost eighteen. He had gone alone to see an American movie called *Boys Don't Cry* at a seedy movie theater. It occurred to Ashok that he shouldn't have gone to see that kind of movie there. A man sat down beside him and after a little while slipped his hand between Ashok's legs. Ashok waited, unmoving, praying it wouldn't go further, and then took the five-minute intermission as an opportunity to run. The man shadowed Ashok as he ran into the bathroom and tried to follow him once he left it. After he lost the man in the crowd, Ashok took a new seat in the darkened theater. That night, feeling his sense of order and calm shaken, he buried himself in a book.

Ashok had not yet learned about sex. But he knew men were not supposed to touch him that way. When he grew up, a government study would find that one in two Indian children—boys and girls both—had been sexually abused. But this was much later, and Ashok had mostly forgotten about the incidents by then. And yet still he could not talk to girls. He just wanted to be at home with his books and his writing. Any day, he'd prefer to be with Martin Amis, who wrote that fiction was "the only way to redeem the formlessness of life." Fiction made him feel safe.

Ashok decided to give up on the marriage search. He remembered
when he was younger, watching scenes in Tamil and Bollywood
movies, which had made marriage seem simple and light. The Tamil
hero would touch the girl's arm, and the girl would say, in a hokey
sound effect, *"haaa-aaan,"* and the studio audience would laugh. Or
the Bollywood hero would dance and sing to her in exotic locales,
like Fiji, Switzerland, or Morocco. Now, it was obvious marriage
was nothing like that—that it was instead a complicated and heavy
affair. Though Ashok was no longer picky, it seemed harder than
ever to find a match.

But then, a profile had come along: a girl named Nada who
lived in Bangalore, who was Tam Brahm and worked for a British
company. In her photos she was good-looking, with an easy smile,
prominent nose, and fair skin, almost like a *firangi*. She and Ashok
connected over the website and later talked on the phone. A visit to
Bangalore was scheduled. A visit to meet her parents was scheduled. When there was a match, the process moved forward quickly.

Before he flew to Bangalore, Nada told Ashok, without a hint
of embarrassment: "When you come down to see me, I might have
pimples."

"That's okay," Ashok said. No superficiality was going to stop
him now.

But when he came down to see her, her skin was clear, and she
told him she had paid for a miracle treatment, along with other
information Ashok found too private to share with a stranger. As
they sat at the local Café Coffee Day, she told Ashok how much she
liked to steal. "I mean stealing small stuff, like when you check in
and out of a hotel. From the lobby, things that would escape notice," she said. She told him she did it for fun. When they went out

to eat, she grabbed a toffee from the host stand of a restaurant and whispered to Ashok that she'd stolen it. "You can't really steal things if they are free," Ashok said dryly. He tried to focus on how Nada had appeared when he first saw her, driving up on her scooter in a Western-style top and capri pants.

Later, they went to Cubbon Park, which was so green in contrast to Bangalore's pollution that it was called the "lungs of the city." Sitting under the thickets of trees, Ashok tried to ask her about books, but she did not read. They had little to say to each other, and Nada played with her phone. Ashok's eyes were drawn to the cheap, clunky jewelry on her arms. His thoughts about her weren't very charitable, but he was determined to press on.

Ashok and Nada got engaged on a rainy day in August, in a big hall attached to a three-story house, which seemed to Ashok like a mansion. His parents had rented it from a landlord they knew. Before the big day, Ashok had met Nada's father, with whom he found he got along better than his daughter. The two talked of Tamil poetry. *It's going so well between the two of us,* Ashok thought, and wished Nada was as intelligent or well-read. After this, Ashok had kissed Nada in his apartment in Mumbai, and it was a decent kiss, not sloppy or clumsy. But then she had begun talking again.

As the engagement date approached, both of them tried to pretend they felt something, sending sappy notes over Gchat.

Nada: Just 4 more days ☺ . . . Are you tired? Because you've been running through my mind all day.

Ashok: can never be tired of you. But yeah, generally, I am.

Nada: love you sooooooooooooooo much

Ashok: Love u 2 bits

Nada: 2 bits?????????

Ashok: It's an expression.

Even the sappy notes didn't work.

A day or two before the engagement, Nada sent Ashok an e-mail, and he was surprised to find she was as reluctant to get married. "I see no great chemistry between us," she wrote. "Do you want to take it forward?"

Ashok wrote a long e-mail in reply, insisting they could make it work. He worried this was his last chance to get married, and if this didn't work out, he'd die alone. It didn't matter if their connection was a stretch. He couldn't afford to let her go.

"I have a feeling that everything will be alright," he wrote. "Our crazy frequencies match. Our involvement in our families . . . The occasional trespass (eating non-veg or getting a tattoo), all these are what I think will make us a rare couple in an otherwise humdrum Brahmanical clan . . . As you rightfully said that not everything is going to be perfect in a relationship."

Some one hundred people came for the engagement party, including most of Ashok's close relatives and family friends. There was a three-course meal, with *puri* and *bhaji* and *subzi*, and afterward, chai, coffee, and sweets. There was no meat or alcohol, since the purity of the Vedas had to be maintained, along with the reputation of a Tam Brahm's piety. Ashok's family brought Nada expensive silverware and fine clothes. The priest spoke, Carnatic music played, and a date was fixed for the wedding. Through all of it, Ashok felt in a daze. In total, his father had spent a mind-numbing forty thousand rupees on the ceremony.

When it was all over, Ashok panicked. *Oh my god,* he thought. *This is not the girl. And my dad has just spent a lot of money.*

As the wedding date grew closer—only a few months away—he was of two minds: marry her and save his father's name, or call the wedding off and pretend it never happened. Ashok decided to honor his father. He would marry her. He had to.

The following month, Ashok and Nada broke up over the phone.

Nada initiated it, saying she had feelings for an ex-boyfriend, a boy who was not a Tam Brahm and whom she had met on her own. But first she had gotten philosophical with him. "Hey, Ashok," she said. "You touch your heart, ask yourself this question if you want to get married to me, and tell me how you feel about it . . . I feel we are not connected. And if we get married despite this we might end up fighting a lot and getting divorced within a year."

The word *divorce* hit Ashok. *I don't want to get divorced. I don't want to fight,* he thought. A marriage was supposed to last seven lifetimes, and divorce was to be avoided at all costs. Once he heard the word *divorce*, he knew their engagement was over.

When Nada told her father, the man fell off the cot he slept on, broke his arm, and dislocated his shoulder.

Ashok dreaded telling his father. But Ashok's father already knew, because Nada's father had written him a terse e-mail that said the marriage was called off, with "mutual incompatibility . . . the reason for the cancellation."

Once, after another failed match on Bharat Matrimony, Ashok's father had shouted at him: "Ashok, you're just a WASTED guy, you can't FIND a girl."

This time, his father did not shout. Instead, he flew to Mumbai to comfort his son, fearful of the effect the broken engagement might have on him. He knew boys did *pagal* things over failed engagements: they castrated themselves, jumped in front of moving trains, and hanged themselves from trees. And so the entire time Ashok's father was in Mumbai, he kept spouting encouragement: "You DON'T have to feel bad for yourself. Things will work OUT for you." And: "Don't worry, Ashok. You will find a GIRL. It's just a GIRL you're looking for, not the Holy GRAIL. The right GIRL will come along." And, the one that discouraged Ashok most of all: "You're NOT doing badly enough yourself. You have a JOB and a studio a-PART-ment."

What a joke. Ashok thought he might die alone in his apartment with his stacks of books and unfinished novel.

But after Nada, he began to write. He had written before, but not like this. Before, his sentences had been funny, optimistic, even blithe. His novel had hung together through its show-offy quality, verbal loops and hoops, and mimicry of great writers he'd read. Now he wrote to get through the fog. Soon, the families in his novel became more dysfunctional, the language more honest, and themes existential. Ashok felt an urgency to write in a way that he hadn't before. There was a mismatch in the tone of the novel from beginning to end, but Ashok did not care. Life was just as uneven.

♥♥♥♥♥

Parvati didn't know how it was possible, but she had almost reached the end of the master's degree. The last year had been far different from the other three, because it had been filled with Joseph. They worked together, drank cups and cups of milky *chai* and South Indian filter coffee, and, after that first kiss on the anniversary of his ex-girlfriend's death, surreptitiously made out in the lab after the other students went home. They never went further than kissing, though sometimes Parvati wanted to. This was why she never let their day trips turn into overnights. On campus, where boys and girls weren't allowed in each other's dorm rooms, it was impossible for things to get out of hand. And so Parvati and Joseph took long, leisurely walks across campus, often pausing under the school's ancient banyan tree. It was a tree so old that no one could identify the original roots, which had long ago disappeared into the ground.

And they went into the city, where they ate crispy *sada dosa* and went shopping, and Parvati spent money on herself for the first time. She even bought a designer handbag, a lavish purchase her father would never permit. Like many fathers, he railed against the increasing consumerism in the country—how young people did not save and spent more than they earned on new gadgets, cheap clothing, and afternoons at the mall, like the young people in the West did.

When Parvati and Joseph took day trips, they often rode buses to faraway places, such as Pondicherry, the French-settled city by the sea. Around this time, they also watched the movie *Up* together. When the montage played of Carl and Ellie's relationship—first marriage, then a house, then dreams of babies and travel, and, best of all, growing old together—Joseph said this was how their life would be.

Before school ended, they wanted to have one last excursion: to watch the sun rise over a Chennai beach. It wasn't something Parvati could experience in Trivandrum, or Joseph in his hometown, because both cities were on the western side of the country.

They stayed up all night in the lab, and very early in the morning, Parvati, Joseph, and another friend took a rickshaw to the beach. Joseph wore his Western jeans rolled up at the bottom, while Parvati wore a golden *kurti* the color of the morning sun. As the sun rose, they marveled at the array of hues in the sky and sea. As the light spread, it was infectious. They took goofy pictures: of Parvati pretending to hold the sun in her hand, their friend trying to swallow it, and Joseph jokingly pushing Parvati into the ocean. They played barefoot in the surf until the sun rose all the way. And they shared *chai* and *idlis*, and Parvati wrote her name in big, looping letters in the sand, then photographed it to remember.

After college ended, Parvati was offered a job with an international auto company in Bangalore, which was just an hour plane ride west of Chennai but felt nothing like the wooded campus at school. Many international auto companies were opening up plants and offices in Bangalore, the country's tech and business hub. Meanwhile, Joseph planned, as he always had, to go back to Germany, where he would earn his PhD in a small university town. They talked of Parvati moving there to join him later, maybe after a year or two. They talked of all the things they would do in Germany together, though Parvati didn't know if they were being serious or playing pretend. Whenever Joseph brought up marriage, Parvati told him she wasn't sure. She knew her parents would never agree. Perhaps they would even disown her. Some parents went so far as to kill their daughters for marrying the wrong boy, though Parvati knew her parents were not capable of that. Perhaps she could convince them—her sister first, then her mother, and finally her father, who had always distrusted other religions—that a Hindu Brahmin–Catholic union could be decent and good. But this, she knew, was wishful thinking.

At times, Joseph grew angry that Parvati seemed unwilling to fight her parents to get married. But in the end they always let the conversation move on.

On the last day they had together in Chennai, they visited a Hindu temple in the oldest part of the city, and then Joseph took Parvati to the station. As she climbed inside the train, he stowed her luggage by her seat. "Good-bye," he said. They were surrounded by hundreds of other travelers and knew they could not kiss or hug. Instead they shook hands, like strangers.

There were a lot of famous train farewells in the Bollywood films Parvati had grown up on. In *Dilwale Dulhania Le Jayenge*, by far the most famous of these, both the boy and girl end up getting on the train.

Joseph promised to come visit her in Bangalore before leaving, but this felt to Parvati like the end.

"Good-bye," Parvati said, and as the train pulled away without him, she steeled herself not to cry.

❧❧❧❧❧

On day one in Bangalore, Parvati felt overwhelmed. She had moved into paying guest accommodations with nine other working women, all of whom seemed unfriendly. Her rent was expensive, and she had no Internet or phone connection; her SIM card from Chennai did not work. It was easy to remedy these problems in the city, but she had never lived on her own.

But then Joseph had come to visit before he left for Germany, and together they bought spices and utensils for the apartment. She started work at the auto company, where she liked her colleagues and the work. And she became close with one of the girls in the house, a girl who was sassy and silly and reminded her of Rachel from the American TV show *Friends*, whose reruns everyone her age seemed to watch. After a few months, Bangalore began to feel like home.

Joseph had decided to spend three months teaching down south in Kottayam before he left for Germany, and during that time he often called Parvati. *Too often,* Parvati began to think, because any time she went out in Bangalore he'd ask where she was going. At night, when she was trying to sleep, he said he needed to talk. And when she had lunch with colleagues or friends he now grew suspicious, saying, "You just had coffee, why are you having lunch now?"

Her parents already called every day to ask what she was doing. She did not need Joseph to do the same thing. *It's like since I moved to Bangalore I have no breathing room,* she thought, and was surprised at how frustrated she felt.

Joseph came to visit her a second time before leaving the country, and this time he tried to show his affection in public, the way couples in Germany did. Though they were in India, he argued that Bangalore was a progressive city—India's Silicon Valley—and that few people knew them there. He would take her hand, sit very close beside her, or put his arm around her in a rickshaw—gestures Parvati began to hate. *It's like he's trying to control me,* she thought, just as at IIT Chennai, when he made her promise to text him every night before bed.

Now, if she made a new friend, Joseph objected, saying she

shouldn't see the same person more than once. Parvati told him she wouldn't but felt confused. Joseph had always been right about everything, but now she had the feeling he was wrong.

To her surprise, she began to count down the days until he left for Germany, when he'd have to sign on to Skype to ask her where she was or where she'd been.

From Germany, Joseph pestered her to tell her parents about him and ask their permission to marry. Sometimes, Parvati thought she should. She missed him. Over the phone, he would talk of all the places they had gone together in Chennai. He would tell her of all the places they could go in Europe. He'd send her pictures from Germany—of a shop bursting with color, or of Germans eating giant wheels of cheese. Parvati knew that young people with means often went abroad to work or study, and she thought maybe she should too.

But when Parvati applied for a position in Germany and didn't hear back, she felt not disappointment but relief. The balance of power had shifted since IIT Chennai. The farther away Joseph was, the more he clung to her. And she didn't like how it felt.

Still, the next time she went home to Trivandrum, Parvati decided to tell her mother about him. She couldn't keep the secret anymore. Her mother didn't even know Joseph existed, though her sister did. Sometimes, Parvati's sister supported the affair, and other times she told Parvati she was foolish. At home in Trivandrum, as Parvati waited for the right moment, Joseph texted her: Did you tell?

Finally, as she packed her bags to go back to Bangalore, Parvati began, her voice tentative, "*Amma*, I'm in love with this guy." She told her mother he was a Christian, and that she didn't know what to do. "What do you think?"

Her mother's fury was immediate and fierce. This was the moment when all the years of careful rearing fell apart. "If you don't want to marry this guy, why did you even bother to tell me this story?" she said. "You could just have finished it yourself."

Stunned, Parvati began to cry.

"Never talk about this again. Don't tell Dad. Let's just close this topic. And forget him," her mother said.

With that, the conversation was over.

The next day, at the airport, Parvati's mother looked at her daughter and smiled. Perhaps it was a kind smile, but more likely it was coercive, meant to ensure her daughter did as she was told. "Just remember what I said. Close the chapter," she said.

Parvati relayed her mother's response to Joseph, who told her she hadn't approached it the right way. He said he was going to e-mail her dad and ask for her hand in marriage.

Parvati knew her father would say no. Like many Hindu Brahmin fathers, he believed a girl should marry not only within her religion but also her caste and *gotra*. And she knew that Joseph asking for her hand by e-mail would infuriate him. Her father was a man who valued propriety, and this was not the way it was done.

Back at work in Bangalore, Parvati couldn't focus. She sat at her desk at the auto company and grew fidgety, and then listless, waiting for her father's call to come.

But it was her mother who telephoned, and told Parvati that her father was not angry but heartbroken. She said he was so upset to receive the e-mail that he could not speak. She said she was worried about how sad he was and how many feelings were in his mind. This was not what Parvati had expected.

Parvati's sister called next, and said that their father had also called her. "It's better not to tell you what he said," she told Parvati. "Horrible stuff. Anti-Christian."

Parvati didn't want to know.

Later, her father would tell her that he'd responded to Joseph, that he had written a clear, unequivocal: "No."

But Joseph said he never got a reply and wasn't giving up.

Parvati would never know who was telling the truth.

After the e-mail from Joseph, Parvati's father vowed to marry her off without delay, and her parents set up a BharatMatrimony .com profile. Though Parvati was Malayali—born, proudly, in the state of Kerala—her family's roots were in Tamil Nadu, and so her profile was placed in the section for Tamil Brahmins. Her father quickly identified a suitable Tam Brahm boy. He was in the United States, working for a big tech corporation, and, luckily or unluckily for Parvati—whom the astrologer warned had terrible stars—the US boy's horoscope matched her own.

Not long after, Parvati's bosses in Bangalore told her they were sending her to Sweden for work. When Parvati told her father, he jumped at the opportunity. He said the Tam Brahm boy from the United States could meet her in Sweden, and that he would come along. Parvati called Joseph to tell him about the impending meeting, and Joseph said he'd also meet her there; it was just a short flight from Germany.

It's like a bad movie, Parvati thought, but she didn't find it funny. She ran through terrifying scenarios of what might happen when she, her father, the US boy, and Joseph all converged in the same city.

As the date of the Sweden trip approached, Parvati felt a loosening on her hold with reality. She began to cry while she walked to work, talk to herself, and write long diary entries and burn them. If one of the girls at the guesthouse spoke to her, Parvati would say darkly, "There is no point in this life." But when a colleague spoke to her at work, she tried to give a calm response. She tried to smile. She thought she should try to hold it together at work, at least.

In these months, Parvati also remembered old South Indian movies she had watched as a child—how the men were always in charge, and any woman who raised her voice was a villain. Watching these, she had believed men should do the thinking for her.

Now she pleaded with her father: "Please don't do this to me. Give me some more time." But Parvati's father told her that time had run out.

She did not go to Sweden. Instead, she told the auto company she'd quit if they sent her there. She told herself she'd have a breakdown. She told her father the trip had been canceled. And she asked her sister's husband to call Joseph and tell him to leave her alone. She stopped answering his calls, texts, chats, and e-mails. At night, she began to see snakes in her dreams. When she was a child, Parvati had been terrified of snakes. When she dreamed of them now, she also felt afraid.

The astrologer had said there was a problem with her stars, and with one star in particular, a star associated with snakes. Now, her parents were doing *poojas* to the snake gods to offset it. They said the *poojas* would help ward off sin, which was in danger of attaching to Parvati. If it did, the astrologer said she might never marry or have children. And she was supposed to marry the US boy.

But Parvati hated talking to him. She found him naive and overly nice, in a way that suggested he was being fake. In spite of his job at a big tech corporation abroad, which many girls would admire, she didn't find him at all impressive. When they Skyped with her sister and brother-in-law beside her, she spent the entire call making funny faces he couldn't see. Parvati's parents assured her that marriage came first and affection would follow. But Parvati didn't think she could ever love the US boy. When she thought of Joseph, she missed his smell the most.

"I don't want to proceed," she told her sister, who told her father, who shouted into the phone. Parvati was twenty-five now and should already be married. Her father and the US boy's parents fixed a date in late November for their engagement.

On one call, Parvati told the US boy about Joseph. In telling him, she thought it might dissuade him from marriage, since it was shameful for a bride to have had a past affair. And if it did not dissuade him and she was forced to marry him, at least the truth would be out in the open. But she made him promise not to tell his parents, because she knew how it would be received. He swore to her he wouldn't.

Soon after that, Parvati's parents went to visit the boy's family, who also lived in Trivandrum, to plan the engagement. When they arrived, his family presented a long laundry list of demands for the ceremony. They insisted that Parvati's parents go to a specific store in Bangalore to get her *saris* stitched. They maintained that they be the ones to place the garlands during the ceremony, which was tradition anyway. They asked that Parvati's parents book rooms for all their family members at the pricey Taj Mahal Hotel. And at the end of the conversation they said, "You should understand we're doing a favor for your daughter."

Joseph. Their son had told them. They knew.

When Parvati's mother relayed this to Parvati afterward, she also told her that her father had acquiesced to everything.

Later, the US boy called Parvati, and Parvati confronted him. "Did you tell about my past to your parents?"

"No, I didn't say."

"Why are you lying to me?"

He grew angry and said, "I don't know what to tell you."

Parvati despised the US boy then. "I'm getting a headache just talking to you," she said, and hung up.

The next day, the US boy defriended Parvati on Facebook, and his relatives did the same. Parvati's father called her and told her, sadly, "I think we are just calling this off."

Parvati was quiet on the phone. But afterward she rounded up her friends and colleagues to celebrate. And that night, she slept more deeply than she had in months. For the first time, no one would be calling her from Germany or the United States or Trivandrum. In

Hindu philosophy, there were three forms of consciousness: waking, dreaming, and deep, dreamless sleep. After deep, dreamless sleep came *turiya*, pure consciousness, which was for the liberated. That night, for the first time, she felt free.

❦❦❦❦❦❦

Ashok found Mallika on the site himself. She was about his age, lived in Mumbai, was a big deal in Bollywood—or so her profile implied—and was into art and books and movies. She seemed street-smart and sure of herself, qualities Ashok thought he lacked. She seemed nothing like Nada, with her cheap bangles and stolen toffees, except that of course she was also Hindu and a Tamil Brahmin.

They met first at a restaurant along the sea, and later at her apartment. In her flat, Ashok was startled to find a three-level cabinet packed with liquor: foreign whiskey, Smirnoff vodka, and Kingfisher beer. He knew most of the country did not drink, and especially not Tam Brahms; the Vedas said intoxicants destroyed the intellect. Mallika offered Ashok milk tea instead and invited him back a second time to drink flavored vodka. The process rolled forward, and he went to New Delhi to meet Mallika's mother. Over tea at the rotary club, her mother told him, "You're the kind of guy my daughter has been wanting to marry. She has seen a lot of guys who are silly and immature. But you seem all sorted." She seemed not to care that he was past thirty.

As Ashok got to know Mallika, he thought that perhaps the guys she had dated had been more than just immature or silly. She was sure-footed and street-smart, this was true. But she also seemed distrusting, as if there had been an incident in her past, and now every man could be a potential offender. When Mallika came to visit Ashok at his apartment, he offered her a mango, but she said she didn't like mangos, and so he offered her an apple, which she accepted only after watching him take a bite. When he kissed her and tried to go further, she recoiled, as if he were going to hit her. But then she had surprised Ashok and invited him to live with her—just for two weeks—as a kind of experiment before marriage. Ashok couldn't help telling his father.

"As long as it's in Bom-BAY, where we don't have any FAMILY members, go accumulate as many experiences as you WANT to," his father said. "But DON'T breathe a word about it to ANY-one." Emboldened, Ashok bought a packet of condoms and packed them along with his book, Salman Rushdie's *Joseph Anton*, and his flute, which he had taken up to play classical Tamil music. Mallika was a Bombay girl, and Ashok assumed Bombay girls were up for sex before marriage.

But when he arrived, Mallika told him, "Okay, Ashok, although I've agreed to live with you, there will be no sex." After this pronouncement, she went into her room and closed the door, leaving Ashok to sleep on a mattress in the hall.

For two weeks, Ashok lived at Mallika's, during which time they hardly spoke to each other. When he tried to initiate conversation, she ignored him or spoke in short sentences. Soon, he didn't care to keep trying. Instead he practiced his flute and read *Joseph Anton*, which chronicled Rushdie's life under *fatwa* and the dissolution of not one but three of his four marriages.

"I'm not feeling quite right about this," Ashok said on the last day, after entering Mallika's room. "Do you think this is what we should be doing?"

"Ashok," she said. "When you see me, do you feel like talking to me?"

Oh, thought Ashok, and he steeled himself to talk about the trauma in her past, to listen and unburden her, though he didn't want to. He wanted to go home.

"You have this face about you that is very busy," he said, finally, "not encouraging people to say nice things to you. It's like you have 'fuck off' on your forehead."

"Yeah," she said, and seemed unsurprised. "I guess I have that."

After Ashok moved back to his studio apartment, they spoke just once more on the phone, and that was it. As Ashok finished *Joseph Anton*, Rushdie told him, unhelpfully: "It was always women who did the choosing, and men's place was to be grateful if they were lucky enough to be the chosen ones."

After Mallika, Ashok's parents began to send his profile to divorcées.

♥♥♥♥♥

Joseph was engaged to be married. After Parvati heard the news, she quit her job at the car company in Bangalore and got a job teaching engineering in Trivandrum, where she'd live with her parents.

Before he got engaged, Joseph had sent her a final e-mail, saying he was "waiting for a positive sign" from her, but Parvati hadn't written back. Now she wished she had. He had also sent her a photo of the girl, who stood in a gazebo in the picture, looking sweet and small and innocent. After Parvati saw the photo, she went into her company's conference room and cried. The girl he was marrying was a Christian.

Now, Parvati had a month off before starting her new job in Trivandrum, and she tried her best to distract herself. She spent time with a girl in her Bangalore guesthouse who was loud and funny and loved to gossip. One night, they went out to a movie, and afterward Parvati saw Joseph had called. Later, he called her again.

"The date of my marriage is fixed," he told her. *Fixed*. In that moment, Parvati realized that she had not believed he would go through with it. She had expected the wedding to be called off, and for him to come to Bangalore and take her away as his bride.

"But I've called off my engagement," she said, the words tumbling out. "Is there a way we can be back together?"

He paused, and said, in his cautious way, "I don't think so. I have said yes to this girl and she is a very nice girl." Parvati was silent. He went on: "She was supposed to get engaged to another guy, who turned out to be a drug addict. So her parents are scared, but they've found me okay, and I've given my word. I don't want to break her heart."

If Joseph had given his word, Parvati knew he wouldn't break it. Quietly, she hung up the phone.

Joseph got married in January, after Parvati had moved back to Trivandrum and begun teaching. On the day of his wedding, she went to the charity house with her parents and distributed clothes to the poor. She knew Joseph would have liked that.

Not long after, Parvati picked up the novel *Balyakalasakhi*, or *My Childhood Friend*, which was about two kids who fall in love but whose parents won't let them marry. As the story progresses, the girl gets married off to someone else, but the boy never finds a bride. They live separate lives, grow old, and die.

It was a beautiful book, written in plain and colloquial language by the Malayalam writer Vaikom Muhammad Basheer. As Parvati read it, she felt that the novel became her real life, and that her life became the fiction. After she finished and emerged from the spell of Basheer's writing, she felt a little better about Joseph. *Just because you fall in love with someone doesn't mean you have to marry him,* she thought. *It is not the end of your life.*

It was said that after Basheer wed, he was institutionalized twice for mental illness, for paranoia.

Or perhaps, she thought, *it was better not to marry at all.*

❧❧❧❧❧

The following month, when her sister and brother-in-law sent her the profile, Parvati thought little of it. Her family had been inundating her with online profiles, and she said no to every single one. Girls were being inundated across India, because as the matrimonial ad section in the paper had gotten thinner, the old aunties who did the arranging had learned to navigate the Web. The online marriage market was expected to triple in the next few years. Bharat Matrimony, the site Parvati was on, had recently run an ad in which a girl came home to be told by her mother that a boy was waiting in her bedroom—scandal—only to reveal that a boy's online profile was open on the computer screen. But though Parvati was lonely, the loneliest she had ever been, she wasn't interested in any of the profiles. None of them compared to Joseph.

No, no, no, she thought now, as she sat in her room in Trivandrum, looking at the profile open on her laptop screen. It belonged to another Tamil Brahmin, who, though he had grown up partly in Trivandrum, now lived up in Mumbai. He had a boyish face and a natural look. He looked like an average Tam Brahm—like, in fact, her father. *He is not looking good,* she thought. *I'm never going to say yes to this guy.*

The next day, her father brought her several engineers' profiles, boring men, men who'd ensure her life would be tedious and small. Parvati saw he was going to force a marriage to one of these men soon, and she'd be powerless to stop him. That night, she revisited the profile her sister and brother-in-law had sent.

The boy still looked like her father. She moved on to his stats. From her parents' perspective, a weak prospect. This made her look more closely. Weak point 1: master's in English. (Not an engineer, lawyer, or doctor.) Weak point 2: height, five feet ten. (In Parvati's family, short. She was almost as tall.) Weak point 3: age, thirty-three. (Too old; Parvati was just twenty-six.)

She saw this was the kind of boy who might upset her parents, and felt a flush of excitement at the prospect.

As she scrolled farther down the page, she noticed extra text at the bottom, a personal note he had written for the girl, not her family: "I would give a free hand to my partner, and expect the same from her." She paused. She liked the sound of this. He didn't seem like the kind of boy who would keep tabs on her every movement.

The next day, trying to keep her voice casual, Parvati told her sister and brother-in-law: "This seems to be an okay profile." It was one of the first signs of interest she'd shown. And so the wheels of marriage were set quickly into motion: her brother-in-law informed her father, who, despite Ashok's age and height and occupation, took their horoscopes to an astrologer. Parvati accepted this news passively. She didn't expect the match to move forward. Out of the dozens of boys her parents and sister put before her, there had been few matches, because of her bad stars. And, despite her recurring dreams about snakes, she did not believe any amount of *poojas* to the snake gods would fix that.

Improbably, Parvati and Ashok's stars matched.

ILLUSIONS

Maya and Veer, 2010 to 2014

"Once your lips were rosy, Krishna,
now black as your skin they're tainted . . .
O God! God! Krishna, go away."

—*Jayadeva,* The Gita Govinda

J anu," Veer said. "His name will be Janu."

Janu would be born the year the census was gathered, which would find that the ratio of girls to boys born in the country remained too low. It would find that the number of married people was falling and divorces were rising. And it would tally India's population at 1.2 billion, so that one in six people in the world were Indian now. Janu would be named after Veer's grandfather, who had worked hard all his life and sung old Hindi ballads to Veer as he lay dying. He would also be born the year Maya would meet Subal.

The name *Janu* was derived from the Hindi word *jaan*, which meant "life." Veer thought the name sounded strong, like his own; *Veer* meant "victorious." It was unlike Maya's name, which came from the Sanskrit and had a complex and double meaning, suggesting both "magic" and "illusion." The concept of Maya was tied to the Hindu belief that the whole world was an illusion. Like how the ocean looks blue but isn't—it just looks that way because of how the sea absorbs the sun. The sky looks blue but isn't either. The concept of Maya suggested that the things to which we attach ourselves are like a mirage in the desert. They are beautiful, enchanting, even magical, at first. But in the end they are an illusion. The person who understands this becomes freer and edges closer to the truth of the universe.

Maya loved the meaning of her name, but Veer wanted a name more like his own for the baby. Like most men, Veer was hoping for a boy but didn't say so aloud. Based on the scan, which showed broad palms and feet like his own, Veer was certain they were having a son. It was illegal to learn the baby's gender, because too many girls were still aborted.

The doctors assured Maya her pregnancy would be easier this time around. It had been three years since she married and two since her miscarriage. This time, the tests did not detect ovarian cysts. Still, a few months before the birth, she flew to her parents' house in Hyderabad, which was considered safer, and was tradition.

Janu's due date was in January, not long after Veer's birthday. Veer flew to Hyderabad so that he and Maya could spend the birthday together, as they had years before, when she bought him a ticket with her treasured books and gold bangles. The baby was expected in a couple weeks. After the celebration, Veer planned to fly to Africa for an important work trip that had been postponed after he'd suffered several epileptic attacks. He had managed his epilepsy since childhood, but it sometimes reappeared in adulthood when he worked too hard. He promised Maya he'd be back in time for the delivery. "You won't," she said, getting upset. "Stay. You won't be here for your son's birth."

But at Maya's checkup that day, the ob-gyn said neither of them was going anywhere. "The baby has a very low heart rate," the doctor said. "We have to operate right away."

Instead of the rhythmic, steady *dhakdhak dhakdhak dhakdhak*, 100-plus beats per minute, the baby's heart sounded like a slow, uncertain *dhak . . . dhak . . . dhak*.

"Look, it's my husband's birthday," said Maya. "Can we come back later?" She knew she was being selfish, even reckless, but she couldn't help herself. *I want to have one last quiet day with Veer before the baby is born,* she thought. She wanted them to be able to celebrate the birthday. The doctor grudgingly told them to come back for a sonogram that night.

By the time they returned to the hospital, Maya had begun to feel uncomfortable. When she lay down on the hospital bed, she was wheezing. After they did the sonogram, several nurses ran up to Maya, wheeling a stretcher. "Lie down. We need to operate right now."

"Where is my husband?" asked Maya.

"He is with the doctor. We're taking you there."

The heart rate had gone very low. Normal for babies was over 100. The heart rate on the monitor read 25.

Maya remembers what happened next in fragments: A gown. An oxygen mask. A needle as long as her arm. A strange, sudden pain, way deep in her bones. The doctor yelling: "Don't. Move." They had to insert the needle four times because she kept moving. "Your baby's heart rate is falling by the second." The voice was very far away. The strange pain again and again, followed by a numbness. The first cut of the C-section, and the sensation that she was being unzipped from the inside. "Where is *Kancha*?" she asked. Veer was let in just as the doctor was about to pull out the baby. He didn't watch the operation, because he worried it would have set off his epilepsy.

"What do you want—do you want a boy or a girl?" the doctor asked, as she reached down to lift out the baby. She directed the question to Maya. "I want a girl. But it's a boy," said Maya.

"It's a boy."

The doctor slapped him hard on the behind, and Janu began to cry. He had silky hair just like his father and big, stormy eyes like Maya. He had a good heart rate and a smooth complexion despite the appearance of jaundice. Veer was certain Janu had been born early so that he was there to witness his son's birth. And so they were born on the same day. He already felt a special connection to his son. He thought Janu looked just like him.

Maya was told to stay in the hospital for five days for observation. "Just don't leave me," she begged Veer, though she didn't think he'd leave his new son.

"No, I won't," Veer said, but after a day, or two, or five—they remember this differently—Veer left on his flight, certain that Maya was stable and in good hands at the hospital.

The stability turned out to be fragile for both of them. Maya soon developed postpartum depression. She could feel almost nothing for Janu. She didn't even want to hold him. She begged to be allowed to leave Hyderabad and fly home to Mumbai. At home, she thought she'd go back to normal.

Back in Mumbai, Veer suffered an epileptic fit, and then another. Maya was sure it was because he was overworking himself and she was not there to call him to come home in the evenings. He also skipped meals when she wasn't there to cook.

Maya was supposed to stay at her parents' house for several months, but by March she had returned to Mumbai. After she came home, her depression receded and she found herself wanting to hold Janu all the time. She was certain that she had never loved anyone or anything as deeply as she loved her new son.

Veer's epilepsy also calmed down. He came home early so that he could help get Janu ready for bed, and he left for work later so that he could play with him in the mornings. One day, Veer joked to Janu, "Who do you love more, Mom or Dad? Raise your right hand for Mom, left hand for Dad." Janu raised both tiny hands, and Veer and Maya laughed together.

Early on, Janu slept in a crib. But one night he tried to crawl out of it, and Veer woke up and caught Janu's head in his hand. After that, they stopped using the crib, and Janu slept in the bed instead, nestled between both parents. Many children in the country slept with their parents; it was said this was why Indian men were closer to their mothers than their wives. Veer had slept in bed with his own parents until he was twelve. Some of his happiest memories were of sleeping beside his mother, who had always made him feel safe and calm.

As a child, Veer thought his mother was the most beautiful and perfect woman on Earth. Unlike most parents he knew, she never hired a tutor for him but took his dictations herself every day after school. On top of that, she gave him two hundred rupees' pocket change every week, which most mothers didn't do, and which he didn't think he deserved. He always stowed the rupees in a white box along with coins he'd collected.

She died the night of Prime Minister Rajiv Gandhi's assassination, when Veer was just fifteen. It happened after a long battle with cancer and much suffering, but still he could not accept that it was true. Curfew had been imposed on the city, because Rajiv Gandhi—who took office after his mother Indira's assassination—had been killed by a suicide bomber, and police said it was not safe to go outside. Veer and his family defied curfew and went out to see his mother, who had fallen into a coma, anyway. In the hospital, Veer spoke to his mother as if she were awake. When she was pronounced dead, Veer had an epileptic fit.

And after she died, Veer never opened the white box again. It still contained the last two hundred rupees she had given him. He never collected coins again either. He promised himself he'd never love another woman, a promise he kept until he met the other Maya, his distant cousin of the same *gotra*, who had been kind and warm just like his mother. But then she had also left him.

Now that Janu had been born, Veer began again to think about death.

Or rather, money and death, and whether Maya would have

enough money to take care of Janu if he dropped dead. This was a new kind of worry—not the frantic, acquisitive mode he knew so well but a gnawing concern he'd never felt before. He was also diagnosed with diabetes, which only compounded his fears. And every moment he spent with Janu increased the anxiety.

Veer saw a lot of himself in Janu. Their hair tufted across their foreheads in the same direction. Janu's feet had the same raised arches, and Veer sometimes rubbed them in case they hurt like his own. At night, he sang Janu old Hindi lullabies, and in the morning crooned new Bollywood pop songs as he got him ready for the day. The old songs were poetic, heavy; the new ones were simple and light.

Every day that Janu grew bigger, Veer worried more about money.

For Maya, the year after Janu's birth passed quickly, with no time for such anxieties. Between the baby, the lost sleep, and the housework, she hardly had a free moment to think. And before what seemed like no time it was almost Janu's first birthday, and Veer's thirty-sixth, for which she knew she should do something special. For days, she surfed the Internet in search for the perfect gift.

Her idea was to get them matching T-shirts, customized, but she couldn't find one in Janu's small size. Finally, she came across a personalized clothing website, still in demo mode, that promised to "design anything, any size, anytime."

When she called the number on the site, a man answered in a baritone voice that was calm and steady. Maya already felt better. "Whatever you want, I can make it," he told her. He said his name was Subal. He stayed on the phone with her for a long time, making sure she had what she needed.

Maya called Subal several more times to talk about the order. They also exchanged a few e-mails to ensure the design and product was perfect. Several weeks later, she received the order, just in time for the big day.

At the birthday party, she snapped a photo of Janu and Veer in their new T-shirts and sent it to Subal, so he could see his handi-work. Both grinned goofily in the picture—Veer all teeth and Janu all cheeks, a miniature version of his father.

ღღღღღ

It was around Janu's first birthday that Maya also proposed to Veer that she go to work. Though she was overwhelmed with the baby, she had an idea, long brewing, to open a preschool, and now felt like the right time to do it. She suggested setting up a franchised school, which would be easier. It would have up-front costs but could make them real money in the long term.

Her school would be nothing like the ones she'd attended in Hy-derabad, where the teachers taught in a mechanical fashion, without any nuance or empathy. And where the children often felt unsafe because a teacher or guard tried to touch them. This happened in Hyderabad, and it happened in Mumbai; perhaps it did in every village and city. In her school, she'd make sure no child ever felt that way.

But from where will the money come? Veer thought. Perhaps he could ask his father. He knew that many preschools shut down within just a few years in Mumbai, a crowded market. And yet he also knew most of the schools weren't any good. He had faith Maya could open something better.

"Let's do it," he said.

With the help of a loan from Veer's father, Veer and Maya bought a two-story villa in a nearby suburb heavily populated by young families. They painted the building in soft colors and hung signs with photos of cherubic children's faces out front. Maya hired about a dozen teachers, all female, and a male watchman who was not al-lowed inside the building. They planned for Janu to be one of Maya's first students and expected to turn a profit within three months.

The preschool was not successful in that time. Not even close. After a year, it was still not profitable, because they had not attracted enough students, and Maya had to ask Veer for more money. But she worked harder to advertise, and, after many months, she got her first full class. After that, the new students kept coming. And coming. Word spread about the new preschool that was different from the others, because it was upscale and clean and did not teach by rote. It combined Indian and international teaching concepts, and the teachers sang both English and Hindi nursery rhymes.

Maya also hired teachers for their level of empathy, so that they could tell her how a child was doing and feeling. She wanted teachers who could guess what was happening at home—such as if a child's parents were divorcing or a man in the neighborhood was a sexual predator. As she did paperwork in her office, she loved to listen to the teachers celebrate the children's little triumphs or find creative ways to assuage their fears. When parents waited anxiously outside the fence at the end of the school day, they were greeted by mostly smiling children. The preschool soon became the most trusted in the area. Before long, Maya and Veer broke even.

As the money came in, Veer felt his worries about death subside. *If tomorrow I have to go and say Jai Shri Krishna, good-bye,* he thought, *I won't be disturbed. I will be at peace.*

Maya was grateful for the money Veer had given her to open the business. But she soon saw his help would end there. She had assumed he would want to talk about the preschool with her. But every time she brought up a problem at the school, he told her, "It's your work, Maya." Or "It's not my thing to be involved in at all."

Okay, so he's not interested even in this aspect of mine, she thought. He was only interested in his own work. *Even this school he doesn't want to have a part in.*

Maya realized why he'd agreed to let her open the school. It was not to support her idea. It was to get her off his back. It was so she would not nag him at work. But she wasn't going to let him off that easily.

6 p.m.
"Please come home, *Kancha*."

"I have to work."

"But Janu."

"I have to work."

"I feel lost here. Can you come home by at least eight in the night?"

8:45 p.m.
"Where are you? I have been calling."

"I'm coming," he said. "Soon."

"Please come, *Kancha*. Just come."

10 p.m.
"Where are you? . . . I need to cook. I need to do all these things. There is a baby."

"I can't make it. You have to manage by yourself."

"But I need you."

"Find yourself a maid," he said. "Do what you want to do."

Veer didn't understand why Maya couldn't see he had to work. Sometimes, it felt like she was a flame that needed constant oxygen to keep burning. Once, he had been attracted to her passion, but now he found it suffocating. He wanted to make her happy, but it seemed like no effort was enough.

He had wanted her to work not just for money but so she wasn't idle. *If you are alone, you are a devil's mind,* he thought. *You have nothing to do so you make up stories about people in your own family, in other people's families, and everything is in your head.* He had thought that when she went to work, there would be less drama between them.

At home, Maya wondered how, in the City of Dreams, she could sometimes feel so alone. Veer had recently told her he didn't believe in romance. He'd said he didn't believe in love. For him, he said, there was one language in Mumbai, and that was the language of money. "Shall I buy a dress with rupees on it to get you to love me?" she replied in a fury.

Sometimes, when Veer did not answer her calls all day, and Maya felt especially alone, she played the song "Dil Hoom Hoom Kare," or "My Heart Is Gasping," from the old film *Rudaali*. The song was sung by Lata Mangeshkar, the most beautiful and haunting of the playback singers, over the sounds of flutes and drums. The film was about a *rudaali*, a female professional crier, of which there were many in Rajasthan, where Maya and Veer's families were from. *Rudaalis* cried at the funerals for the people no one would cry for.

In the film, the *rudaali* befriends a woman whose life has been nothing but misfortune. The woman has suffered so much hardship that she can't cry, not even when the *rudaali* tries to teach her. She doesn't cry even when she realizes her lover is gone.

❦❦❦❦❦

As Janu grew, Veer tried to make things better for Maya. He began paying for a full-time maid named Pallavi, a young and able woman from a nearby shanty. Most middle-class families had at least one servant, if not a maid, cook, and driver, and Veer decided they now could afford a maid, who could help cook, and also a driver. In the morning Pallavi made breakfast, cleaned dishes, and washed the clothes. In the afternoons she folded laundry, swept the house, and put out the trash. She had a slender but strong frame, wore flowery but functional *saris*, and kept her hair tied back in a long braid. She was warm and full of energy and good with Janu. She had a laugh like a bell. After she arrived, the house began to run more smoothly.

Like many maids in Mumbai, Pallavi was married to a husband too lazy to find work. Maya tried to help by giving him a job as a security guard at the preschool, but before long he stopped showing up. Pallavi was not surprised. The two women did not tell each other much about their personal lives, but both knew when the other was troubled. Maya noticed it in the food Pallavi made, which was tasty or badly spiced depending on her mood. Pallavi saw it when Maya and Veer fought in the mornings as she moved quietly about the house. On these days, she sometimes made Maya special green tea or folded her clothes extra neatly. And she always tried to distract Janu from the fighting, by picking him up and singing to him. "Pallavi-*ji*," he began calling her, as soon as he learned to talk. Pallavi would laugh at this nickname, a sign of respect for a maid. She spent as much time or more with Janu than with her own children.

One evening, Veer came home with a BlackBerry for Maya, a gift he thought would make her feel less alone.

Maya downloaded BlackBerry Messenger, an app that promised to "keep you connected with friends and family." There was even a little check mark that showed when the person read your message. Maya thought it would make it easier to reach Veer at work. But it also opened up a new world of conversation, with half friends and acquaintances. Among them was the T-shirt maker, Subal.

On Subal's birthday, Maya sent him a message. After that, they began talking regularly. With the messenger app, it was easy to continue the conversation.

At first, they chatted about their days and their work. He asked what she liked and didn't like. Then they began talking about family. As they spoke, Maya found him charming and perceptive and saw that he gave good advice. She began to ask for his guidance on small matters, and then bigger ones, related to her preschool or Janu. After several weeks of messaging, she found herself confiding to Subal how often Veer was away.

Before long Subal also told Maya about his wife, how they'd had a love marriage across religions—he was a Hindu, and she a Catholic—which hadn't been an issue. But he said there were other problems. On Facebook, Maya found a photo of his family: a rotund little boy, a stout little girl, and a wife who was commandingly tall. Maya thought she was unpleasant-looking, with a shrewd smile and a horse-shaped face, though she did not tell this to Subal.

As the weeks passed, Subal also began to ask Maya more personal questions—probing ones she didn't want to answer. She wanted to remain somewhat of a cipher to a man she assumed she'd never meet. But she'd already told him some things she hadn't told her closest female friends or family, whom she couldn't always count on not to judge her.

One day, months after they'd started exchanging texts, Subal implied in a message that Maya was just a typical Indian housewife: a woman who stayed at home and didn't know much about the world. As Maya read his message, she was overcome by a fierce, almost irrational fury. *That bastard,* she thought, and was surprised by her anger at a man she'd never met. *I'm going to show him who I am.*

For the first time, Maya sent Subal a photo of herself. In it, she wore glamorous sunglasses, a pastel pink blouse, and a short navy blue skirt. She stood barefoot in the surf in Goa, a region of white sand beaches and coconut trees. Veer had taken the photo. She sent it just as Subal took off on a plane home to Mumbai after a business trip. She wanted it to be the first message he saw when he landed.

As Subal climbed into a rickshaw outside the airport in Mumbai, he opened the photo. He looked at it, and looked again. *Could this really be the person I've been talking to?* he thought.

She was petite but shapely, and her hair was thick and unruly.

Her skin was nearly as pale as the inside of a dragonfruit. But what struck him were Maya's eyes, which were bright but sad and lined in dark *kajal*. She was a strange mix of the simple beauty of the girl next door with the mysterious glamour of a dance-bar girl.

He typed a message: Should we meet?

Maya read the message. She was twenty-eight. Janu was one and a half. The photos on the wall across from her desk showed him at different ages; over time, Janu's eyes had grown bigger and his hair longer and wavier. There were still henna swirls on the linoleum floor from the Ganesh Chaturthi party. The painting of Krishna and Radha, two lovers on a swing, still hung above the kitchen table.

Maya typed a response, hesitated, and then sent it.

❦❦❦❦❦

On their fifth wedding anniversary, Veer forgot all about it. Or ignored it. Maya had flown from Hyderabad to Mumbai to be home in time to celebrate, but when she arrived, Veer didn't mention the date. All day, he said nothing, until Maya texted him at work: Happy anniversary then.

Do you want to do something? he wrote back.

They made dinner plans, but Veer didn't make it home until ten. When he finally walked in the door, Maya felt something snap in her. *We can no longer ignore the elephant in the room.*

In the weeks that followed, Veer didn't worry much about their colorless anniversary night. But it was all Maya could think about. At home, her thoughts ran. *There's nothing happening here. That formality thing doesn't even exist.* At times her resignation turned to a savage anger. *Fuck this man. I'm not going to bother myself about it anymore.*

Maya and Veer began to fight whenever he was at home. Most days, they fought about banal, insignificant problems, like how warm the *chai* was or why Pallavi hadn't shown up to work. But there were also bigger stressors: problems related to Maya's preschool and Veer's trips to Africa. Fights over how Maya needed more help caring for Janu. The most wounding questions—like why they had not had sex in almost a year, or why Maya made Veer feel like a wayward husband—flowed just under the surface but were not voiced aloud.

Though they fought regularly, they tried not to shout in front of Janu. But Janu, who was almost two, was a precocious child, and it was possible he understood more than they realized. Sometimes, after they had a particularly bad fight, even with lowered voices, Janu would wet or soil his pants.

Finally, Maya confronted Veer over dinner, as he sat eating under the painting of Krishna and Radha ecstatic on the swing. In a quiet, steady voice, she said she wanted a divorce.

"There's nothing between us, no physical relationship, no mental and emotional relationship," she said. "Do you want to move on?"

Maya knew that a divorce could cause her to lose her job, her home, and her reputation. She could even lose Janu; under the Hindu Minority and Guardianship Act, the natural guardian of a child over five was his father. While it was true that Mumbai's unwritten rules for women were changing, she knew women could run into trouble if they overestimated the progress the city had made. More women were asking for divorce, but they never seemed to get the alimony money they were supposed to, and many were still so stigmatized they could not get or keep work. They lost friends. They lost family. They lost their money and property if they were in their husband's name. But Maya decided it was worth the risk.

After she spoke, Veer looked at her evenly, as if they were discussing cold *chai*. And then he said, "Take a year, Maya. Wait it out another year and then see how you feel. If you still feel that way, then you can leave."

The clock with Hindi script ticked behind them. Veer spoke again. "And you can leave Janu with me."

Janu.

His name had the desired effect. Maya got up and began clearing the dishes.

The reasons a Hindu man or woman can ask for divorce are enumerated in the Hindu Marriage Act of 1955: religious conversion or entering a religious order; lack of cohabitation or lack of contact for years or death; an unsound mind or other mental illness; rape, sodomy, or bestiality; leprosy; adultery . . . and, as of an amendment in 1976: cruelty and desertion.

Maya saw that none of these applied to them.

In a year's time, an amendment would be proposed to the Hindu Marriage Act allowing for divorce on the grounds of "irretrievable breakdown of marriage." But it would not pass, because the populist politicians and the religious men would rail against it. They would warn of the breakdown of the Indian marriage, asserting that love marriages led to divorce. They would say that the world had entered the Kali Yuga, the age of vice predicted in the ancient Sanskrit texts. In the Kali Yuga, people sinned and lusted and left religion, lost their *dharma*, and broke their vows without care. They would point to how homosexuality had already been decriminalized, saying that India was being "disrobed" piece by piece by Western culture.

There was no Hindi or Sanskrit word for *divorce*, because it was said even those who predicted the Kali Yuga had not conceived of such a practice.

Veer did not want a divorce, at least not now. But he thought that the big disappointment of marriage was that a husband and wife did not stay friends. He and Maya had had an uncomplicated friendship before marriage. They spoke openly and laughed with ease. They shared their tensions with each other instead of creating new ones.

When he considered their relationship now, he saw it in two lights: the "frank picture" and the "rosy picture." The frank picture was that on the way home from the office, he often had to think about how he could avoid a fight. The frank picture was that their marriage took up so much time that could be spent working, and they laughed far less than they had before.

But there was also the rosy picture: Maya was not like most Indian women. She did not misjudge people based on her own biases. She was not like the women who sat on folding chairs in hallways, gossiping the day away. Instead, she saw straight to the heart of people and their motivations, with an uncanny perceptiveness. She never gave a sugarcoated view. And she was supportive of Veer, even when he didn't deserve it.

Veer also knew that if he were not married, he might go out drinking with his cousin on weeknights and sleep out. He might drive himself into the ground with work, eat poorly, and his epilepsy could get worse. Maya was a reason to come home at the end of the day. Janu was very much a reason to come home at the end of the day. And on many nights, they still made each other laugh. The idea of divorce was unfathomable to him, at least when Maya still depended on him for money. He could not shirk that duty.

But when Veer imagined life in the seaside shack, with a shop on the first floor to keep him busy, he didn't always imagine Maya in it. He didn't even imagine Janu there, who would be almost grown by then. Instead he imagined waking up alone to the sound of waves. He told himself he didn't want to force Maya into his dream.

✿✿✿✿✿

After Veer asked Maya for another year, she thought that maybe she had been mistaken, and that he did care for her after all. But then she found the messages on his phone. Maya remembers that Veer was in the shower, and she was in bed with a fever when she picked up his work cell phone to call a doctor.

A text from the other Maya was on the screen. Disbelieving, Maya began to scroll through Veer's messages. She found many messages from the other Maya, though they seemed to be forwards from Veer's second phone, so they didn't include the original messages he'd sent her. In her messages to him the other Maya called him *"jaanu."*

Jaanu. "Darling." Like the English word: "baby."

Such as: Jaanu, I'm out of balance, I'll call you in a little while.

"What is this?" Maya asked when Veer came out of the shower. She showed him the texts on the phone.

"There's nothing," he said.

"She's calling you 'baby' in the conversation," said Maya. "That's a little unbelievable."

He was quiet.

"You call her right here in front of me."

"I'm not going to do that."

"Call her."

This wasn't the first time. The year after they'd married, Maya had seen call logs that showed Veer was talking to her from the time he left work until the time he got home. Then, Maya had said, "Go ahead and talk to her, but don't hide it from me."

"I'm not talking to her," he'd said, and she let it go.

Now, Maya saw that she'd been foolish. They hadn't been talking as friends, or even as two people who once loved each other. They talked as if they were still intimate. Veer took his phone back, but later Maya sent the other Maya, who she knew was engaged to be married, a message from her own phone. Maya told her that what she was doing was not right.

The message she received back was impudent; the other Maya said she'd never understand what they had.

Maya, furious, replied: Let's do one thing. I'll forward these messages to your fiancé that you sent to my husband. If he understands then I'll understand.

The other Maya did not reply.

Maya showed Veer the message she had gotten from the other Maya, the one that said she'd never understand. "As long as I'm your wife I need to understand what's going on here," said Maya, trying not to panic.

"I think you're overreacting," he said.

To Veer, this was not cheating. He maintained he had only met the other Maya twice in his life. He had never seen her again after she'd ended things, which was many years ago. Yes, they texted now and again. Yes, he still loved her. He still thought of his relationship with her as the most perfect it could have been. But that also meant it was in the past. Their relationship was forever caught in amber. And he was married now.

Eventually, Maya dropped the argument. She did not know what else to do. And she did not text the other Maya's fiancé. *Let at least one marriage be intact,* she thought. But her thoughts about Veer ran like a tape. *Did I force him to marry me? Is he ever going to get out of loving this girl?*

She saw now that the other Maya was the love of his life. And she thought she understood why. Veer valued family above all else, and the other Maya had sacrificed their relationship for her family. The other Maya was the virtuous one, while she, Maya—who had risked her relationship with her father to marry Veer—was immoral. She was like the girl who eloped in the film *Omkara,* who also defied her father. In the film, another character asks: "How can anyone trust a girl who betrays her own father?"

Veer had never trusted her. Never loved her. Never would.

And, if that were the case, then Maya thought she might as well give up *thoda compromise* altogether. She would no longer compromise her ideals, and that meant no longer following the old religious rules, such as not eating meat, not cooking with garlic or onion, or being unclean during her period. She no longer owed him anything.

꘎꘎꘎꘎꘎

A month after Maya asked Veer for a divorce, she had to go for a three-day training course to Powai, where Subal, the T-shirt maker, had his office. After he had asked to meet, Maya put him off for many months. But they kept messaging, moving from talk of their daily lives to deeper, more personal subjects. When Maya mentioned she would be in Powai, Subal offered to pick her up and drop her back home. She hesitated but told herself there was no harm meeting once.

It was Maya who saw Subal first. From the side of the car, at an angle where he could not see her, she saw his brushy mustache and shock of sandy gray hair. *What am I doing here?* she thought. She noticed his thick stomach. *Why can't people just take care of themselves?* She considered turning around. But he was searching the sidewalk for her, and she noticed a brightness in his eyes. Her phone rang.

"Where are you?" he asked.

In Subal's memory, it was raining that day, and Maya was holding an umbrella as she spoke to a friend across the street. She wore a gray T-shirt and jeans. She looked beautiful and young—too young for him. *Could this really be her?* he thought. Maya doesn't remember any rain, or an umbrella, only that she had been talking with her friend. When she climbed in Subal's front seat, she folded her legs underneath her and sat back, trying to act relaxed.

On the ride home to her suburb, which was more than an hour in traffic, Maya and Subal didn't talk much. The conversation wasn't stilted, but it didn't have the easy rhythm of their messages. Subal kept noticing how warm she was in real life. She smelled good, strange; she wore men's cologne.

"This is on your way home, right?" Maya asked.

It wasn't. Subal lived in Thane, which meant he'd have to drive an hour north to drop her off, farther north around the city's sprawling national park, then south to Thane. He'd make a giant loop, covering almost all of northern Mumbai.

When they arrived at her apartment complex, driving coolly past the nosy guard at the gate, Maya said, "Do you want to come upstairs and take a coffee?"

He said he'd just like to come use the bathroom.

Janu was upstairs with Pallavi. When Subal came in, Janu tottered over to him. Maya watched, amazed. Janu was not very friendly with men. Like many Indian mothers, she had taught him not to be. And yet he had welcomed Subal without fear. She went into the kitchen to rummage for something for Subal to take home and brought out chocolates for his children. She noticed how tall he was, almost a foot taller, and how when he spoke it filled the room.

That night, Maya told Veer that a man had driven her from Powai to home, then back to Thane. "Is that guy okay?" said Veer. "And are you?"

When Maya went to Powai for her second day of training, Subal asked if they could meet again so he could show her something. "Okay," Maya said, but thought: *What am I doing?* A married woman did not fraternize with married men, much less allow them to take her places. Subal wanted to show her Chhota Kashmir in Goregaon, a secluded area spread over four thousand acres, with lakes and gardens and paddleboats for two. Chhota Kashmir meant "Little Kashmir," and it did look a little like that beautiful valley region whose beauty was overshadowed by politics and conflict. Maya felt nervous as they walked around. *What does he want from me?*

Finally, she ventured aloud, "Why have you brought me here? Do you want to kiss me?"

"What if I say yes?" Subal said.

Maya felt drawn to him—his low voice, easy smile, and eyes that gleamed when he spoke. But she didn't like this setup: two married people in a clichéd landscape of seclusion, having the kind of cheap conversation that appeared in romance novels. "It will ruin every-thing," she said, her voice flat.

"But I like you more than a friend," he persisted.

"But I am not comfortable," Maya said, and she knew it was time to go home.

The next day, Janu fell sick, and Maya used the excuse not to go to the third day of training in Powai.

❦❦❦❦❦

At night, from the inside of Maya and Veer's apartment, the bass of car stereos could sometimes be heard from the street, pumping out old Hindi ballads and new Bollywood songs. Lately, all the drivers had been playing the soundtrack of *Ishqiya*, and especially the song "Dil Toh Baccha HaiJi," which meant "My Heart Is a Child," and whose instrumentation sounded foreign and hypnotic. Bollywood was always making metaphors about the heart: *My heart is a child. The heart is a madman. This heart is a thug. The heart is like the sea.*

The distant clatter of aging trucks could also be heard from the apartment, because they often ferried goods after the traffic had died down. And there was the unsettling howl of stray dogs that couldn't find enough scraps to eat that day.

Veer could fall asleep to the discordant sounds with Janu curled up in his arms. But Maya often sat awake in the living room, look-ing out at the city.

From her perch on the couch, she could make out a cluster of palm trees, encircled by the dozen buildings in their apartment col-ony. Beyond these lay hundreds of intersecting roads, zigzagging cars, and a ridge of hills off in the distance. But the nearby apart-ment buildings were most interesting, because each one contained some twenty windows in a grid. At night, many of the windows lit up, each window like a tiny play. A full scene was never visible, but Maya could catch glimpses.

People went out, watched TV, and had dinner. Husbands sat at the dinner table with their wives and children. In the windows, the husbands always seemed to come home on time. Maya was reminded of an old adage: *The family that eats together stays together.*

In one window, a child was up late, and her mother seemed to be shushing her, then dragging her across the room to bed. In another, a man sat in his undershirt on the couch, his tubby stomach lit by the glow of a TV screen. In a third, plates were being cleared, though the clatter could not be heard from across the way. Maya could see big TVs in some of the apartments and small ones in others, AC units or open windows, the outline of a washing machine or upturned bucket—each an indicator of a family's wealth.

After an hour or so, the lights would shut off, and the sounds of the city's millions would die down. Sleep was necessary if work was to be done and two-bedroom apartments in the suburbs paid for. A light in one room would dim, and then in the next. Families mostly went to sleep together.

But outside the gates of the apartment colony, Maya knew one woman might still be awake. If she was, she'd be standing in the middle of the rubble-filled lane, dressed in a raggedy red *sari*. It was the same *sari* she wore every day. The madwoman in the lane hardly slept.

On some days, the woman picked petals off a flower and scattered them in the road. On others, she sat listlessly on a big rock. Her hair was always wild and unbrushed, and her cheekbones were sharp. Lately, her hair was cut short, like she had had some kind of infection. Her *sari* was often dirty and crumpled at the edges. She looked as if she hadn't eaten in days. It was said that she once had two big flats and a family nearby but went mad after her husband left her for another woman.

Maya wanted to stay awake longer watching the last of the win-

dow plays, but she was tired. After another light shut off, Maya got up to go to bed. A few pigeons landed on the tin-roof porch, making a gentle *"whoo, whoo"* sound at her. She looked back at them for a moment and then shut off the lights to go join Veer and Janu in bed.

❦❦❦❦❦

It was Subal who suggested The Resort to Maya. He had been there for conferences and meetings before. Maya had been to The Resort once for Veer's birthday. Now, she and Subal met there for breakfast, in December, when the air in the city was cool.

The Resort was more magical than Maya remembered: the whitewashed building standing tall against the clear, blue water of the hotel pool, the palm tree fronds dangling in the soft breeze. Subal listening intently to what she had to say, though he was not pushy. She found herself tracing lines in his hands—life line, head line, heart line—and it did not seem like a cheap romance novel at all.

Afterward, they walked back to the parking lot. In the car, Subal leaned over without warning and tried to give Maya a kiss. Maya moved away, and his lips fell on her neck instead. For a moment, they stayed there, his mustache brushing against her skin.

This is bad, she thought, and if it were an old Hindi film, this would be when the playback singer would start to warble, her voice thin and shrill. *I want to go home. But also it feels so good,* Maya thought. *It has been so long.*

If it were an old Hindi film, there also would be no kiss; it would never make it past the censors. And there was no kiss now.

After a minute, she pulled away, and they drove out of the gates past the twisting banyan trees, back toward Maya's home.

The following month, when Janu turned two and Veer thirty-seven, Maya did not get them anything special. It didn't feel necessary, because Veer had been spoiling Janu with plenty of gifts from abroad: dress shirts from J.Crew, pants from the Gap, sneakers by Nike. He brought them back from work trips to China and Qatar, along with branded clothes for Maya. "Top of the line," he'd say. "Best quality." He enjoyed buying items that would last a long time, especially international brands, which everyone in India wanted. Soon, there were so many new outfits Maya had to pile them in Janu's crib, which had barely been used. The apartment was cluttered with everything Janu.

On the walls were pasted marker drawings he had done in pre-school and posters of *Chhota Bheem*, the kid-aged, Indian version of Superman. In the corners were stuffed animals, toy cars, and rolls of Mickey Mouse and Winnie-the-Pooh stickers. On the TV stand, beside the photo of Maya and Veer in Mussoorie, sat framed photos of Janu at three months, six months, and a year old, with his hair falling into his eyes.

Janu had grown into a bright but naughty child who liked to discard his clothes and run around naked or dress in odd costumes he cobbled together from his closet. He loved disobeying Maya especially when it was time for a bath. He listened more often to his father, who was sterner with him. He had a smooth face and shiny hair just like Veer and big, wistful eyes like Maya. The effect was so charming that people stopped her on the street to ask if he was a child model.

Though Maya hung the letters *J-A-N-U* on the wall for Janu's birthday, she and Veer more often referred to him by his nicknames. They called him *"beta,"* which meant "son," or *"bana,"* a Rajasthani word for "little prince." Veer's favorite nickname was *laddoo*, which was a delicious sweet.

When Maya began letting Subal visit her apartment, Janu was almost always home. Janu accepted this new man in his life without question and got excited when Maya said he was coming over. From the beginning, Subal—who had two school-aged children of his own—helped Maya change Janu's diapers and heat up his steamed milk. As Janu grew older, he played game after game with him and answered his many curious questions.

To her family and friends, Maya began referring to Subal as her "best friend." She introduced him to the teachers at her school. She pinned a picture of her and Subal to her office wall. And she informed Veer when she went out with him. She also encouraged the two men to spend time together, and sometimes they did, even without her.

Veer didn't question Subal's role in his wife's life. *If Maya needs a friend, so be it,* he thought. Perhaps it would take some of the pressure off him. *I should give her space,* he thought, and then didn't think about it anymore.

At first, Maya was surprised Veer didn't question this new relationship. But then she decided it was more proof he did not care about her. She was certain Veer stayed married to her out of duty. Duty to her. Duty to Janu. Duty to some antiquated notion of family. Duty, perhaps, to pursuing the goals of any good Hindu's life— *dharma, artha, kama, moksha. Duty, means, pleasure, freedom.* Through marriage, you fulfilled a moral duty, acquired means, and enjoyed pleasure. And in the end, you died and became free.

She considered no longer seeing Subal. She could stop now, before it turned into something. Before she let the attempted kiss slide into other territory. But if she did, she'd be alone again. And Veer would not come back to her. Over the years, she might go wild with loneliness, like the madwoman in the lane.

No. She'd keep her sanity and spend time with Subal when she pleased. Subal, who was open-minded and charming, with his baritone voice and witty comments and his willingness to discuss philosophy, politics, and religion. Subal, who treated her like a companion in the way Veer had forgotten how to do. She would keep seeing Subal even though he'd begun calling her "baby" in

English, which was maybe as intimate as the Hindi word *jaanu*, or "darling."

And she decided she would expand the preschool as another way of keeping sane. Before long, she recruited a vice principal, Ashni, to help her do it. Ashni was smart and clever and spoke frankly. She had an open face, thick hair she wore pulled back, and a motherly but exotic beauty. She was about Maya's age and had a son the same age as Janu. Maya saw in Ashni a future friend.

The two soon became close, and Maya entrusted most of the preschool's daily tasks to her. In addition, Ashni helped Maya retain teachers, which was often a problem at India's schools. Female teachers often left the job after they got married, facing pressure from a new husband or in-laws. Many of these girls were the first in their family ever to go to work. Economists and sociologists debated why more Indian women weren't entering the workforce or were dropping out, but Maya thought she understood. Despite better jobs for women and more women wanting to work, the opinions of husbands and in-laws had not changed. A woman was needed to run the home, care for her children, and cook for her husband's family. She was still expected to live up to the ideal of *pativratya*—of total devotion to her husband.

Though she knew they wouldn't last long, Maya hired these girls anyway. She wanted to give them a chance to see what the working world was like. When they told her they were quitting, she and Ashni would try to coax them to stay. Sometimes, this would work, but mostly it wouldn't. Even if they left, Maya was proud she had given them several months of employment and freedom.

Veer had far fewer female employees than Maya. There was just a handful at his factory. The rest were all married men. But these men's marriages presented their own problems; his factory manager, for one, was always taking leave to go collect his wife from her parents' house, where she went whenever they had a fight. The lower-level employees at Veer's factory, almost all of whom were local men, had their own marital problems. But Veer was proud of how far he'd come with them. He had set up his factory in a tribal area at a time when no one else in Mumbai would. People warned that the *adivasis*, or tribals, were violent. But Veer had not feared them, and instead had come at Diwali time, given them gifts, and offered jobs. Now, more than a decade later, the tribals had acquired skills and were paid well. Still, there was much for Veer to worry about at the factory. Often, he worried how much rain would come. The amount of rain determined the number of people who'd get sick, which in turn determined how much medicine people would buy, and the amount of aluminum foil needed to package it. When there was a high demand for foil, Veer sometimes didn't come back from the factory for over a week or more, not telling Maya where he'd gone. At home alone, Maya often grew anxious, and then upset or angry.

ভেভেভেভেভে

Ever since she was a child, Maya had visited International Society of Krishna Consciousness temples. Hare Krishna temples, which preached an ecstatic love for Krishna, existed all over the world. In Mumbai, the temple was in Juhu, a tree-lined suburb along the sea. Maya wasn't a Hare Krishna follower, but Krishna remained her favorite god, and she always felt a presence when she visited the temple, which she described as a kind of strong vibration. She often gave offerings and prayed for her preschool to continue to do well.

Soon, Subal began visiting the temple with her. They made it a habit to go together every Friday. Subal wasn't a follower either—he professed himself an atheist—but Maya liked that he was willing to come along.

And soon, Subal changed jobs, joining a financial company in the suburbs, so Maya's house was now on his way to work. A crass saying in Mumbai went: *People fuck based on location, because the traffic in the city is so bad.* She and Subal were not having sex. They hadn't discussed it. But still.

Subal began stopping by Maya's apartment almost daily. He would come up for a cup of coffee or just to talk. Or Maya cooked him her specialty, *rajma chawal*, its rich ginger-garlic smell filling the apartment. Often, he sat on the ground in the kitchen playing with Janu, giving him a playful knuckle on the ear. Maya never worried that Veer would come home while Subal was there, because Veer rarely showed up until after dinner. Or he was away for many days at the factory or weeks in Africa.

When Veer was away, Maya often sent Subal meals packed in *tiffins*. It started after he told her that his wife cooked one meal a day and other than that expected him and the children to eat leftovers. Maya was aghast. She knew how much Subal valued food. *Just look at his stomach,* she thought. Maya also considered good food essential for a happy life. *Why do we earn?* she thought. *For food, for shelter.*

Subal and his wife had been married almost two decades, but he told Maya he hadn't been happy for a long time. Once, he implied to Maya that his wife had a man on the side, someone from college, but didn't say more. Even his family knew his marriage was in trouble; they had for a long time. He said he didn't care if it ended or who knew.

One afternoon when Subal stopped by Maya's apartment, Maya had just gotten a call that Janu was sick at school. It was a call she received regularly. Like his father, and like many children in Mumbai, Janu had an array of health problems caused by the pollution.

Subal was sitting on the living room couch next to the porch, where the honeybee hive had come and gone. Maya sat on the couch opposite his. After she hung up, Subal said that they should have sex. Maya looked at him steadily.

"Boss, I need to pick him up soon," she said.

"As much time as I have, I don't care," Subal said.

The *Bhagavad Gita* was clear on the subject of adultery. A wife who slept with another man destroyed the family. The *Vishnu Purana*, another ancient text, said an adulterer was reborn as "a creeping insect" and "when dead he falls into hell." Manu, an ancient Hindu lawmaker, saved special disdain for the female adulteress: "Through their passion for men, through their mutable temper, through their natural heartlessness, they become disloyal toward their husbands, however carefully they may be guarded in this [world]." The consequences were also worse for a female adulteress: a woman who strayed was to be "censured among men," and in her next life "born in the womb of a jackal" and "tormented by diseases." In the old texts, men sometimes kept multiple partners, but a woman who cheated was past reproach.

It had been so long since Maya had had sex.

And Radha was a cheater. This part was played down in the Krishna-Radha stories, and Maya had not considered it before, but it was true. Radha was a married woman when she had met Krishna, and she was still married when he undressed her on the Yamuna River banks. Of course, Krishna was also a philanderer. He snatched away the clothes of all the milkmaids, which was the source of Radha's anguish. But Krishna was a deity and could do what he pleased. Radha was just an ordinary woman, and her infidelity could not be denied. Or perhaps it did not matter when your lover was a god.

According to the myths, Radha was married to a dark, dull-witted man named Abhimanyu. He was apparently no match for Radha's beauty and intelligence, and he did not recognize her great gifts.

The poet Jayadeva wrote of the moment before Radha and Krishna's lovemaking: "The darkness of night deepens, and with it Krishna's passion . . . There's no point in waiting any longer, innocent girl—now is the moment for the tryst."

His language suggested something had been sullied: Radha's "breast had been scratched, streaked scarlet by his nails," and "her eyes were bloodshot from sleeplessness." Her lipstick "was smudged"; flowers had "fallen from her disheveled hair." Even her skirt "had slipped loose from its golden girding cords."

Centuries later, Krishna and Radha's affair had been reduced to metaphor. Now, the pious people said their passion was an allegory of man's desire to connect with his god. They said that Abhimanyu had never existed.

Maybe. Or maybe Radha was a cheater.

❦❦❦❦❦

Veer noticed that Maya now saw or mentioned Subal every day. Pallavi also noticed it, but Pallavi was a loyal maid, and Maya knew she would not stir up trouble. Many maids in Mumbai kept secrets. And Veer did not tell Maya to stop meeting him. *One thing's simple,* he told himself, with the twisted logic he sometimes employed to make things right between them. *If she wants to have her life her own way, then that's the way. It's her choice, why not.*

Since Maya asked him for a divorce, Veer had adopted a harsher view of marriage. He questioned whether it was a viable institution for the modern age. Perhaps the four goals of life could be achieved without marriage, because marriage only complicated life and friendship. But if you did get married, and stayed married, he thought a husband and wife should try to keep the friendship intact. They shouldn't bring up the past too much. They should try to allow each other to be independent and live their life in the present day. And so he didn't say anything about Subal.

On the subject of cheating, he felt different ways on different days. Or at least he expressed it differently. Sometimes, he said that it was more relevant that a husband and wife be happy. If he didn't know about an affair, then he didn't mind. "It is just normal human nature to want to explore greener pastures," he said. If someone had an affair, that was a subject that should be raised at an appropriate time, when both people felt comfortable addressing it. Some of the old books sanctioned extramarital affairs, including the *Mahabharata*, which taught that life was complicated. The *Mahabharata* also said your *dharma* wasn't always easy to find, and that sometimes rules should be bent or broken.

But there was also the *Ramayana*, an epic that taught the opposite, and said that you should always follow the rules and do your *dharma*. In the *Ramayana*, decisions were far more black-and-white. If a spouse wanted to sleep with someone else, perhaps it was better they divorce first. *Not like I'm safe here and playing there,* Veer thought. *It should not be at the cost of the family.*

Sometimes he grew more philosophical on the subject. "Time should only change our selection of things," he'd say, his voice growing sad and tired. "Not the people around us."

♥♥♥♥♥♥

May 8 was a date Maya and Subal would not forget—the day of the Big Bang. May in Mumbai was known for the intensity of its heat, and the day was sweltering. They were back in Aksa at The Resort. The hotel was quiet except for the crash of the ocean waves.

The Big Bang, as in: after so much built-up tension, an explosion of feelings between them. Everything out in the open at last. Out in the open for them but not for others to see.

Afterward, Maya left to pick up Janu from school. She brought him back to The Resort, to a small park beside the hotel pool. For a long time, Maya watched Janu play on the merry-go-round. She looked out at the sea, and then over at Subal, who stood at a distance looking at her. He held her gaze for a long time. While he felt happy, he was also a little unsettled, because he thought he didn't deserve her. And it seemed impossible this could end well.

But Maya felt only at peace. She wanted to hold on to the moment and the calm it gave her for as long as she could.

Like Veer, Subal traveled a lot—often to Jaipur and Indore up north and to Bangalore and Goa down south. After the Big Bang, Maya began sending him flowers everywhere he went.

She had always gone overboard in her affections, for all of her friends, male and female. She loved the *bhakti* poems and the old stories about devotion. And with Subal, she felt compelled—as she once had with Veer—toward a showy, demonstrative kind of love.

Maya went through local vendors to make sure she found the freshest flowers in every city. Later, she also began sending desserts. In Goa, it was chocolate *bebinka*, with its layers of butter and sugar. In Pushkar, it was *kaju barfi*, the native cashew sweet. In each place, she made arrangements so the bouquet would be waiting for him in his hotel room. And in each place, Subal sent her a photo of himself smiling with the gifts.

Sometimes, Maya also sent gifts to his workplace. His team of accountants began to expect them. They would be sitting in a board meeting and a local delivery boy would bring in a dazzling bouquet. At their annual meeting in Jaipur, which more than one hundred people attended, Maya sent a three-tier, sixteen-kilogram cake, which cost her a staggering fourteen thousand rupees. When these deliveries arrived, Subal felt not like a middle manager but a CEO. But as time passed, even her extravagances began to feel routine, and he didn't always send her a photo in return.

Subal sometimes sent Maya flowers—on her birthday, or if there was a positive development at the preschool, which kept attracting more and more children; even Janu had enrolled. Or Subal sent her books, in English, Hindi, or regional languages, several of which Maya knew. Maya gave Subal a copy of Kahlil Gibran's *The Prophet*, one of her favorite books, and on an inside page, she wrote: "To Subal . . . This book has all of life in it." Gibran said that a friend was all of a person's needs answered, "your board and your fireside." He said that in friends you found peace.

Around this time, Maya changed her last name on Facebook from Veer's name to her family name. People asked her about the change. She said it was because she liked her old name better. Veer said nothing about it.

Soon, Subal and Maya began going away together. Subal was not religious, but he knew it was important to Maya, and she convinced him to accompany her to Amritsar, which she had a tradition of visiting every year. The Golden Temple in Amritsar was the central place of worship for Sikhs, a small monotheistic people, but it also held special meaning for Maya, who believed that in some past life she was a Sikh who went to the temple.

On this visit with Subal, the Golden Temple brought up old memories for Maya of having been molested as a child. Maya knew this happened to many Indian children, and so she thought it best to banish the memories. This had mostly worked; she hadn't thought about them in years. But now she worried that there could be a connection between the incidents and her relationship with men. Perhaps these memories explained why she grew too attached or acted so needy. Perhaps this was why she wanted sex more than the average Indian woman. Maybe this was at the root of her unhappiness with Veer. And maybe it explained why, when men came on to her in a sleazy way and she didn't like it, she sometimes flirted back.

For her, the connection had to do with the concept of *hisaab*, the settling of accounts. Everyone had a *hisaab* to fulfill. Her attitude toward men could be evidence of a debt she had to repay. Maybe spending time with Subal was also about a debt. All accounts would be settled, now or later. As she looked at her reflection in the sacred pool, she thought she should feel some kind of dread. But with Subal standing behind her, all she could feel was light.

A few months later, Subal changed jobs again, and Maya was

no longer on his route to work. After starting his new job, Subal learned there were financial issues in the company. Months went by, and he wasn't paid. He worried about how to pay his bills. He discussed his problems with Maya, who began lending him money and even sold off some of her gold jewelry to do it.

Soon, Subal began to visit less. His calls and texts became erratic. Maya noticed that he never messaged her on Sunday, which he said was a "family day." She began picking fights with him about his wife and accusing him of messaging other girls. Subal insisted he wasn't and begged her to hang on. He said he needed to get his life in order, and then things could go back to how they'd been. He told her to remember the Big Bang.

After one of these fights with Subal, Maya went on a whim to the nearby mall, where there was a tattoo parlor. She asked for a treble clef, saying that she loved music. Subal called her as the first ink was seeping in.

"Where are you?" he asked.

"I'm just shopping for my birthday," she said, and told him the store number. When he arrived, the outline of the backward *S* was already imprinted on her arm.

"What are you doing?" he asked, and looked closer. "Oh god, you are mad," he said, and Maya knew he meant it as a compliment.

She was mad, *pagal*. She didn't care.

Around this time, Subal also introduced Maya to his father. Afterward, he thought: *You've finally met your match in madness.*

The tattoo hadn't hurt as much as Maya thought it would.

ভভভভভ

Soon after, it was the tenth wedding anniversary party of Maya's cousin Adit and his wife, Naisha, whose marriage had been arranged. Adit and Naisha were new money, so it would be an extravagant affair.

Maya, who was still in her petticoat, glanced up at the clock. Veer was late, as usual. She wrapped herself in an embroidered *sari* of turquoise and orange and chose gold *jhumkas* that dangled from her ears. She added a deep red *bindi* to her forehead. She took a photo of herself looking glamorous and sent it to Subal. As she set out a tiny black suit and white collared shirt for Janu, Veer finally arrived. He swept in the door singing, throwing out his hands in grand sweeping gestures—trying to make Maya laugh.

"You're late," Maya said, and rolled her eyes, pulling Janu's tiny T-shirt over his head. "Hurry."

Veer disappeared into his room and reemerged in a white dress suit and black collared shirt, the inverse of Janu's. He had his hair gelled the same way.

"How do we look?" Veer asked her, as they struck a pose together: Veer imitating Janu, and Janu imitating what he had seen in the movies.

"We look *too* good only," said Janu, who did a little hip sashay, and Maya laughed and snapped a close-up.

"Let's go, you two."

They were among the last guests to arrive at the party. At the entrance, a larger-than-life-size photo of Adit and Naisha greeted them. The real Adit and Naisha, somewhat smaller and dressed in Indian finery, stood beside it. The room was draped in purple and gold, and a stage was set up for speeches and dancing. Seated women in heavy *saris* commented on "how much *bhabhi* has changed" and "how beautiful she looks in her expensive clothing." Naisha smiled demurely as she greeted her guests, a massive Rolex on her wrist.

After a few minutes, the lights in the hall went down and a slide show began. First came photos of Adit and Naisha in different poses and on different vacations, standing beside their rotund, red-cheeked son. Then came slides with messages typed in fancy cursive, a series of clichés in English: "You are better than precious diamonds to me," a slide from Adit read. And from Naisha: "They say the first year is the hardest for a wife, but you made it a piece of cake."

As the lights came up, Adit stepped onstage. In a shiny *sherwani* suit, he looked out at the audience and began his speech: "When my parents told me to meet her, I told her: 'I might stay in Bombay or go. So I'm not sure.' I said, 'What do you think?' And she said, 'Let's take it step by step. Let's take that approach.'" Adit gazed over at Naisha, who sat, hands folded, beside the stage. "These were words of wisdom. I wish I could be like her," he said, and paused to take a deep breath. "This was an arranged marriage. But it is a love marriage now."

The room burst into applause, and Maya and Veer politely joined in. Adit grinned and held out a hand for Naisha to join him onstage.

Maya used to be skeptical of arranged marriages like Adit and Naisha's. She saw the practice much as the Western world did: antiquated and lacking romance, unfathomable for her own life. She had always thought that love, wild and untethered, should come first. But now she'd begun to think she was wrong. Perhaps it was all a matter of compatibility, and a marriage arranged by the people who knew you best had just as much chance of working. It seemed to Maya that any marriage was a kind of arrangement, or became one. And in this room, after ten years together, Adit and Naisha seemed to be in love.

Maya and Veer's tenth wedding anniversary was only a couple of years away. She doubted that they would celebrate. Not like this. She didn't know what Subal and his wife did for anniversaries. She didn't like to ask.

♥♥♥♥♥

A few days later, Maya stood in front of the mirror, fidgeting. She shifted her weight from one foot to the other and tucked a strand of loose hair behind her ear. She tried on a dress and complained that it made her look fat. She settled on another one: gray, Western-style, and conservative. She slid her feet into plastic turquoise shoes, in case it rained.

They arrived at the restaurant before Subal. He now worked more than an hour away.

"Can you call him and make sure he isn't lost?" Maya asked Veer, and excused herself to the bathroom. "Okay," Veer said, curtly.

When Subal arrived he greeted Maya and Veer with a toothy smile. He adjusted his belt over his ample stomach and sat down as the DJ put on an Indian remix of a European techno song. He pinched Janu's cheek, who ignored him; lately when Subal visited he had been impatient with Janu, which Janu didn't like. Janu made a show of playing with the table settings, taking olives from a platter and dropping them into his water glass. A TV behind them played the World Cup, which India had not qualified for.

After exchanging pleasantries, Veer filled the table in on a recent business meeting. "I'm going to kill the *bhenchod* who is trying to screw me," he told Subal.

"Now or later?" Subal asked, as if calling his bluff. Veer didn't answer.

When the waiter came, Maya and Subal ordered chicken; Veer ordered *palak paneer*. Drinks were poured: Old Monk rum for Maya and Subal and Johnnie Walker for Veer. Janu mixed himself a mock-tail of water, peanuts, and mint leaves, unconcerned with anyone at the table. Maya worried that Janu would ask for chicken in front of his father, but Janu knew better.

"The food is good," said Veer, looking up at Subal, who was chewing on a gristly piece of chicken. Subal nodded, and said, "But Maya's *rajma chawal* is better." Maya giggled and gulped at her cock-tail. Veer looked down at his plate.

After the meal was finished, the adults went out for a smoke. Janu had fallen asleep inside at the table. It was blazing hot that month in the city, and they all were sweating. Veer offered a cigarette to Maya. Her eyes were getting glassy, and her words were running together. They began to talk about marriage, other people's marriages, and Maya said, her voice loud: "What do you all think? Is marriage shit?"

Veer took a long drag of his cigarette, while Subal exhaled. "Partly, yes," Subal said. "But I think later in life you could make a better decision about this, because of the growth and experience of the person."

"But your emotions always stay the same," said Maya, and turned to Veer. Veer sucked hard on his cigarette and glanced toward the window. Janu was curled up on his chair. It seemed that they were on the edge of something dangerous, but talk turned quickly to the World Cup.

Inside, Subal paid the bill, and Veer bent to pick up Janu. Outside, the night air was heavy. Maya began walking ahead, toward Subal's car instead of her husband's. "I'll meet you at home," she told Veer over her shoulder.

Subal and Maya made it home first, and she waited in his passenger seat. After Veer parked, he came up to the car, and rapped his hand on the window. *Time to come in.* Janu was draped over his shoulder. Veer waited as Maya said good-bye to Subal, slowly lifting her purse off the car floor. It was quiet in their apartment complex at that hour, and the sound of the car door closing seemed loud. Without a word, Maya followed her husband and son into the dark.

FIRE IN THE HEART

Shahzad and Sabeena, 1999 to 2013

"On no soul doth Allah place a greater burden than it can bear."

—*The Holy Quran, 2:286*

It was wintertime in the city, cold and gusty, and Shahzad was thinking of leaving his cold storage business. Though business was good—there were no malls yet or online shopping, only open-air bazaars—he often felt tired and weak at work. Years ago, a customer had told Shahzad that working with freezers would make him sick. Now, what the man predicted seemed to have come true. Every time Shahzad left work he felt dizzy and light-headed, though he was still young, not yet forty. Almost forty, and still without a child. He noticed the weakness intensified every time he headed toward home.

But Shahzad didn't want to leave the market, or at least didn't want to leave one person: Diana, a local Catholic woman, and a customer at his shop, who was all fire and intensity. Diana was half-Nigerian and half-Goan and had smooth fat cheeks, siren red lips, and wild, curly hair that framed her face. She wore tight but expensive clothing and worked at a fancy advertising company downtown. Everyone in the market called her "Madhuri," because when she laughed, she looked just like the actress Madhuri Dixit. Diana often came to buy chicken from Shahzad.

Like many men at the bazaar, Shahzad found her attractive and magnetic. But Diana was also something else for him—more than just a pretty distraction. Shahzad had begun to think of her as his good luck charm. When he was around Diana, the market seemed not as shabby, and his chicken seemed to fly off the shelves. The day never seemed mundane or dull.

Over time, Diana had begun bringing cakes to his shop at holiday times, and he had begun giving her a package of mutton every Bakri Eid. She was fond of mushroom and chile curd, so he started stocking these items alongside the chicken. And he began calling her "Madhuri" to her face, telling her she had the same million-dollar smile. After a while, Diana started calling Shahzad on his work phone just to talk or to confide in him about problems with her husband.

Shahzad knew she was married, but had always assumed she was childless, until one day she brought around a fat boy with ringlets like hers.

Soon, she confided in Shahzad that she also had problems with her son, who was fourteen. He played football well but wasn't a good student. He would have trouble clearing his SSC exam, which was compulsory to complete secondary school. She said the son's father was a drunk and couldn't help. Shahzad thought he understood, because his friends had told him that Christians were like this: they needed to drink to sleep at night. Shahzad had never touched alcohol, which was *haram*. Because of this, he felt he was clearer of head and saw how he could help her.

In Shahzad's memory, it went like this: Diana gave money to Shahzad, who used it to pay off an official at her son's school. After that, her son passed the SSC. And Diana gave Shahzad her million-dollar smile.

But then Diana returned, distressed again. Despite passing the exam, her son had not been admitted to Elphinstone College, one of Mumbai's oldest and best colleges. Shahzad soon came up with a plan, which hinged on the "MLA quota." In some schools, there were seats reserved for members of the legislative assembly, who could give their seats to anyone. Shahzad thought that at least one member would give his seat to someone who'd pay. After he made a few calls, he found a willing member, and at the last minute Diana's son received admission. Breathless, she came to see Shahzad at his shop. "Shahzad," she told him. "You've done what my husband could not do."

Next came the line that Shahzad would remember all his life. "If something happens to you, Shahzad, I will die," Diana told him. Shahzad had never felt so lucky.

And that same season, as if she was a kind of talisman, an unexpected opportunity arrived in the form of a baby.

A cousin of Shahzad's who worked with him lost his wife in childbirth. She had gone back to her native village to deliver her baby, and the rural doctors botched her Cesarean section. The mother died, but the baby survived.

Shahzad's extended family shouted at his cousin after the death, just as they had shouted at Shahzad when his uncle died. "How could you send her home? The doctors are not good there," they said. A more pressing question was also passed among them: "Who will look after the new baby?"

"I will," Shahzad said.

He had already begged Sabeena for permission, saying the Quran's warning did not apply, because the boy was related by blood. Even Shahzad's father could not complain.

"*Bas, bas*, let's take him," Sabeena said at last, worn down by Shahzad's persuasions. She was also worried about the future of the baby. *After all, it is a newborn child.*

Together, Shahzad and Sabeena went down to meet his cousin and see the child. They both thought he looked perfect. As they sat with the baby, the cousin's father quizzed Shahzad about his business. But Shahzad did not give the right answers. The old man didn't like how little money Shahzad had in the bank, because Shahzad had spent so much of it on doctors. And he found it troubling that Shahzad planned to leave the cold storage business soon.

For the next forty days and nights, Shahzad and Sabeena did not get an answer about the baby. It was a mourning period, and decisions could not be made. But Shahzad was certain the baby would be theirs. Men whose wives died did not raise children on their own. *Soon I will be a father,* Shahzad thought, and could barely wrap his mind around the thought.

But then the circumstances changed. The family agreed that the sister of the dead wife could marry Shahzad's cousin, a common fix in their community when women died early. Together, they would take care of the child. Shahzad and Sabeena were told their help was not needed.

Diana had not been a good luck charm after all.

Despondent, Shahzad addressed Allah as he knelt down on his prayer mat. *Everybody has a child. Why not me?* he prayed. *Give me a child also. Just one. I'll be very thankful. All of my brothers are having a child. I am the only lonely person.*

Please.

In the weeks that followed, Shahzad grew impatient to see Diana, who seemed to never visit his shop anymore. He needed her energy to offset the disappointment of the lost baby. He forced himself to listen to Sabeena, who told him once again that he couldn't force a child. "Each man's fate is written," she told him, with the same fatalism their Hindu neighbors sometimes employed. It said so in the Quran, verse 57, sura 22: "No misfortune can happen on earth or in your souls but is recorded in a decree before We bring it into existence."

This didn't make Shahzad feel better. He wanted a world in which circumstances could be changed and tragic events undone. And he knew that in the new Mumbai, men could make their own fates, and families did not have to dictate lives. He kept thinking of how his father, who rarely spoke anymore, continued to rule his fate with his silence.

Shahzad tried to comfort himself by thinking of Dilip Kumar, the actor known for tragic roles who played the prince in *Mughal-e-Azam*. Kumar never had a child in real life. Shahzad wondered if even the manliest of actors suffered from a low sperm count just like him. *No,* Shahzad decided, *it must have been a choice.* The choice of a broken heart, because Kumar had fallen in love with his costar Madhubala, and Madhubala's father, like the king in *Mughal-e-Azam*, had forbidden their love affair. Years after the film came out, as her father continued to keep her from Kumar, Madhubala grew very sick. At thirty-six, she died from a hole in her heart. And though Kumar later married, he never had any children.

Shahzad marveled at how life mirrored films and films mirrored life. Except that he and Sabeena did not have an epic love affair. He did not know if they had ever been in love. He didn't think he even knew what that was. He had stronger feelings for Diana, the kind of feelings he'd seen in the movies. A phrase kept coming into his mind about him and Sabeena: *shaadi barbadi.* A ruined marriage. Without a child, he didn't think it could be anything else.

Sabeena did not think of their marriage as ruined. But she had learned that she had to live for others, not herself. Shahzad's mother lived to take care of Shahzad's father, and Sabeena lived to care for Shahzad and his mother. *What is inside a woman dies when she marries,* Sabeena thought. *We have to sacrifice our wants and our feelings, from morning until night.*

And: *Sometimes you find happiness, other times not.* When she told Shahzad this, he felt ashamed. He would hang his head and say, "My family is like this—what can I do?"

Sabeena remembered back to when she was a child, which felt like many moons ago. She remembered how she would laugh all the

time with her father, making *masti* and telling jokes. Lighthearted-
ness didn't seem part of her personality anymore. Life went ahead
anyway.

She still thought about what her father had said about Kashmir:
Madhubala, anywhere you want to go, you can go in a marriage. But that
was silly. Trips required money. Kashmir was for the movies. And
Shahzad's family was so conservative that she rarely left the house.

At the beginning, life and marriage had seemed limitless, stretched
ahead like the shimmering line of the sea. She and Shahzad went
on trips. They spent money as if it would not end. They did lots of
favors for each other. *It was a very good, very beautiful life,* she thought.
But now the wave had come crashing down. Her mother-in-law,
with her increasing demands, Shahzad so busy and stressed, and
then the medical test that had determined their future and possibly
made her husband go mad. Since then, they rarely did favors for
each other.

But if she drew a line back from every problem in their marriage,
she saw that it almost always pointed at Shahzad's father. Privately,
she had begun calling him "the Dictator." Shahzad's mother—young
and beautiful and full of promise—had been weighed down by the
Dictator's madness, and now she sought to weigh others down.
Shahzad had been scarred in childhood by the Dictator's words, and
in adulthood by his silence; now he was mangling their marriage
too. The question of adoption, though entangled with their faith,
was really made impossible by the Dictator, who lived his life by the
old, harder ways. How far could one man's hurt travel?

Sometimes, Sabeena wished that the Dictator would die.

ଏଏଏଏଏ

By the next winter, Shahzad had left the cold storage business. His
hands were losing circulation. His arms shook just pulling a chicken
out of the case. Though he bought a hair dryer to blow hot air on

his hands after removing a chicken, especially in the cold, it did not help much. Still, he did not want to leave Byculla Market altogether, which would mean leaving Diana.

And so Shahzad began selling live chickens in the market. His father leased him a narrow, enclosed walkway in the middle of the bazaar, which Shahzad quickly realized was the wrong space in which to raise a bird. Perhaps his father had known that. There was almost no ventilation in the passage. The chickens began to die before Shahzad could sell them, collapsing from heat exhaustion and then suffocating from lack of air.

Shahzad decided it was time he made his own contacts in Byculla Market. Many Muslim men in the area were builders, and he soon found his way into real estate. Ever since the economy had opened up a decade ago, Mumbai held the promise of limitless jobs. It was one of the largest cities in the world, and getting larger, as more and more people moved in—thousands every day. And so real estate was a booming business. As a real estate broker, Shahzad could also do what he did best: win people over with his honesty and good nature. No one distrusted the earnest broker in the ill-fitting clothes.

But though he and Diana still saw each other around the market, she had recently stopped speaking to him. It started after Shahzad saw Diana's husband with another woman and had run straight to Diana's workplace to tell her. He burst into her office and breathlessly delivered the news, even though her secretary was in the room.

Later, Diana admonished him: "Why would you tell me that in my office in front of other people?"

Ever since, Shahzad had been looking for a way to patch things up. He knew Diana lived in a small, one-bedroom kitchen apartment, even though she earned good money and could afford better. He was sure he could find her a nicer flat. And he thought he knew just the neighborhood: at Mira Road, a far-north suburb with mangroves by the sea. After much persuasion, Diana agreed to take a look.

The day Shahzad showed Diana the flat at Mira Road was one of the happiest of his life. There was a wide creek, tall, marshy grass, and a clear view of the sea. On the suburb's coastlines, the mangroves' roots stretched into the water. The flat, though still under construction, promised to be huge, and Diana loved it. They came back downtown very late at night. *This day was just like a picnic,* Shahzad thought.

But the picnic ended after that. In Shahzad's memory, Diana gave him money to book the flat, somewhere between one and two *lakhs.* The following month, work on the building was canceled. Construction was like this in Mumbai: *pakaa* one day and canceled the next, due to a building collapse, the industry's rampant corruption, or a builder caught skirting the rules. Diana was furious with him. Shahzad tried to reassure her, telling her about another flat by the same builder near the city's naval dockyard. If she went with the same builder, he promised she wouldn't lose a rupee. But Diana's husband did not want to live there; now that he'd seen it, he wanted Mira Road. And at the dockyard, the property cost more. This time, Diana would have to take out a loan, which she did, because otherwise she would lose the money she'd put down.

After the paperwork was done, Shahzad called her to check in, as he often did, but Diana did not want to talk with him. "Now you don't call me," Diana said. *"Kya?"* Shahzad asked, certain he must have misheard. "Shahzad, you're a broker. I'll give you your 1 percent, but then it's over."

Shahzad grew angry. The usual brokerage fee was 2 percent. He had done so much for her, and now she was not only ungrateful but also trying to cheat him. He felt as if he'd been used. "You give me 2 percent, that's what everyone is giving," he said, his voice rising.

In the end Diana gave him 1 percent, and after that did not answer his calls.

Instead, on the day of her move, which was just before Christmas, Shahzad watched from afar as she carried her baggage to a taxi; Diana's old apartment was just across from Byculla Market. Distraught, Shahzad could not do any work. A builder friend patted him on the back, saying, "Why are you worried? You'll get many other girls." But Shahzad did not want other girls. He wanted Diana and her million-dollar smile.

Shahzad continued to try to call her after that. Again and again he dialed her number, which he had memorized. Then he started showing up outside her work, at the café she went to for coffee, and in the restaurant where she ate lunch. If Diana saw him, she ignored him, perhaps growing disturbed at how often he was popping up. Shahzad knew he was stalking her but couldn't help himself. He had seen men chase women like this in the movies. Eventually, the woman always gave in. *No* really meant *yes*, or *keep trying*. After many, many calls, Diana picked up, perhaps afraid of what would happen if she didn't.

"Whatever is there, let's forget it and just become friends," Shahzad said in a rush.

"I don't know," she said, and hung up the phone.

After Diana moved, Shahzad felt his world had grown dark. He realized that she had used him to advance her son and to get a nice flat. Even Bakri Eid, the "festival of the sacrifice"—for the cutting of the goat, cow, sheep, buffalo, or camel—one of Shahzad's favorite holidays, did not cheer him up.

For several days around the holiday Shahzad felt sick, weighed down by work and daily life. He didn't take any meetings or show his clients flats. When Shahzad's brother asked him to go visit their grandfather's native place to arrange some paperwork for the family property, Shahzad begrudgingly agreed. The village was a forty-minute boat ride away or a rocky three-hour drive in heavy traffic. He couldn't stand the thought of getting on a boat feeling as he did, and so he took the three-hour taxi. As they drove past the winding *ghats* near hilly Panvel, he felt even worse than before. At first, he assumed it was just nausea from the car ride or his depression over Diana. But, passing Panvel, Shahzad had a sudden sinking feeling that something was not right. It was a feeling he couldn't shake even after he arrived at the village. He completed the paperwork and returned home anxiously to bed.

Several weeks later, Shahzad was at the train station when his cell phone rang. The call was from an old childhood friend, who used to go on the Sunday drives to Chowpatty. "See the headlines," his friend said.

Shahzad ran outside the station to buy a paper. There, on the front page, was the headline: a karate champion in Mumbai was dead.

Atif.

Shahzad came home crying. His best friend. His strong friend. His braver and better-than-he friend. His only true friend, if he was being honest with himself. The clients and builders and shopkeepers and Diana—they were all friends because they wanted something. Atif had never asked anything of Shahzad. He had only given, never taken.

"It's God's will, *O,*" Sabeena told him. She wanted to comfort Shahzad but did not understand how it was already Atif's time. Atif was still young, not yet forty.

The next day, Shahzad went to see Atif's parents. In Shahzad's memory, this was the story they told him: Atif had a niece, a Muslim like him, who fell in love with a Hindu boy. The girl and boy ran away. Atif, the strongman of the family, was asked to find a way to stop the marriage and went to the police station to ask for help. Several officers followed him in jeeps to track down the girl. But when they reached the boy's house, the girl already had a red *tika* on her forehead, which was worn by married Hindu women. Atif called his wife and said, "She's married. It's too late."

Shahzad found it strange that Atif would have agreed to help prevent an interfaith marriage, which were only becoming more common in the city. After all, Atif himself had run away with a Jain. But his family told Shahzad that the boy was uneducated and the girl was underage. Under those circumstances, Atif must have found it his duty.

It's too late. Those were Atif's last words. After that, the police put the boy in the passenger seat of one of their jeeps to take him to the station, while Atif sat in the back with the constable. The girl was placed in a second jeep. Atif's family's hypothesis was that the boy was afraid, because the girl was underage, and he could be put away in jail for many years. As they drove past a tree, the boy reached across the driver and grabbed the wheel, turning it toward the tree. Perhaps his plan was to make a break for it. But the jeep spun out of control, tumbling down a hill, into a *ghat* outside Panvel. The boy emerged with only a fracture. Atif and the constable were dead.

Atif's family told Shahzad they believed there had been a conspiracy. *Why was the boy sitting in front? Who puts a criminal in the front and the constable in the back?* It didn't make any sense.

Atif's death appeared in the paper late, because of Bakri Eid. During the festival, a time of celebration, the family held the news. But Shahzad realized now, looking back at the date of the accident, that it was the very day he'd passed the Panvel *ghats* with a sinking feeling. He thought he must have somehow sensed that his best friend was dying nearby.

The family told Shahzad that as Atif tumbled into the *ghat*, he'd been doing *namaaz*. Shahzad cried harder at this. Of course he was praying. Atif had always been a better man than he.

After this, when problems arose at home or with Sabeena's family, Shahzad sought to prove himself as worthy a man as Atif. He wanted to be known as a man who could be called upon in times of crisis to fix problems.

Shahzad found his moment after Sabeena's brother, who was known to be hot-tempered, married a girl who kept a lover, and there was an incident on their first night of sex. It was not clear whether Sabeena's brother had been rough with her, or if she had refused sex because of her lover, or whether something else happened altogether. But the rumors flew. People gossiped that Sabeena's brother was gay, which was a black mark in their community. They whispered that because of this he could not perform.

Shahzad went to Sabeena's brother. "Didn't you break the seal?" he asked. He said he had. Shahzad told others in the community that Shahzad's brother had performed, and wasn't gay, but the rumors persisted. Shahzad had the idea to take him to a fertility clinic. The doctor measured Sabeena's brother's sperm count, which was very high. Shahzad couldn't help but feel jealous. *Wow,* he thought. *God has shown me this report I wanted to see for myself for so long.*

"Now no one can talk badly against you," Shahzad told him. He called Sabeena to tell her the good news. "He can be strong now," he said, and he was right. The community accepted the report as evidence her brother was straight, and Sabeena felt proud of her husband.

But within a week, the girl asked for a divorce. The decision was up to Sabeena's brother and the community, because Muslims had their own laws that governed marriage and divorce—laws that had been in place even before Partition. Efforts to create a uniform civil code in the country had been unsuccessful; each time, the government was accused of violating religious freedom. And so it was Sabeena's brother and the community that granted the divorce, claiming extreme circumstances had warranted it. Even the Prophet had said divorce was an occasionally necessary evil. The girl was blamed, while Sabeena's brother was considered an *innocent divorcé*.

After the divorce went through, Sabeena's brother quickly found a new wife. His position in the community was secure. Shahzad was proud of his role in safeguarding it. But he also couldn't help thinking back to the doctor's report. *It is no wonder he could marry again so quickly,* he thought. With a sperm count that high, a man was capable of anything.

A few weeks after his marriage, Sabeena's brother and his docile new wife came to Shahzad and Sabeena's house for a meal. Sabeena bustled around the kitchen. She rarely had the opportunity to serve her extended family at home. But before long Shahzad's father appeared.

"Why did you all come here?" he shouted from a corner of the room. "Who called you?"

As Shahzad's father stood and glared at them, Sabeena's brother and new wife stayed silent.

"Go away," Shahzad told him, finding a voice he did not know he had. "You are mad," Shahzad continued, his shaky voice growing stronger. "You don't know anything about how relations are. You go inside."

Surprised, Shahzad's father retreated. But the meal was already ruined. "I'm very sorry," Shahzad told Sabeena's brother. "No, don't worry," he said, as they stood up to go. "I know your father, Sabeena told me."

After this incident, Sabeena was dejected for days, and Shahzad made it a point to get her out of the house more often. He was sorry he hadn't done so more in the intervening years. They began going to Chowpatty Beach again, though not by scooter, because in all those years Shahzad's driving had not improved. Instead they went by taxi, with the windows down, so they could feel the fresh air.

At Chowpatty the water was dirty with the debris of past festivals and neglect. Garbage collected at the place where the Arabian Sea met the sand, and the water was unsuitable for swimming. And yet many couples went parking at Chowpatty, because the breeze was always cool after a scorching Mumbai day. The view of the city was also magnificent as the darkness set in. By this hour, the lights of Marine Drive began to gleam like pearls, a sort of mirage that gave the road its nickname, the "Queen's Necklace."

One night, as Shahzad and Sabeena sat at the beach's edge, looking out at fellow beachgoers, they considered their life together. It had been a hard stretch of years, but Shahzad thought maybe things were getting better. *It is so nice to do timepass like this,* he thought.

Sabeena also felt content. She had always loved Chowpatty, and now, with the breeze on her skin and the wind pulling at her *dupatta*, she felt at peace. They didn't need to speak. It was enough to sit in silence, gazing out at the churning sea.

The beachgoers that night were mostly teenage couples, looking carefree as they stood on the sand eating *falooda*, *kulfi*, and butterscotch *ice-gola*, the liquid streaming down their arms. But dozens of kids also ran along the beach, circling the balloon sellers and other toy hawkers and digging deep holes in the sand. They screamed with excitement as they rode the miniature Ferris wheel. And they begged their parents for *ice-gola* or to go swimming in the murky water.

As Shahzad watched the children, he felt a rising anxiety, more than usual. He could not bear to look at them and hear them laugh and scream.

"Let's get out of here," Shahzad told Sabeena. "Please."

After that, they did not make the trip to Chowpatty Beach again for a long time.

❦❦❦❦❦

Shahzad began visiting doctors again. They all gave him the same report as before—low sperm count, no other problems—with the exception of a female doctor, who had a different take. "Your body is perfect," she said. "Maybe it's your brain."

The female doctor recommended seeing a psychiatrist, which was becoming less taboo in the city, though suicide remained a crime and confidentiality was poorly regulated. The government had begun warning that many millions of Indians needed counseling and weren't getting help. Shahzad decided to see the psychiatrist but not tell anyone outside of his family. The doctor was a handsome, thin man with a beard, a fellow Muslim, who gently asked Shahzad what was on his mind.

"How can I forget her?" Shahzad blurted out.

Diana. He had not meant to say her name. But then he told the doctor everything, ending with how their friendship fell apart.

He also told the doctor about being childless. He talked about the shame he felt around his neighbors and the burden of not being able to give a child to Sabeena, which sometimes felt too much to bear. And he went back further, to his uncle's death, their fight, and how everyone had blamed Shahzad. "If you think about it this way, it will come again and again in your mind. The fact is we will all go inside someday," to heaven, the doctor said.

Shahzad told the doctor about the hand washing too, how he did it compulsively, often before or after eating. He told him how he still felt the dirt from his uncle's grave beneath his nails. Sabeena had begun to complain because Shahzad asked her to scrub the house even when it was clean. After Shahzad finished talking, the doctor prescribed him a multipurpose drug for depression, anxiety, and obsessive-compulsive disorders. "It will calm your mind," the doctor said. "Just for now. Come back again, and next time I will reduce it."

A few months after Shahzad started the medicine, Sabeena noticed a change in him. He seemed less anxious. He began sleeping better. And he washed his hands less frequently. He even told goofy jokes more often, such as: *Husband: Do you know the meaning of wife?*

*It means "without information fighting every time!" Wife: No, darling, it
means "with idiot forever!"* After telling a joke, he'd laugh his infectious laugh until Sabeena joined in. She suspected he was also growing more confident, because, after years of trying, his real estate
business was thriving.

Shahzad mostly showed flats to local Muslim families. But being
downtown also put him in contact with dozens of *firangis*—from
England, France, the United States, and all over the world. As India's economy expanded, expats had begun flooding in. Shahzad
made friends with many of them, winning them over with his off-
color jokes, florid style of dress, and oddly accented English. "He is
an Englishman now," Sabeena joked to the family, as he spent more
and more time with *firangis*. But Shahzad had been fascinated by
foreigners since his school days, when he'd studied French and first
learned English. Sabeena's English had never come as easily.

As a real estate broker, Shahzad was not always good at his job.
He arrived late to show houses, and keys often went missing. He
showed people flats that didn't fit their specifications. But he saved
himself, as he always had, by being more honest than the other men
in the business.

Shahzad felt that showing flats showed him the whole world. He
found flats for rich women and poor men, for Hindus, Muslims, and
Catholics. One day, he found a house for a man who had transitioned to become a woman. Shahzad was familiar with *hijras*, which
he also knew as eunuchs, a common sight on the streets of Mumbai. As far as he knew, these men were not really men and liked to
parody women. They also cursed you if you did not pay for their
blessing. But the woman he found the flat for was different. She
lived like any other Muslim and was married to a man. And she had
very specific needs for Shahzad: a dark house with plenty of privacy.
She told Shahzad she had been teased as a child in Mumbai, gone to
America to transition, and was now back to care for her mother. She

worked as a makeup artist in Bollywood, where being transgender was more accepted, but otherwise did not go out in public much. She did not want neighbors watching her. Shahzad took her request to heart and found her the most private house he could.

Before long, Shahzad expanded his brokerage business into a tourist business, offering all-India package tours or Mumbai *darshans*. He asked the *firangis* to meet him in his dingy office, which was on the second floor of a convenience shop in the Colaba tourist district downtown. He often started his *darshans* with a slum tour of Dharavi, once Asia's largest slum and still India's biggest, and where his family had property. There, the foreigners could feel a mix of pity and awe at all the poor, resourceful people and take photos of young, wiry men at sewing machines or bent old men treating leather in a tannery. They were always amazed that these goods would find their way West. Afterward, Shahzad took them to the *dhobi ghats*, where they marveled at the endless rows of laundry and at how even the poor wore well-pressed clothes. Next, to lighten their mood, Shahzad brought them to the Bollywood studios, which he visited with the help of the transgender makeup artist. At the studios, the foreigners laughed at the dance numbers, calling them "cheesy," and compared them to old Hollywood movies before they evolved beyond song and dance. To finish, Shahzad took them on a night tour of Marine Drive and Chowpatty, where the lights of the Queen's Necklace gleamed. Often, they spent the whole day getting in and out of an air-conditioned car, which blocked out the heat and stench and poverty but cost a whopping four thousand rupees to rent for the day. Shahzad was amazed by how foreigners lived.

But then, in 2008, the terror attacks on Mumbai happened, and the foreigners stopped coming. On Shahzad's TV, a newscaster said that men were on the ground with guns in Mumbai, in multiple locations.

Leopold Cafe, where all the tourists went for beer, was among the first targeted. Eight people in the café were killed. Two bombs also went off in taxis in the suburbs; downtown, young men wielding AK-47s opened fire in Mumbai's famed Victoria Terminus, not far from Shahzad and Sabeena's home. As they sprayed bullets across the open hall, commuters screamed and ran and fell. At a Jewish center, the gunmen took hostages. They tried to enter a women and children's hospital, but the nurses had turned off the lights and locked the doors to confuse them. The gunmen also stormed the Taj Mahal Hotel.

The Taj sat, proud and opulent, across from the Gateway of India, on the shore of the Arabian Sea. People described it as a wedding cake, with seven tiers of Gothic windows and hanging bays in tan and cream. The hotel employed some 1,600 staff and boasted 565 bedrooms and 11 restaurants. It was where dignitaries and rich *firangis* stayed, but it also had a grand lobby where anyone could sit, which Shahzad sometimes liked to do.

Terrorist attacks were not a rarity in India, but this one was different. It was larger in scale and ambition. The gunmen had entered the city on a rubber dinghy at a fisherman's village, not far from the Taj, as if attacking the city was easy, like a joke. And they targeted the places foreigners liked to go. The attack also took place over Thanksgiving in the United States, and so for three days Americans watched their TVs in horror as Mumbai was under siege. The terrorists took out men, women, children, rich, and poor. When the shooting and explosions ceased and the police had caught or killed the gunmen, the newscasters announced that 164 people were dead. The majority were Indian, but among them were some two dozen foreign nationals, six of them American.

After the attacks, the foreigners stayed away. No one wanted to visit Mumbai, city of horrors. No one wanted to tour the slums or even play bit parts in Bollywood for a day. Shahzad's brokerage and tour guide businesses suffered. But he was hopeful the tourists would return. And he held on to the *firangi* customers who stayed in Mumbai, though some of them talked about leaving. They said that a coordinated attack like this would be the first of others.

India held Pakistan responsible for the attacks, but Pakistan denied it had played a role. Rumors flew that sweets had been distributed in Pakistan to celebrate the siege. But that same year Pakistan had forty terrorist incidents, and Shahzad knew there was plenty of blame to go around. Mumbai's attacks, which began on November 26, became known as 26/11—like 9/11, which took place in America seven years before. And extremists were still trying to plot attacks on American soil. To Shahzad, it seemed that attacks could now happen anywhere, in rich and poor countries alike. This idea scared him—that violence was possible even in the places you would not expect.

ღღღღღ

It was after this that the Dictator got sick. First, he stopped wanting to eat. Then, he was unable to clean Byculla Market. At his hospital downtown, the doctors could not figure out what was wrong. Shahzad's family went to another hospital, and a third, until they were told it was cancer.

For more than twelve months, the Dictator was confined to his bed. This was a difficult year, not as much for Shahzad, who often came home late from work, but for Sabeena, who took on the role of her father-in-law's maid and live-in nurse. Her days were already overscheduled, with endless laundry to clean, meals to make, and prayers to perform. Now, on top of all her duties, she also had to tend to the Dictator's health and whims. When his appetite returned, he demanded food from Sabeena at odd hours, calling out in the middle of the night: "Cut me an apple!" and "Make me fish!"

Sabeena always did what he asked. But she worried about Shahzad's mother. It was a fine line to walk—tending to her father-in-law's needs while not making his wife jealous. She worried Shahzad's mother would grow upset.

One day, as Sabeena sat next to Shahzad's father to keep him company—though his company was very poor—Shahzad's mother became suspicious. She looked at Sabeena beadily and shouted: "You are making like you are a sweet dish at my husband, a *gulgule*."

Sabeena controlled herself and did not reply. If she did, she knew there would be a fight. Later, she and Shahzad laughed about it, whispering in their bedroom in the dark. *Gulgule! Like a sweet dish.* Her mother-in-law was a genius.

Before long it was Bakri Eid again, and Sabeena had to help Shahzad's mother with the preparations. After the cutting of the goats, and after the women cooked the meat, the men went out to distribute the leftovers to friends and family and the poor. A few hours after Shahzad had gone out, Sabeena got a call from the police.

"Your husband has been in an accident," an officer said. "It is a bad accident. Come to the hospital right away."

Sabeena, always the picture of calm, began screaming. It felt like the moment she had learned of her father's death.

Together, Sabeena and Shahzad's mother ran to the government hospital where Shahzad had been taken. When they arrived, Shahzad was unconscious, with stitches zigzagging across his head.

They were told Shahzad had been on his scooter coming back from Byculla Market when he collided with a Parsi man's car. It was unclear who was at fault. But it was lucky it had been a Parsi, because Parsis, a tiny community of Persian origin, were known to be wealthy and conscientious. True to type, the Parsi man paid a visit to the hospital with his mother and father and even offered Shahzad's family a watch or money as compensation. Though they were likely trying to avoid a police case, Shahzad's family found it extraordinary they showed up at all.

Meanwhile, Shahzad was not waking up. The whole night, Sabeena and Shahzad's mother lay on the floor beside him, crying and praying for his recovery. They both slept in their *salwar kameez*, the folds of their dresses serving as blankets, and their *dupattas* too-thin pillows.

In the morning, Shahzad opened his eyes.

"What are you doing here?" Shahzad asked his neighbor, who had come to the hospital after hearing the news, and now stood over his bed. Shahzad turned to Sabeena. "What happened to me?" he asked.

"You're in a hospital," Sabeena said. "You had an accident."

"You've just fallen from the bike and gotten a little hurt," Shahzad's mother said, gruff again now that it seemed her son would get well.

And then Shahzad remembered. He had been out distributing meat on his scooter when he had seen Diana. Diana, whom he once distributed meat to every Bakri Eid, before she cut him out of her life. She had been sitting in a taxi. Through the window, he could see her fat cheeks, red lips, and cascading dark curls. He had blinked and then her taxi was gone. He'd been rattled but drove on to Byculla Market to give his lawyer a package of meat. After that, he'd headed toward home. And then he had seen Metro Cinema looming before him—he was close to home now—when the Parsi man's car appeared. That was when everything went black.

Diana, his good luck charm. And now look where he was. It was not Diana but Sabeena who had come to see him. It was Sabeena who slept in her clothes on the floor. Later, when Shahzad got home from the hospital, his father shouted at him: "I told you not to go on the motorcycle. Why were you driving?"

Even Shahzad began to wish his father would die.

It was a searing hot day, six months after, when they got the call.

The Dictator wouldn't make it until morning. At the same time, the world's seven billionth baby, Nargis, was born, an Indian baby chosen symbolically to represent the country's swelling population. Every minute, fifty-one babies in India were born. Every minute, ten people in the country died. The doctors said the Dictator had stopped swallowing food, even after they had put a hole in his throat.

But before this, Shahzad's father had done something unexpected. He had told his wife he was sorry. He'd begun crying and said, "I made a mistake. I never looked after my children." He even showed his hands, as if in a sign of apology. "I treated you all bad, I did not treat you all good."

He did not say this to Shahzad, but his mother told him afterward, which was enough.

The apology reminded Shahzad of a moment in *Mughal-e-Azam*, when the Emperor Akbar seeks his son's forgiveness. Akbar tells his son he is not an "enemy of love" but "a slave of my own principles." Perhaps Shahzad's father had been a slave to his illness or his cruelty.

Now, Shahzad and the family crowded around the bed, where his father lay, unmoving. After a little while, Shahzad thought he saw a small movement beneath the sheets. "See, his stomach is still there. He's breathing," Shahzad said. "No, it's the ventilator," another family member told him. "He is already gone."

When he heard this, Shahzad began to cry. He didn't know what he felt. He couldn't say that he was happy or sad. It was a strange mix of emotions he did not recognize.

People offered words of comfort: "He was in bad pain," "His soul will be blessed," and "He will be at peace." These platitudes helped a little.

For forty days after that, the family sat in mourning. Shahzad did not go to work, and no one went out except for the necessary shopping. There was a big marriage in the extended family, but they did not attend.

Sabeena felt lighter the moment Shahzad's father stopped breathing. At long last, they were free of the Dictator.

❦❦❦❦❦

The change in Shahzad was just as dramatic. After his motorbike accident, his balance had worsened and his gait became more uneven. But after his father's death, his posture corrected itself. He grew his mustache into a manicured goatee, like some Westerners did, and even went to the salon to maintain it. His hair was now always hennaed, and he wore better-fitting and more expensive clothes. All of this made him look younger, and even the women in the family commented that he had grown more handsome.

After his father died, Shahzad had realized the obvious. At long last, he could adopt a child. A child would no longer be considered an outsider.

When Shahzad approached his mother after the mourning period, she insisted he still adopt within the family, a baby that could take his name. But Sabeena now said she wasn't sure she wanted a child at all. She felt old—they were both past forty now—and it seemed to her too late. Shahzad dismissed this, saying he was as full of energy as the day they met.

Shahzad's mother presented another idea. They had distant relatives who lived in a hut on a hill in Kalyan, a faraway suburb at the end of the Central Railway line. A woman had given birth to a baby boy, but she was sick and did not have the money to care for him. "She's got TB and must be dying, so you can go adopt that child," Shahzad's mother said.

And so Shahzad took the long train ride to Kalyan. When he entered the hut, it was obvious the baby boy was also sick. He seemed to have a fever. Perhaps he had already caught his mother's TB. But

Shahzad still thought the baby was good-looking. He could even sense a trace of mischief in him. He prayed with the baby as the boy fell into a twitchy sleep on the floor.

The woman was very thin, and the bones on her face were sharp. There was no food in the hut, and she said she couldn't afford a doctor. Kalyan, a popular resting place for new migrants to the city, had few doctors anyway. The woman and her husband and father had come from a fort city several hours east, but now the husband was gone.

Shahzad felt uneasy. His manicured, hennaed beard, shaded glasses, and city clothes stood out amid the harsh poverty. No one else in the area spoke English. The woman was making him tea, even though she was ill, and had no idea why he'd come.

The woman's cell phone rang. It was Shahzad's mother, calling to do the telling for him. After the woman hung up, she faced Shahzad. "I understand what you want," she said. "But first you have to ask my father."

Shahzad knew just a little about the woman's father—that he owned a mutton shop but never seemed to have any money. Later, he learned that the man was a gambler, which was illegal but common, and that the man lost his money playing cards.

When the old man appeared inside the hut, the woman told him about Shahzad's plan to take her baby. "No," the old man said, without hesitation. "I have only one grandson, and he is the last. I cannot live without him."

Shahzad nodded and turned to go. He wasn't going to fight an old man. But the woman's father stopped him, motioning to his lower body. He lifted up a pant leg and showed Shahzad that his skin was raw and peeling. Whatever the affliction was, it looked as if it had never been treated. The man also pulled out a broken cell phone. He said the phone was more important than his leg. He did not mention his daughter's illness. Shahzad took the man to the repair shop and pushed two hundred rupees into his hands. "Give me one hundred rupees more, I need it," the man said, and Shahzad did. He could not wait to get on the train back home.

"We don't want it," Shahzad's mother said, after he told her what happened. "He's a gambler, he will always be out for money." Shahzad knew she was right. Even if the old man gave them the boy, he was certain to appear regularly—on the boy's birthday or during Ramadan or Eid, along with the other poor people—to ask for money for every ailment and problem. He might even demand the boy back when he was grown.

But maybe he wouldn't. For a brief moment, Shahzad considered stealing the baby. He could take him to a doctor. The boy could have a better future. And the chances of repercussions were small. Poor people almost never went to the police or to court against the rich, because the outcome rarely worked in their favor.

No, Shahzad thought. *This is not the way to become a father.*

With regret, he gave up the idea, and on future Ramadans and Eids, when the boy came to their house with the other poor children to ask for money, Shahzad noted with relief that he had survived, but also that he hadn't grown up to be good-looking.

❦❦❦❦❦

The Dictator's death set other events in motion: most important, the inheritance of an enormous tract of family property in Dharavi, a half-hour train ride north of home. It was the slum land where Shahzad used to bring the *firangis*—some twenty thousand square feet of it—and he inherited it along with more than a dozen other family members. Dharavi had one million inhabitants per square mile and a churning economy all its own. It was part dumping ground, part living space, and part swamp. It had countless satellite dishes and cell phones but few toilets. Shahzad's cousins took a survey of the land and immediately declared it a headache.

For one, the property was not in good shape. At the entrance there was a dirt-filled field, which doubled as a rough cricket *maidan* where young boys liked to play. Beyond that sat hundreds of makeshift dwellings. A narrow lane, which ran between the dwellings, was filled with hanging laundry, running children, squatting women doing wash, and men hanging out in *dhotis*. These slum dwellers had not paid rent in years, and it would be difficult for Shahzad's family to collect it now. Surrounding the living spaces were heaps of rotting trash, dirty water running from pipes, squawking chickens, tied goats, three-legged dogs, and tiny kittens pawing at the remains of food. Big-beaked crows sat on Dumpsters eating pilfered meat. And at the very end of the property sat the remains of a burnt-out tannery.

The second, and much bigger, problem, was that when Shahzad's cousins went to visit the land again, they found a goon had moved to take control of the property. The goon was associated with a local but powerful right-wing political party that had previously led attacks against the city's migrants. Shahzad's family worried that he would hurt anyone who tried to reclaim the land.

But Shahzad was not afraid. Instead, he saw an opportunity. This was his chance to prove himself a hero. And if he could keep the land and then sell or rent it to a builder, they'd all be rich. Though in bad shape, the property was valuable—as the goon and his party recognized—because Dharavi occupied five hundred acres at the center of Mumbai, and Mumbai was running out of space. If Shahzad got rich from the builder, he could also afford to adopt a child. He'd be so rich no one would dare stop him.

Through his brokerage business, Shahzad met with several builders and found one willing to pay twenty-eight *crores*—an incredible 280 million—rupees to build on the land. The builder said he would do all the construction legally, through the city's major project to clear and redevelop slum land. The project promised slum dwellers free apartments in exchange for their shanties so that luxury towers could be built in their place.

It was possible that when it came time to build, some of the slum dwellers would be obstinate about moving. Shahzad had heard stories of slum people who were ungrateful for their brand-new apartments, objecting to the isolation, lack of community, and Western toilets in the new flats. Some slum dwellers even begged to go back home—to homes that no longer existed. The builder promised Shahzad he knew how to handle this. But first Shahzad would have to get rid of the goon.

As Shahzad plotted his next steps, his perspective of himself began to change. He began to see himself as a big shot in Dharavi, a would-be slumlord with lots of land. He concocted wild plans for a show of force against the goon. In the meantime, he visited the property and put up a giant sign with his name on it, warning: "Trespassers will be prosecuted." He told himself he wasn't afraid.

Over the course of his visits to Dharavi, Shahzad grew close with the people who lived there. He got to know them and their stories—the girl who spoke English and worked in marketing but lived in a decrepit hut to save money for more schooling; the fat, lazy men in undershirts who roasted chicken *tikka* and hung out on plastic chairs all day; and a hunched-over man named Pinya, who was once a big man in Dharavi before he got hooked on moonshine and drank all his money away. Out of all of the slum dwellers, Shahzad liked Pinya best. He often gave him money to do small tasks, such as fetch *chai* or share information he'd learned about the goon, though he knew how Pinya would spend the money. Every so often, slum moonshine was made wrong and killed dozens of people. But Pinya was hooked and drank it anyway.

Shahzad also got to know a security guard the goon had hired, a boy so young he couldn't grow a mustache. The boy had come to Mumbai from up north after suffering a bad breakup. If this was the goon's security guard, Shahzad thought he didn't need to be afraid. Emboldened, Shahzad set up shop in an old office in the center of the property and taped a picture to the door of him standing with members of another local political party. He hoped it would scare away the goon and any other interlopers.

After several months, Shahzad and his family met the goon in person. They gathered twice in fancy flats—the goon's choice—to negotiate over the family land. Both times, Shahzad and his family rejected the unfair terms the goon offered, though they worried that violence would follow.

The more often Shahzad visited Dharavi, the more the slum dwellers grew to like and admire him. Even Binky, the floppy-eared slum dog, perked up when he came around. Shahzad took the time to ask after their families, gave them small amounts of money, and never collected rent. They greeted him in obsequious tones, commenting on how *bindaas* his Western-style blue jeans and fake Gucci belt were or inviting him into their shanties for dinner. As Shahzad waved at them, he sometimes imagined that he was royalty, a real *shahzad*, and that this was his fiefdom. Which, in a way, it was. Here was a property that bore his name. A property worth twenty-eight *crores*. And here were people that owed him something and whose futures were in his hands.

With his new swagger, Shahzad began to respond differently to strangers when they asked if he had children. He no longer hung his head and said *"Nahi, nahi,"* in a small voice. Instead, he began to play pretend.

This did not work with his neighbors or the people in Byculla Market, Crawford Market, or Bhendi Bazaar. These people all knew better. But if he and Sabeena went to a wedding or birthday party with guests they did not know, there Shahzad could lie. Sabeena had been the one to suggest this. "Who's going to question you?" she said.

Shahzad lied with confidence and gusto. "How many children do you have?" a wedding guest would ask. "Two children, one boy, one girl," Shahzad often replied, "and they're very good-looking." The wedding guest would nod in approval or say, *"Allah ki marzi."* "It's God's will." This always made Shahzad feel good.

Sometimes, Shahzad got confused. At the last wedding he attended, he told a guest his daughter was six years old after first saying she was seven. "Oh? I thought you said seven?" the keen-eared guest asked. Shahzad saved himself by telling the biography of his niece Mahala and nephew Taheem as if they were his own children. He told the guest in detail about their hobbies, friends, and high-quality Catholic primary school.

"Ah, good school, a convent school," the wedding guest said appraisingly, and Shahzad smiled with relief, and let the conversation move on.

Mahala and Taheem had still been small when the Dictator died. In the years since, they had grown up to be bright-eyed, buck-toothed, and full of energy. They were so close in age people thought they were twins, a ball of energy split into two humming parts. They made the joint family home younger, louder, less predictable and staid. After they started school, they'd become even livelier.

In the evenings, the kids would run from one room to another, finding Sabeena to ask what she was cooking for dinner or tracking down Shahzad to tell him what they learned in school that day. Mahala was the more talkative and mature of the two, while Taheem often got scolded for his mischief. They had reedy voices and expansive laughs, and they were almost always playing.

Shahzad had gone to see Taheem when he was born, which was at Ramadan time. He had looked thin and small and perfect in the hospital bed. Shahzad had also visited the hospital after the birth of Mahala, whose skin had been very black, like a poor laborer's child, but he had still found her beautiful. *At last I'll have some company,* he thought when they were born. But it was only now that they were older—old enough to hold conversation—that Shahzad realized how much they'd changed in him.

They called Shahzad *"buddhi baba"*—big father—and Sabeena *"buddhi ma."* Though Taheem was often naughty with his father, he would mostly listen to Shahzad. If Taheem told Shahzad he got into a disagreement with a Hindu boy at school, Shahzad would admonish him: *"Chup! Pagal hai tu.* Hindu-Muslim differences are very bad for children." On weekdays, after finishing his homework, Taheem would come into the living room in the morning and call out, *"Buddhi baba,* put on the TV." Every night, they'd watch *Maharana Pratap* together, a show about a Hindu Rajput king who fought against the conquests of the Muslim Mughal emperors, including Emperor Akbar of *Mughal-e-Azam,* who had been a real-life king. After watching their epic battles, Taheem would sleepily shuffle off to bed.

On the weekends, while Taheem's father worked and his mother cooked, he and Shahzad watched cricket and made bets against each other. "Thirty rupees," Shahzad would call out, as India played New Zealand, Sri Lanka, or, most important, Pakistan. If he lost, he'd joke with his nephew, "I won't leave you, I'll get you in the night." Taheem would always run away giggling. Or they played cricket outside, and Shahzad would bowl for his lanky nephew. He threw the ball over and over until Taheem connected, hitting it all the way into the lanes of Crawford Market.

Mahala and Taheem's parents had had a love marriage. Farhan, who was nearly forty, had been teaching classes in the trendy suburb of Bandra when he met Nadine, his much-younger student. Nadine had a tiny frame, a baby face, and deep dimples. He was immediately smitten. Farhan told his family, "I will marry this girl only, or I won't marry anyone." Though Nadine was much younger, she and Farhan were from the same community, and so her father had given in. At first, even after marriage, Nadine had been enamored with Farhan, who was a learned and well-spoken man. He had read the entire Quran and many of the Islamic scholars and poets. He could even quote Rumi, the Sufi mystic and poet, offhand. But as time went on, Nadine saw that Farhan was not making much money. He stopped teaching and took up a job as a mobile phone technician. It was an unglamorous and low-paid position. They rarely went on vacation or out to eat in hotels.

Sometimes, Nadine complained to Sabeena, telling her older and wiser in-law that what she had expected and what she got were not the same. But Sabeena had heard all of this before; she had also gone through some of it herself, in her own way. Once, Nadine complained to her sister that Farhan did not buy her jewels, but Nadine's sister had not been sympathetic. "It was your choice only, according to your choice you have done," her sister said, and Sabeena privately agreed. She felt that Nadine was behaving foolishly.

But Sabeena also knew that when a woman chose a spouse on her own, she was often young and didn't know her own mind. And then she became upset later, because her husband did not meet her expectations. Love marriages seemed to be built on expectations. Even Sabeena had come to marriage with expectations, but she had also known she would have to adjust. It was something Nadine didn't understand. Because of this, Nadine had *bhadaas*, or what Sabeena called "fire in the heart"—which could only be quenched by acting out, shouting, gossiping, or crying. Nadine got out the fire by talking about her marriage with Sabeena. Shahzad, who maybe also had *bhadaas*, got it out by taking action at Dharavi.

❦❦❦❦❦

Shahzad was spending more and more time at the family property. With each day that passed, he felt closer to securing it and becoming the family hero he'd always wanted to be.

There had been some complications. The old owners of the burnt-out tannery on the land had started a legal battle with Shahzad's family. They were being helped by the local goon and, improbably, by members of Shahzad's own extended family. The goon was now going around offering checks to Shahzad's cousins and aunts to buy out their shares, for far lower than what the property was worth. Shahzad had to keep calling his relatives and warning them not to accept the scam money. He assured them that they would make not *lakhs* but whole *crores* of money from a builder in a legal deal, if they could just wait a little while.

Shahzad was now fighting the tannery owner in the Mumbai Court of Small Causes. Long ago, it had been the court where Gandhi and Jinnah, the founding fathers of India and Pakistan, famously started their practice in law. Now, it was where sticky matters of tax and property were adjudicated. In the courthouse, a great, old colonial-era building, the cases moved lackadaisically, as if in an earlier time. In some rooms, documents were stacked to the ceiling. Court peons pasted decisions on paper using toothbrushes and sticky glue. It was no surprise to anyone that the general backlog of court cases in Mumbai numbered in the hundreds of thousands. But Shahzad was confident he would win the suit, because of how the tannery owner had let the land go. Today, the property was a thick jungle of grass, a crumbling stone wall, and a buzzing of fat, malarial mosquitoes. Downy ducks paddled in a small pond. Nature had long ago won the battle.

That said, Shahzad worried about the goon's continued involvement in the property. He hadn't forgotten the violence the party sometimes employed. The attacks against North Indian migrants in the city were still fresh—shop windows smashed, taxi drivers beaten till they bled. Shahzad had nightmares he'd be killed by the goon in the night. Even Sabeena, though she did not know all the details, began to fear for Shahzad's safety. Whenever he was at

Dharavi, she would call his cell phone and ask: "O, how long until you come home?"

With his focus on Dharavi, Shahzad's belief that Sabeena could still raise a child at last had begun to subside. His days were filled with court appearances, slum visits, and builder meetings rather than medical appointments. Yet his feelings of inadequacy were directed elsewhere—to his manhood—because as he had gotten older, he had not been able to make love to Sabeena the way he had before.

When the performance problems started, Shahzad talked about them with his friends, the men he knew from Crawford Market and Bhendi Bazaar. They laughed and told crude jokes, which he did not mind. It made the problem seem less serious. Soon, they even came up with a code word for Shahzad's manhood.

"How is *babubhai*?" they'd say, jabbing each other, laughing at the idea of using *bhai*, a term of respect, for a sexual organ. "*Babubhai* is working or not?"

"No, *baba*," he'd say, shaking his head sadly. "It's not working at all."

The men also had developed a code word for porn, which was strictly forbidden in Islam, *haram*. Of course they all watched porn, or "blue films" anyway; these videos were now available and shareable on their mobile phones. When they talked about the videos they'd call them "BP," for "blue pictures." Later, the code word evolved from "BP" into "Bashir Patel," who was a member of Mumbai's legislature. *"Bashir Patel bhejna mera mobile pe,"* one man would slyly request of another, and soon, a video message popped up on his phone.

Shahzad thought these films were having a negative effect on Indian society. He read that India had some of the highest porn traffic in the world, and that at the same time sexual assault numbers were rising. He worried that the kind of uneducated man who stared at women in trains, or groped or "Eve teased" them on the street, was growing more aggressive from seeing these videos. *It is because of all the naked women always playing in their minds,* he thought.

But Shahzad also watched porn, and felt little shame about it, though he did not tell Sabeena. Once, she found a gel he had been using to watch porn and asked him: *"Yah kya hai?"* "It is *babubhai*'s tonic," he told her, laughing, sure she wouldn't understand. But she did, because the Haj Committee had warned pilgrims that year not to bring such gels or pills to Mecca. She only shook her head. Still, Shahzad did not tell her about the photos of big-breasted girls he kept on his phone, in a secret subfolder called DIA, after Diana.

One day, a nephew of Shahzad's, who was just out of university, found out about the porn and the code. "Have you met Bashir Patel recently?" he teased his uncle. Shahzad, growing red, feigned innocence. *"Kya?"* he asked. "What do you mean?" Shahzad thought that boys must be growing up faster now because of the Internet. Taheem, who was in the room, and just eight years old, asked, "Who is Bashir Patel?"

"Just a person going to stand election," Shahzad said, and left the room. From his bedroom, he could hear his older nephew laughing.

After that, Shahzad did not talk to his friends about his performance problems anymore. Instead, he began to visit doctors again, who told him that after forty, any man could have trouble performing. His low sperm count didn't help, nor did his anxiety. But they said that half of all middle-aged men in India suffered from the same problem. This didn't ease Shahzad's mind. If he couldn't be a father, at least he should be able to perform.

Sabeena didn't care how Shahzad was in bed. She would have told him this if he asked her. She had grown older now and felt it in her body. She didn't want to be made love to like a teenager anymore. There may have been times she wanted to have sex and Shahzad couldn't. But the Quran was clear on this point: a woman had to love, honor, and obey her husband, no matter what came.

The Quran also said that Allah never placed a burden on a person greater than they could bear. And in her community, it was the men who ended marriages, pronouncing *talaq*—"I divorce you"—three times, as Muslim personal law prescribed, though some women were challenging this practice now.

But Sabeena didn't want to be like the women in the West, who in the morning were married and in the evening divorced, or who took a lover on the side. She didn't want to be like the women who drank to keep themselves from being sad or to fall asleep, who wore short clothes or showed cleavage to attract men, or who didn't look after their parents or in-laws as they grew old. And who did not know how to find strength in the best place of all: in God. She also didn't want to be like the sex-addled women she'd heard about, who loved their husbands for what happened in the bedroom.

Still, Shahzad was becoming obsessed with this new problem, and Sabeena knew it was her job to stop him. She knew where this road led. She asserted herself, telling her husband in a firm, raised voice that he was acting *pagal*. But this only further upset Shahzad. He became convinced that Sabeena was becoming more assertive because of his problem in the bedroom—because she thought he'd become weak. She already controlled the house, and he worried soon she would control him. Many women in Mumbai controlled their husbands now. And so Shahzad continued to make appointments with every doctor he could, but none of them seemed able to help him.

After Shahzad came home from another upsetting appointment, where the doctor told him nothing could be done, he carried on an inner monologue with himself: *I am not gay. I have good hair. They say, "You are a perfect man." They say, "Everything is normal." Except this.*

Except everything down there. It had been the problem from the start.

Would it have been different with Diana? he wondered. *No.* Diana had not loved him. He had wasted so much time being focused on the wrong things. The wrong woman. If only he and Sabeena could find a way to begin again, to go back to that cold and drafty room where he'd first seen her and Sabeena had not yet raised her eyes to his.

SKYWATCHING

Ashok and Parvati, 2013 to 2014

"*My womanliness. Dress in sarees, be girl*

Be wife, they said . . .

Choose a name, a role . . .

Don't cry embarrassingly loud."

—Kamala Das, "An Introduction"

Ashok's father called him at work, unable to wait until his son got home. There was a profile Ashok had to see. Her name was Parvati, and, despite her bad stars, her and his son's horoscopes were compatible. This was what mattered in life, and in marriage; that same year, a Hindu saint called for the opening of a university in India to study astrology. "The stars are already MATCHED, Ashok," his father said. Also important was that Parvati was the daughter of a prominent engineer.

"I'll look later, *Appa*," Ashok said.

When Ashok got home after midnight, he unhurriedly opened the profile on his desktop computer. He clicked through her photos one by one. *I'm not too interested,* he thought. Thick hair, open face, natural look—a typical South Indian girl.

He scrolled farther. Parvati's bio said she graduated with a master's degree from IIT Chennai (*okay, smart*), that she played the violin and could sing and draw (*artistic*), and that she was working as a teacher in Trivandrum (*kind*). It wasn't the worst profile he'd seen.

"Okay," Ashok told his father the next morning, though he wouldn't allow himself to get hopeful. "Let's see where it goes."

In Trivandrum, Parvati's mother sat her daughter down and said, "He's thirty-three, don't you think he's a little old for you?"

"No," Parvati replied, smugly. "You know it's better not to judge."

When Parvati picked up the phone a few days later, she was surprised by the warm and friendly voice on the other end. It sounded nothing like the boys her father had introduced her to—boys who kept stammering and letting out uncomfortable peals of laughter. "Hi," this voice said, casually, as if he had known her for years. "I'm Ashok. In Mumbai." She could tell that he was smiling on the other end.

He also had an accent unlike any she had heard before. It sounded British but also Indian. It made him sound intelligent. He named the paper he worked for, one everybody knew and read. He made little money there but told her he was working on a novel. Parvati was impressed.

As they talked, Ashok told her about how he was learning the flute, and Parvati spoke of her Carnatic singing, an on-and-off-again hobby since she was young. "So you can sing and I can play the flute," he said. "Yeah, we'll see," said Parvati. She couldn't decide if his enthusiasm was endearing or too much.

"If on seeing you I don't like you or vice versa, we should be free to say no."

"I agree."

After that, Ashok and Parvati Skyped with both sets of parents. It started off poorly, because Ashok's father was so excited he kept interrupting his son. "*Appa, Appa*, it's not like that, let me talk," Ashok kept telling him. As the two bickered, Parvati and the rest of her family just stared at the screen.

But then the parents let them talk alone, and Ashok played his *bansuri*, a North Indian flute with a sound that was strong and low. Though Ashok wasn't an experienced player, and his notes and playing were uncertain, Parvati found his posture confident, almost sexy.

"It's good to put a face to your name," Ashok said when he finished. "Your photo on your profile doesn't do you justice." Over Skype, he could see the pretty heart shape of her face, the warm flush in her cheeks, and how her expressions were more in her eyes than her mouth. For the Skype date, she had put on a green *salwar kameez*, rimmed her eyes with *kajal*, and even straightened her hair.

"I'm not photogenic," she said.

"Well," he said, and, to add a drawback of his own: "I work in the evening at the newspaper."

"That's okay," said Parvati. If she married him, she realized, she could have every evening to herself. She could live far away from her father and his demands. Her father would agree to the marriage—anything to get her away from Joseph—but inside he would regret that she was not marrying another engineer, a man closer to her age, or a man with money.

They kept talking on the phone, and after a couple calls, Ashok started calling Parvati "dear." They still had not met in person, and this nickname unnerved her. "Don't call me that, it's weird," she told him. "You use the word *dear* when you know someone, not with a stranger you've called twice."

"But *dear* has lost its meaning by now," said Ashok. From the *Oxford Dictionaries*: *Old English* dēore, *of Germanic origin; related to Dutch* dier *"beloved," also to Dutch* duur *and German* teuer *"expensive."* Ashok knew theirs would be an expensive wedding, more than his engagement to Nada had cost.

"But you don't even know me," Parvati said.

March 2013, Gchat:

Ashok: Do you have a deadline or are you under pressure to say yes?

Parvati: My parents suggest I should be able to decide by talking twice

or thrice though that is not my way . . . I thought I'd decide by gut
feeling this time

Ashok: What is your gut feeling?

Parvati: Not sure . . .

Ashok: I believed in arranged marriages. The discovery of the other
person

Parvati: I believed in love marriages

Ashok: No good-looking handsome seniors?

Parvati: Well . . . no Brahmins

Parvati still hadn't told Ashok about Joseph. She wasn't lying
when she said there'd been no handsome Brahmin seniors. She
worried that Ashok would react like the US boy and tell his family
about her past affair.

At the same time, Ashok had only told her a little about his
failed engagement with Nada. He worried that if he told her more,
Parvati would leave him just like Nada.

"Hey, Ashok?" Parvati asked, as she rode a train back home
to Trivandrum after a weekend trip to Alleppey, a southern city
of backwaters. "How come, Ashok—you're thirty-three, good-
looking, you speak really well—how come you didn't fall in
love?"

Ashok sat in his Mumbai apartment studying the photos she
had texted him from her trip. In the first, she had captured a typical Kerala-style home, sun dappling its thatched roof, the grass
flooded with light. In the second, she'd photographed a kelly
green house with a bright red and blue roof and an apricot-colored
kurta hanging on the line. The whole scene was reflected in the
backwaters, a perfect mirror image. In the third, she'd taken a
photo of sagging Chinese fishing nets suspended over the water.
Again, the scene was reflected in the water—a lovely composition
of land, backwaters, and sky. He was astonished by how beautiful

her photos were. She also sang and drew so well. She did not seem like an engineer.

"Oh, you know, I'm a Tam Brahm," Ashok said, trying to make his voice sound indifferent. He hoped she would leave it at that. "What about you? Why didn't you find a guy?"

Parvati paused and looked out the window. The train sped past rivers and clusters of spindly coconut trees. "I've got something to confide," she said. "I have this huge history and . . . I'm trying to get over it."

She told Ashok all about Joseph, about Chennai and Germany and Sweden and the e-mail Joseph sent to her father. She told him about the US boy and her breakdown and move back home.

When she finished, Ashok said: "But if you had a thing, if you had a guy, you should have gone with him and not worried what your parents thought of it. After all, it's your life. You should be the one to decide."

Parvati was bewildered. This was not what Tam Brahm men said. Tam Brahm men saw past affairs as shameful and believed that parents were the ones to choose.

"It's too late, and now that guy is unavailable," she said, a little bitterly. "Where were you last year?"

Ashok laughed at this, but then grew serious. "What's past is past, and I think we should move on, Parvati. Let's just think about our future together."

"Hmm," Parvati said, her voice wistful. He could tell she liked what he said.

E-mail from Parvati to Ashok, May 2013:

Subject line: ♥♥♥

Ashok!!! Ashok!!! Ashok!!

Today I poured down my worries to you. My past.

E-mail from Ashok to Parvati, May 2013:

UCA, would you want to visit Mumbai before the wedding?

UCA, meaning "under certain assumptions." Ashok had come up with it. Assumption: if they met and didn't like each other, they wouldn't take the marriage forward.

❦❦❦❦❦

Once, when Parvati's father invited a boy over to see her, she had made no effort to dress up. Her father was furious. "Why are you dressed so bad?" he shouted. "Is this a way to dress when people come to see you?" He went on: "Your mom looks better than you. She's looking as if she is the bride, and you are the servant girl wearing a bad *salwar*. You better change into something nice." She had gone upstairs and changed.

This time, with Ashok coming with his parents all the way from Mumbai to Trivandrum to meet her for the first time, Parvati took care to dress well. She put on a green *sari* with a red border and golden thread, the kind you might wear to a reception. She put in her contacts and rimmed her eyes with *kajal*. She even went to the spa to get her hair done. Before he arrived, she found herself looking in the mirror again and again.

When Ashok walked through the door, she could tell her effort had the desired effect. *Oh my god,* he thought. She was far more beautiful than he had realized on Skype, with her fair olive skin, eyes the color of honey, and thick, dark hair that fell around her face. But she was also cute and nerdish. The combination had an impact.

"We finally meet," he said, gazing at her.

"Yes," she said, and smiled. She was also surprised. In his pictures and on Skype Ashok had seemed very bookish, with his glasses and slicked-over hair. In person, he was that way, but also very handsome in his pressed white shirt. Mostly, Parvati noticed his face. It seemed like there was a lot of light in it.

A line from *Hum Dil De Chuke Sanam*—a film about two men who loved the same girl—said that if you kept looking at someone a certain way, then you would fall in love. Both Ashok and Parvati had seen the film more than once.

Parvati didn't speak much during his visit. *This is actually a show,* she thought, and looked at the ground, as prospective brides on display were supposed to do. She worried that if she spoke, she might say the wrong thing.

But it didn't matter, because everyone else did a lot of talking. Ashok's mother chattered to Parvati: "I saw your horoscopes, I gave it to an astrologer, he said you will have a lot of healthy kids." Parvati mutely nodded.

Meanwhile, Parvati's father was going over next steps, though Ashok's father kept interrupting him, speaking loudly as he always did when overeager. He kept praising Parvati's father to the assembled crowd: "The man is VERY methodical, took his TIME, but made sure to get a HOROSCOPE, THEN a meeting. He got the job DONE." Though Parvati's father preferred to speak in Tamil, Ashok's father kept speaking in English. Parvati could tell her father found Ashok's father's behavior absurd. He was still going on: "MARRIAGE is a GOOD thing. TWO PEOPLE getting MARRIED is a BETTER THING. And between a GIRL AND A GUY even BETTER." He was so agitated he had stopped making sense.

The couple was sent out alone. As Parvati drove them over to the local Café Coffee Day, Ashok talked on and on about Mumbai. She saw that he rambled the same way his father did. "Bombay is a place you're going to fall in love with. It is very open, welcoming of people from all over," he said. "Bombay has been very nice to me. People from Bombay are very nice. It's more cosmopolitan than Trivandrum. Also you can make friends easily."

When is he going to stop talking? thought Parvati.

When is she going to talk? Ashok thought, and babbled on.

As they got out of the car, Parvati realized Ashok must have thought she was a small-town girl, with a small-town mind-set, who had never lived in a city before. She cut in, "Ashok, I was in Bangalore for almost two years. I like to be independent. Any place can be a strange land. If we are a good match, then it will be okay."

"Okay," he said, and his phone rang. It was his father. "Is everything going WELL, Ashok?"

"We just got here," Ashok said. "We haven't even had a sip of coffee. Don't put a gun to my head."

"You've known each other for TWO MONTHS. You've CHATTED. WHY are you HESITATING?"

Ashok hung up the phone.

His father called back. "WHEN are you GOING to come BACK?"

"*APPA.* We'll start home in another ten minutes."

It seemed unfair that his father was acting like this. After all, his father had married his mother only after they had dated for eight long years. They met when she was just fifteen. Both had been smitten. But her parents had not approved and had promised to disown her if she went through with the marriage. And so Ashok's parents had dated, and deliberated, and dated some more. When at last they married, his mother's parents had kept their promise. They did not come to the wedding and never spoke to their daughter again. They even cut her out of their will. But Ashok's mother and father had had almost a decade to think about it and did not regret their choice. *Eight years,* Ashok thought. And now he wanted his son to agree to a girl after just thirty minutes.

"We need one more day," they told the assembled family.

Ashok's father lost his temper. He began to shout at Ashok, who told him, firmly, "Dad, we'll tell our position tomorrow."

"WHY do you need one more DAY, you've been TALKING, now you've MET her, this is not how you should ACT, not when we've come ALL the WAY from Thrissur."

Everyone stared at Ashok's father.

Am I saying yes to the wrong guy? thought Parvati. She thought of Joseph, and how much more serious he was than Ashok. She considered how Ashok would behave more like his father as he aged. But then she remembered the line on Ashok's profile about giving his partner a free hand and expecting the same from her. She decided she had to trust him.

Ashok and Parvati were told to go upstairs and decide right then, not tomorrow.

"This isn't romantic, not with the way my dad is acting," Ashok said, as they stood facing each other, each on one side of a doorframe.

"It's okay," Parvati said. "That's how parents are."

"So we've met, and I feel this is going to be a positive thing," Ashok said, looking Parvati in the eye. Somehow he was certain she'd say yes. "So it's a yes from our side."

Parvati looked back at him. Earlier that day, they had hugged, and she had noticed that Ashok did not smell at all like Joseph. In that moment, she knew she would never love like she had loved Joseph again. Life with Ashok would be wholly different. But this was the life she'd been offered. And maybe, someday, she could also love him.

"It's a yes for me too," she said, keeping her voice even. "I like you. And I feel like we'll be happy together."

They walked down the stairs together and Ashok told the assembled family, "We've made a decision. It's a yes from both of us."

They sat down to a proper South Indian meal: rice and *dal* and *sambar,* to celebrate the union of two Tamil Brahmin families. Someone asked them to stand next to each other, and all the relatives nodded and clicked their mouths in approval: "*Haa,* yeah, he's a little bit taller."

ღღღღ

UCA, would you want to visit Mumbai before the wedding?

In May, Parvati visited Mumbai for an interview at IIT Bombay, where she could get a PhD. The city was not like Ashok described it. Not outside the airport anyway, where a sea of taxi drivers stood chewing *paan* and speaking in rough Hindi. They reminded Parvati of every villain she'd seen in the Bollywood films.

But then she spotted Ashok in the crowd, grinning as he held his long *bansuri* over his shoulder. He looked happy here, so maybe she could be too.

On the first day of the trip, which Parvati had made with her father, she noticed how skinny Ashok was. Perhaps it was that everything was bigger here: the new residential skyscrapers that towered over the city, the huge, multilane freeways and expressways that cut across town, and the colossal cable-stayed bridge that linked the suburbs to the downtown—its cables the shape of an upside-down *V* in the sky. The bridge's wires could span the circumference of the Earth; this was exactly how vast the city felt. *He is looking so puny, and I so heavy,* she thought. *Should I reduce or ask him to fill up?*

To Ashok, Parvati hadn't seemed heavy down south, where all the Tamil girls had a belly. She was not at all large, just of average build. But in Mumbai she somehow seemed plump compared to the thin, modish city girls—girls who wore lipstick and heels, straightened their hair, and went out to clubs in tiny tops and tight jeans. He worried that they would not look good in photos together and told himself he should start lifting weights.

On the second day, when the sun was high in the sky, Parvati took Ashok's hand as they were crossing the road, just to see what it felt like. Parvati's father was walking ahead of them, and Ashok was surprised. For a moment, Parvati brought Ashok's hand up close to her chest. When her father turned back to them, they hurriedly detached.

On the third day, Parvati had her interview at IIT Bombay. She and her father were staying at a guesthouse on the campus. It was her father's plan for her to get a PhD in engineering there. PhDs were cheaper in India than abroad, and it would be the perfect way to anchor her in Mumbai. Parvati had not had a say. Parvati's father had come around to the value of women working, but on his terms. If she got in, she would begin attending in the fall, just after she and Ashok were married. Now, as they waited for her interview, Parvati, her father, and Ashok sat talking over coffee on IIT Bombay's campus, which looked a lot like IIT Chennai, with the same banyan trees, wide promenades, and scatter of school buildings.

"Hey, Ashok, why don't you have a car?" Parvati asked. It was a casual question, perhaps just to make conversation, but Ashok felt ashamed. There was no reason he shouldn't have one; the Tata Nano, the world's cheapest car, had come out in India that year. And he knew Parvati had grown up with a car at home, plus two scooters. He wished Parvati's father wasn't sitting there, waiting for his answer. "You don't really need a car in Mumbai," Ashok began. "There are trains, buses, rickshaws—"

"But why can't you drive?" she pressed. *This is a real weakness in me,* Ashok thought. He knew what a car meant: status, privilege, freedom. He didn't make enough money to afford one. But he promised himself he'd buy her one someday.

The engagement came soon after, in a big hall in Trivandrum, where Ashok and Parvati sat on the floor with a mountain of sticky-sweet *laddoos* between them. They were surrounded by piles of fruits, some of them expensive and out of season: apples, grapes, even tender plums. Parvati wore an eighteen-yard blue *sari*, and Ashok had on an expensive blue dress shirt. They both wore garlands of white carnations around their necks. As Ashok grinned and talked with ease to the party guests, Parvati watched him, not knowing how to feel. At the end of the ceremony she sang a Carnatic song about Lord Vishnu, protector and preserver. Ashok had already performed in his confident but unpracticed way the "Raag Desh," a romantic nighttime song. He had wanted to accompany Parvati with his flute, but it had been too hard to pull off. Parvati thought the songs had come out better separately.

That night, after the ceremony, Ashok tried to take Parvati's hand as they walked out from the engagement hall. "This is Trivandrum. This is not Bombay," Parvati said, and shook him off. "If you hold my hand at this time of night, people will come and bash you for taking advantage of a girl." "But what is wrong? We're engaged," said Ashok. "Not here, Ashok," she said. She had been in Trivandrum long enough to know. "And if they see me smiling, then it means I'm a different kind of girl." Frustrated at her prudishness, Ashok dropped her hand.

What if this doesn't go well? What if we decide to call it off because of some fight? thought Ashok. There was still time before the wedding. Time for everything to go wrong.

In the months between the engagement and marriage, Ashok's thoughts ran. He thought of the last engagement, and of Nada's last-minute call. Parvati could phone anytime now and say she was still in love with Joseph. She could say that if she and Ashok got married they might end up fighting and get divorced. Or she might not get into IIT Bombay, and then she'd have no good reason to come. She would call off the wedding, his father's name would be beyond repair, and he would never marry.

But Parvati was accepted to IIT Bombay and moved in July to the city, where she planned to stay in a campus hostel until their wedding day. She arrived with her parents and her baggage at Kurla, one of Mumbai's most chaotic train stations. Ashok had booked them a taxi from the station, hoping to impress her father. As her parents unloaded her bags, Parvati took note of the scene before her. The station was filled with trash, stray dogs, and limbless beggars. The signs had dried *paan* spit on them. When a train arrived, men and women hurled their bodies onto it—pushing, shoving, and shouting obscenities at one another. In the rush to get on, many people were left behind on the crowded platform. Some who made it on hung off the side of the train cars or sat on top, risking electrocution.

A nearby overpass was also under construction, adding to the chaos and noise. But Parvati was thrilled. She could not wait to leave sleepy Trivandrum behind. As she got down from the train, she placed her hand into Ashok's, who squeezed it as a welcome to the city.

After Parvati's parents left to go back to Trivandrum, before the wedding, it began to monsoon in Mumbai. It always monsooned in the city in July, but this year the rain was heavier, harder. Meteorologists blamed it on El Niño or a subtropical westerly jet. Parvati had seen enough Bollywood films to know that the monsoon in Mumbai led to romance: shared umbrellas, wet *saris*, the dreamy way the trees and seashore glistened in the rain. When Ashok came to see her at her hostel, he found her bags packed for an overnight stay.

"Oh," he said, looking up at her, surprised. "I wanted to ask you, but I was not sure if you would want to come."

"You're the only reason I came to Bombay," she said. "So I just want to be with you, and get to know you."

When they left the hostel it was still pouring, the kind of rain that covered everything in mud. The kind that splattered *kurtas* and ruined *chappals* and exasperated the city's maids, who clucked at all the work they had to do. The rain soaked through Parvati's jeans to her skin, but she did not mind.

Ashok's apartment, in a busy eastern suburb, was neat and clean and compact. Parvati liked him better for it. She imagined them living together in just a bare single room and found herself charmed by the thought. She decided she wanted to try kissing him inside the cozy apartment as the rain beat hard against the window. But then she remembered when he'd surprised her with a kiss in Trivandrum, and how his breath had been awful. She'd told him, prudishly, "You have to brush your teeth twice." "Do you think couples sharing a toothbrush is romantic?" he had joked back, trying to save the moment. "No," she'd said, unsmiling. "It's unhygienic."

Now, inside his apartment, Parvati said, "I'll kiss you only if you brush your teeth." He did, and they kissed, and it was better. Afterward she used his toothbrush without shame, and even felt that he was right: it was romantic to share.

"Hey, Ashok," Parvati said. "Let's take a shower together." Her jeans were soaked, and it was chilly being wet, but that was just an excuse.

What will this be like? Ashok worried, as he had with the Gujarati girl as they danced in his living room.

The shower was very small, and the two of them filled up the space. As the water ran, they hugged each other. Parvati was ready to go further. Forget the *kanyadaan* at the wedding; plenty of women were given away not as virgins. But Ashok seemed uncomfortable. He had not expected a girl from a conventional background to be so forward. He worried she was only acting this way for him. *I don't want to take advantage of her,* he thought. And he didn't want to do anything that could ruin their chances of making it to the marriage hall.

His unsureness endeared him to Parvati. "You go," she said, after he had finished washing. "I'll take some more time." Ashok kept Pears brand soap in the shower, the blue kind that smelled of mint extract. When Parvati smelled it afterward, she would always think of that night.

After they got out, Ashok started making his bed on the floor, still thinking that he should not presume.

"Why are you doing this?" asked Parvati, who got down on the floor to sleep beside him, and it was settled. They lay awake for a long time, talking and hugging, as the rain pounded down outside.

For the next few weeks, Parvati came to stay with Ashok on the weekends. In August, just before their wedding day, Parvati bought Ashok a small red wooden car for his thirty-third birthday, shaped like a Rolls-Royce from the 1930s. She hoped it would show him that she didn't mind that he didn't have a car. Forget status and privilege. She also drew a homemade card. When she got to his apartment, she handed him the model car and card and said, "We're not going to get a car, so let's have this." Afterward, she gave him a big hug. But Ashok didn't say anything, not even thank you.

I thought he would think it was romantic, Parvati thought, but it was clear he didn't. She felt stupid about the gift, the card, all of it. She realized Ashok was not the kind of guy who would quote her scenes from movies like *Up*, the way Joseph had. He was not the kind of husband who would be romantic.

♥♥♥♥♥

On the day of the wedding, Parvati woke up annoyed. The beautician began her work at 3 a.m. sharp, because the first ceremony was to begin at 5:30 a.m.—the early time chosen by an astrologer. Parvati fidgeted as she was caked with makeup, draped in gold jewelry, and wrapped in a nine-yard red and gold *sari* her mother had chosen. She hated wearing the color gold, which felt ostentatious and gaudy. *I feel like a clown,* she thought.

When the ceremony began, Parvati was kept to the back at first,

while Ashok looked out at the crowd. Parvati came from a prominent family, so some three thousand people had shown up. Ashok
did not know most of them. *Her family came out in droves,* he thought,
and was upset that he did not have more guests there.

The wedding officially began with a *pooja,* followed by the cus-
tom of the bachelor pretending to leave for Varanasi, saying he did
not want to get married and instead would become a wandering
ascetic. Ashok, bare-chested except for his *yajnopavita,* or sacred
thread, and wearing a *dhoti,* acted the part, holding his stick, begging bowl, and copy of the *Bhagavad Gita,* a book that discussed
the self, nature, and God. "I don't want to get married," Ashok
said, though his voice was halfhearted. Parvati's father, also bare-
chested, his sacred thread also crossing his chest, replied with more
vigor: "No, there's a girl waiting for you. Don't give up everything.
Just take a look at my girl, and you'll change your mind."

Ashok did, and told the crowd that he had decided to get married
after all. He and Parvati exchanged garlands of roses, marigolds,
and jasmine. Parvati's face shone as she smiled, and Ashok saw how
beautiful she was when she was happy. There were white carnations
in her hair. She was weighed down with bloodred bangles and gold
jewelry. As Ashok smiled back at her, he decided he didn't care that
she had more guests there. He was proud that his extended family—
who had witnessed his failed engagement to Nada—was here to see
him make it to the marriage hall. Now that they had exchanged
garlands, he and Parvati were said to be two souls in one body.

The wedding lasted six hours and was filled with tradition and
ceremony. They performed one ritual in which Ashok bent down to
touch Parvati's feet in respect, which was the tradition Parvati liked
best. They also did the *kanyadaan,* in which Parvati's father symbolically gave away his virgin daughter. At last came the most auspicious
time, when they were required to physically tie the knot—three
knots, in fact—on a gold necklace with three threads, for which

Ashok's mother had bought a big jewel. As Parvati sat on her father's lap for the tying, he smiled out at the crowd, looking confident and happy. His hands rested on Parvati's shoulders. Just for a moment, Parvati looked back and gave him a knowing sidelong glance—a look that was captured by the photographer. It was an expression that said that although he had won, she had won too, because, like many women now, she was marrying a man he didn't quite approve of.

Then Parvati looked forward again and lowered her head as was expected. Soon, a priest began chanting *mantras* in Sanskrit. A *nadaswaram* played, its sound as celebratory and loud as a trumpet but reedier. It was an instrument of good fortune, and together with the *mantras* it built the emotion in the room. As the music swelled, Parvati closed her eyes. As Ashok tied the knot, she could feel him standing close beside her. *For once, I'm not going to be lonely anymore,* she thought, and hoped this would be true. *It's going to be the two of us, through thick and thin.*

Their honeymoon, in Coorg, was to be a trip of firsts: first time to the land of coffee plantations, first vacation together, and—they both hoped—first time they'd have sex.

It was the year Ashok turned thirty-three and Parvati twenty-six. It was the year India launched its first mission to Mars, whose position in either of their star charts could have made them unmarriageable. And it was the year astrologers predicted vulgarity and Western influence would spread like a virus, infecting Indian youth, and a leading politician proclaimed that women who drank liquor and wore jeans were bad for Indian culture. Parvati packed her favorite blue jeans for the trip, and on their first night in Coorg drank wine for the first time ever. As they ate a meal in a treehouse restaurant, she grew tipsy, and then they kissed as if they were not in India but some Western country far away.

To them, the name *Coorg* sounded magical. Coorg was also called

Kodagu, but the Anglicized version had stuck ever since British officials treated it as their getaway. The Brits had also dubbed Coorg "the Scotland of India" for its rolling mists and hills. Ashok marveled at how just two days ago they'd gotten married in front of three thousand people, and now they were on a sprawling coffee plantation, almost entirely alone.

The next day, Parvati woke up to her period. She had bad cramps and worried that it would ruin the trip. If she were at home, she'd be untouchable. But Ashok told her that was silly; no one believed that anymore. He suggested they spend the entire day in bed. They ordered all the food they could off the room service menu: vegetarian soup, fried rice, *palak paneer*, *chapati* breads, ice cream, and cake. Ashok told the server, "*Chalo*, bring them all." Their plates came heaped up high like a mountain.

The next night, Parvati felt better, and they went out to the private pool beside their cottage. Parvati wore just her panties and a bra, her wedding henna still dark on her hands. Ashok stripped down to his boxers. As they swam, they kissed, but Ashok didn't try to initiate having sex. He would wait for Mumbai. Instead, he taught Parvati how to float, and they stayed in the pool gliding on the surface for a long time, even though the water was cold. The next day, Ashok took a photo of Parvati on a swing near the cottage wearing blue jeans, a blue *dupatta*, and a seductive eye-smile for the camera.

When they returned to Mumbai, it was the last day of the festival of Ganpati. The streets from the airport were crowded with processions. Massive elephant-headed idols were carried in the air, on horseback, and on floats through swelling crowds. People sang and danced and drummed for Lord Ganesh, god of new beginnings, remover of obstacles. It was as if the entire city were celebrating their union, and their ability to make love, at last.

♥♥♥♥♥

Sex between them wasn't clumsy at first, not the way Ashok thought it might be. But it did become smoother over time. *You don't hit the ground running,* he told himself, remembering one of his father's flash card idioms, as they had sex the first time in the bedroom of their new apartment, just after their honeymoon. *You walk, you limp a bit, then you jog, you hit a stride.* Soon, they were having sex two or three times a week, and Ashok was amazed at how comfortable it felt. They didn't care if the lights were on or off. They didn't worry about how their bodies looked. And they always fell back to talking right after sex, about what took place at his office or her lab at school that day. Or sex segued right into banter, with her making fun of how excitable he got around groups of people, like he had at their wedding, or him jabbing her for how spoiled she acted because of her wealthy upbringing. He secretly found this behavior sexy.

But Parvati didn't think they were hitting a stride. To her, it seemed that their sex didn't have passion, at least not like she had seen in the movies. She didn't like that they transitioned from making love to talking of trivial matters. And she thought the way they had sex felt almost mechanical. With Joseph, she was sure it would have been different, electric. But she was married to Ashok now.

And she was in Mumbai, not Germany, in a north-central suburb that looked a little like Trivandrum. It was greener and less smoggy than the rest of the city and built along an artificial lake. Crocodiles sometimes basked in the sun there, and bird-watchers came to find jacanas, kingfishers, and cormorants. The lake's water, though long ago declared unfit to drink, was a deep, even blue.

Because it was a kind of oasis of calm in the city, their suburb was filled with *firangis* and wealthy Indians. Many of them lived in one apartment complex, a set of ornate, neoclassical high-rises that towered over the suburb's downtown. The high-rises had romantic names like Florentine and Eva. But Ashok and Parvati could not afford to live in the towers, and so they'd moved into an anonymous-looking cooperative complex up on a hill instead. Ashok got them into the complex by telling the society board they were newlyweds. Their apartment, on a high floor, seemed to them spacious and airy.

Parvati worked hard to make the apartment feel like home. She started in the living room, where she hung their marriage photo, which showed her enveloped in deep folds of red and gold, and Ashok, bare-chested, grinning beside her. In the kitchen, she stuck Post-it notes with recipes dictated by her mother to the wall so she could cook the kind of elaborate meals Ashok's mother had at home; this was the measure of a wife. In little corners of the house, she placed sentimental trinkets: the model car she'd bought for Ashok, a lucky lotus flower made of glass, a statue of a little boy and girl holding hands. On their wooden altar, she placed Ram and Sita, the stars of the epic *Ramayana*, who had fallen in love at first sight.

In the beginning, Parvati would also stay up late, until Ashok got home from his night shift at the newspaper, so they could watch TV and gorge on ice cream together. Every day she brought home a different flavor from the Naturals ice cream shop down the road: tender coconut, *anjeer*, mango, or papaya pineapple.

She felt like she was playing house, and it was working. She thought it'd keep working as long as she didn't think of the past too much. It was like in *Yeh Jawaani Hai Deewani*, a Bollywood film that came out just before she and Ashok married, when one character warned that memories were like a box of sweets. If the box was opened, you couldn't eat just one piece.

But sometimes, Parvati needed to be alone and think, and went up to the terrace of their apartment building to do what she called "skywatching." She had done this as a child in Trivandrum, gazing up at the sky as her father told her and her sister all about the stars and solar system and helped them identify Venus and Mars. Now, as she lay on her back on their cool marble roof, she tried to see stars or spot a comet. But she could not see anything because of the heavy pollution in Mumbai.

Mumbai was light polluted from its traffic, signboards, and brightly lit offices and residences. It was air polluted from the number of vehicles, road construction, and open burning of fuel and waste. It was so polluted that living in Mumbai was said to be equivalent to smoking four packs of cigarettes a day. It was said to cause respiratory symptoms, heart and lung disease, and premature mortality. Parvati sometimes dreamed of another life—of moving out to the country, even—where she could see clear skies.

There were other moments that broke the spell of being newly married, when Parvati realized she did not really know Ashok. After a visit to his family in Trivandrum, where he told each of his relatives how wonderful they were, he disparaged them in private to Parvati. "But—what are you doing?" she asked, surprised at his duplicity.

"I was talking to my grandma. She is eighty-seven years old," said Ashok. "There is no point in telling her something bad."

At first, Parvati couldn't get past this. But as she thought about it, she realized this was something that wouldn't change. She knew she couldn't keep listening to this false praise for the rest of her life. From then on, she left the room when the praising began.

❦❦❦❦❦

The week before her first exams at IIT Bombay, and just a few months into their marriage, Parvati told Ashok she needed a break.

"Sure, *Chiboo*," said Ashok, using Parvati's childhood nickname, which she'd always hoped her husband would use someday.

And so they took off for Matheran, a hill station east of Mumbai with sweeping vistas of the plains and valleys. They took a train partway up the hill and rode horses the rest of the way up. It was peak season, and the whole of Matheran was packed with tourists. Their hotel, which looked seedy, was full of nervous couples and rickety furniture. It was difficult to get a moment alone.

The next day, they decided to get up at sunrise, 5 a.m. But when they got to the top of the mountain, it was still dark, and a lone *chai-wallah* told them that in December the sun didn't rise until six. And so they sat quietly and drank tea in the dark, watching as the local people woke and swept and walked to their baths. It reminded them both of the south, and Ashok began to speak of his childhood in Tenkasi.

In Tenkasi Ashok had gone to a Protestant school just before the new millennium, and the pastors had read to the children from the book of Revelations, warning of the water and the deluge. In Tenkasi Ashok dove into a pond that was twenty feet deep, although he couldn't swim. His friend had dared him, and for long seconds he sank under and under, his mind going blank, until his friend had pulled him out, laughing as he choked up water. In Tenkasi his father had quizzed him and his brother from the flash cards: "What does it mean when you say you have HATCHED a SCHEME?" "Okay, tell me the meaning of *through THICK and THIN*." Ashok would always try to answer first.

Ashok also told her about his years in Chennai and Trivandrum, though he omitted the part about the *chai-wallah* and the man in the movie theater. Instead he told her about how his father moved from business to business, and when the business flopped and the family had almost no money, they were forced to move again. As he spoke, Parvati regretted having talked so much about growing up wealthy in Trivandrum—about the car and scooters, having *chai* brought to her in bed, and a fancy case for her violin. She began to see Ashok differently.

Ashok asked Parvati why she had needed a trip away.

"*Chetan,*" she said, using the Malayalam term of respect she had taken to calling him, a kind of distancing nickname he didn't quite like. "My past is coming back to me and giving me a lot of trouble. So I am not able to focus at school."

Ashok nodded, but Parvati knew he didn't understand. He couldn't, because she wasn't telling him everything. She didn't tell him that nothing felt right—not engineering school, not Mumbai, not him. *I was not supposed to get married to this guy,* she thought, as the orb of the sun crept over the mountains.

Some days, Parvati felt a strong aversion to this new life they had constructed in Mumbai. On those days she missed Joseph and wanted nothing to do with Ashok. She hated playing house.

"I want to take a break from school," she said now. "Take leave for a little while."

"Okay, *Chiboo*, you go ahead," said Ashok. "Take a break."

But on other days, she knew she was the problem. On these days, Parvati felt grateful to Ashok and almost loved him for allowing her the room to be confused. He had not even hesitated in supporting her decision to take time off from school.

They filled the rest of their trip to Matheran with activities. They rode horses, climbed a mountain, and went rafting along with other nervous, newly married couples. In each photo from the trip, Parvati attempts a smile. After they returned to Mumbai, they sent the photos to their parents, and Ashok's father wrote a glowing e-mail to Parvati: "Both you and Ashok look so happy, so young . . . I am very happy for you. DAD."

Shortly afterward, Ashok's aunt and uncle came to stay. Like Ashok's father, they could talk for hours. But unlike him, they mostly spoke about themselves. The last day they were in town, Parvati went to the mall after school to find a book to read at a coffee shop—anything to not go home to them. She picked up Amitav Ghosh's *Sea of Poppies*, which was about the colonial opium trade and the people it hurt, and she read and read, until she stopped on a page that ended: "It was useless, she knew, to be seized by regret now, on the very night when her fate had been wedded to his . . ."

That night, as Ashok's aunt and uncle talked endlessly about themselves, Parvati had nothing to say. *I am listening to them and falling sick,* she thought. The next morning, she woke up with a bad cold and fell back to sleep. The aunt and uncle woke expecting breakfast. They pestered Ashok, saying, "We are here, we want our breakfast and then we need to go. How can she be sleeping?"

Ashok tried to shake Parvati awake. "They want some breakfast. Do you want to make it?" he asked.

"No," Parvati said with a groan, and rolled over. Since the wedding she had gone back to sleeping almost ten hours a night, like she had at IIT Chennai when Joseph was away.

Ashok made coffee but soon ran out of milk. He offered to make *dosas,* but his aunt said she'd make them herself. They left indignant that Ashok's new bride was so uncultured she couldn't be bothered to get out of bed.

When Parvati woke up at around 9 a.m., she sleepily shuffled into the kitchen. "Is there any milk at home?" she asked.

"No, you have green tea," Ashok said, his voice tight. Later, he confronted her. "You could have at least got up and said hi or something. What's the harm in at least making tea? They were just going to be here for a day or two. You could pretend to like them."

"I'm sorry," she said, surprised to see Ashok angry. "I wasn't feeling well, and I needed to sleep for longer."

Ashok's expression softened. "If that's the case, then fine," he said, and in his easy way let the incident go. Neither he nor Parvati brought it up again, but after that, Parvati was certain his family had branded her as unfit to be a household girl. She told herself she didn't want to be one anyway.

On New Year's Eve, Parvati woke up feeling hopeful. Exams were over, IIT Bombay was finished for the semester, and she'd applied for a break from school after that. Maybe she wouldn't go back at all. The promise of freedom thrilled her. Outside their cooperative complex, puppies had been born. New high-rises were going up. New Western chains were opening across Powai. New, new, new. That day, Parvati cleaned the apartment, even the places that were hard to reach. She bought a small chocolate cake and made a hand-made poster that said "Happy New Year."

But when Ashok came home, he looked at the cake and poster and said, "Oh, wow, Happy New Year," and then, "Let's go to sleep." It was not yet midnight, but he was exhausted from work. He also didn't like New Year's. *One more year of resolutions you'll never keep,* he thought. Ashok felt that one part of him was still a child, while the other was as cynical as an old man.

The next day, Parvati started a diary for her time off from school, writing in a small green and maroon floral notebook: "January 1, 2014. First New Year after marriage. Nothing much but cut a cake and then went to sleep."

January 2014, Gchat:

Ashok: Let's decide not to continue with the PhD
Parvati: Not ready for PhD. Chttn I feel so stupid
Ashok: Chill maadi

Parvati: Chttn ur my sunshine . . . one of the rare ppl who has told me
not to keep lot of options except to opt to be myself.
Ashok: U are making me blush ☺

> **Parvati:** When i told yes to you at my place in tvm when u came to see
> me i said yes to everything about you . . . Good or bad . . . I might
> murmur stuff i don't like because it's new to me . . . Once I get
> used . . . My yes will take its full form literally.

> **Ashok:** OUOUOUOYIU.

Parvati and Ashok sometimes were more affectionate online than in real life. Online, they could try out what they wanted to say without the in-person rejection. Online, they could test out the kind of couple they wanted to be.

In the official paperwork requesting Parvati's leave, Ashok wrote that his wife was having a difficult time adjusting to their arranged marriage. He did not need to provide details because this was a problem even the stodgiest university bureaucrat could understand. After some deliberation, the leave was approved.

Parvati spent the first month of her break rearranging the furniture in the house, cooking her mother's recipes without much success, and sleeping long hours in her baggy pajamas. She tried Gchatting Ashok, but he was often busy with work. And so instead she loaded Joseph's Facebook page and clicked through photos of him and his Catholic wife.

First was a photo of him and her in a pristine green field, her arms wrapped around his stomach. Next was a photo of them with her family, all dressed in fancy *saris* and *kurtas*. After that they were pictured on a campus in Germany wearing winter jackets and on the ground a light dusting of snow.

On a few occasions, Parvati talked to Joseph over Skype. They spoke tentatively at first—so much time had passed—but then the conversation became more natural. When Joseph asked Parvati about her marriage, she told him everything was good. She could not bring herself to ask about his wife. On one call, Joseph told her that he'd heard the ancient banyan tree at IIT Chennai, the one whose roots went deep into the ground, was going to be cut down. He said the students were agitating against it. After Parvati hung up from these calls, she often felt depressed.

When Ashok came home from work one night, she was crying. "I have no way to figure this out," she said.

"You have to," he told her. "You can."

Parvati just kept crying.

"What's happened in the past, let's put it behind us," Ashok said. "Let's bury it and move on. To live a life together you have to focus on the future."

"I know," she said. "I know." But along with the weather of Mumbai and Trivandrum, she kept the weather of Berlin on her phone.

She called her sister many times during her break, even though her sister was busy with work, her husband, and a new baby. Sometimes, Parvati cried and ranted; other times she hinted at suicide. "There is no point in living anymore," she said. She blamed her sister for not supporting her relationship with Joseph. She blamed her father for keeping her from marrying Joseph and pushing her to go to the IITs, when so many other women were choosing their work and husbands. "Don't be like this," her sister said. "It is you who have tortured you the most." She reminded Parvati that she had chosen Ashok and her school program. And then Parvati blamed herself. By the time Ashok got home from work, Parvati had cried herself to sleep.

February 2014, Gchat:

Parvati: Do you feel any comm gap between us . . . I feel u don't want to listen or u r getting bored . . . I feel I am bothering you

Ashok: I want to listen to you . . . Seriously . . . I was writing and you were unloading

Parvati: So I have to keep some time off to tell u about what bothers me

Ashok: I have the fear that if I don't continue writing I might not reach anywhere

Parvati: Chttn I don't think I have ever disturbed you while u r at work writing

Ashok's novel about the dysfunctional couple was not being written. Parvati's emotions were taking up most of his writing time. In the mornings before work, when he used to write, he often found her crying. He would sit down and they'd talk, and a whole morning was lost, and then another. At night, after work, when the house was quiet, he was mostly too tired to write.

February 2014, Gchat:

Ashok: [If I see you cry] I will also break down . . . That is a sight I can't take

Parvati: Sounds like I am always going to be alone when I cry

Weeks into her break, Parvati began to draw again. This time, she didn't sketch Hindu gods and goddesses or dancers of Kathakali but instead drew celebrities from American movies she and Ashok watched together. She drew Jennifer Lawrence, Emma Watson, and the cast of *Friends*. She watched YouTube tutorials that instructed her on how to draw lips, mouths, and eyes, instructing her to "break up the major planes into minor planes," "look at the landscape surface," and "make sure to observe all the angles." She began to think that drawing was a bit like engineering.

She also started riding the train with Ashok to work downtown so she could visit the galleries in Kala Ghoda, an art district shaped like a crescent moon. In Kala Ghoda, time seemed to move slower than the rest of the city. The architecture was colonial, Indo-Saracenic, and neoclassical. The cafés had high windows and were expensive and airy. The streets were wide, but little traffic entered, and a person could walk for long minutes uninterrupted. Today, Kala Ghoda looked like how people described the old, colonial Mumbai, when the city hadn't yet become overpopulated, and when you could still pluck mangos from the trees.

Parvati's favorite gallery in Kala Ghoda was the Jehangir Art Gallery, which invited visitors to come in and talk to the artists. The gallery's art included soft watercolors of rural areas, bronze sculptures of Hindu gods, and neon acrylics of proud village women. After Parvati visited, she often went home and drew for hours. As she did, she began to feel more like herself.

Soon, Parvati focused her efforts on drawing portraits, and specifically on eyes. She had heard that the eyes were the most difficult part of the body to capture, because they expressed the most feeling. Kamala Das said eyes were like a "white, white sun burning." An Indian yogi had said the heart smiled through the eyes. The beloved Sufi poet Rumi had said the same. Rumi had also said, "Rub your eyes, and look again at love, with love."

As she drew, Parvati began to give Ashok more space, and as she did, she noticed how he came back to her.

February 2014, Gchat:

Ashok: I was thinking about how I rolled on top of you and you rocked me clasped between your legs

Parvati: That's what you're thinking about?

Ashok: Yes chikki that's true

Chikki, an Indian sweet, made of groundnuts and jaggery. *Chikki*, the color of honey, and of Parvati's eyes. Parvati had cut her hair during the break, shorter than she'd ever worn it. Ashok told her it looked "naughty and impish," because few Indian girls wore their hair short. When they had sex now, they tried new positions, even put their mouths on each other.

Parvati got better, Parvati got worse. Whenever she had a bad meltdown, Ashok called it a "crying jag." One day, he heard Parvati crying so loudly he knew it was going to be the worst jag she'd had yet.

From the *Oxford Dictionaries*: *Jag—a sharp projection . . . Origin— Late Middle English (in the sense "stab, pierce"): perhaps symbolic of sudden movement or unevenness.*

The jag started after Parvati got off the phone with Ashok's family members. As she spoke to them, she realized how foreign they still felt. She hadn't chosen them, not really. She hardly knew them. And she didn't feel connected to them at all. The more she thought about it, the more upset she got. After hanging up, she went inside her room and began to sob.

"What's up, *Chiboo*?" Ashok said, coming into their bedroom.

Recently, someone had told him that the name of their suburb meant "drama" or "hysterics" in the Gujarati language. *My life since moving here has been all drama and hysterics,* he thought.

Parvati looked up at him now. *Who is this person?* He was just a blank space. A space barely filled in over the last year. He was a stranger, one she had traded for her father.

"Why are you crying?"

"It's about my past," Parvati said, weeping now, though inwardly she reproached herself to stop.

Ashok sat beside her, not knowing what else to do.

"Ashok," she said finally, "if I go into one of my phases, don't ask me what is the reason for my crying."

"Okay," he said.

"I cry even when you aren't here."

"That's really something to worry about," he said, and left to go get his phone to tell his editor he needed the day off.

Ashok sat hugging her as she cried. After that, they went to sleep, even though it was the afternoon. When they woke up, the apartment felt hot and stale, and it had grown dark outside. A car would have been a welcome distraction, but of course they did not have one. They decided to take a walk, meandering through the suburb's downtown, past the D-Mart grocery store and the new Starbucks. When they got back to the apartment, Ashok turned on a Malayalam movie, which he thought Parvati would like. Soon, she began to talk over it.

"I should not have wept so bad. It must have scared you, Ashok," she said.

"It's fine," he said. "You had to. But your weeping made me very worried." Sometimes, Ashok felt afraid of his new wife.

"I won't cry from here on out," she said, her voice solemn, as if she were making a promise. "I'll deal with it in a way which is more mature. We'll talk about it."

"Okay," said Ashok, though he wasn't sure the promise could be trusted.

ღღღღღ

In April, Ashok bought a car.

He'd worried about not having one for months. He knew Parvati's desire for a car was linked to her desire for him. In all the films—Bollywood, Tamil, Malayalam, even American and British—men took women out on long drives in their cars or on their motorcycles. It was how they fell in love. "You are *that* kind of girl who wants to . . . take long romantic drives," he teased Parvati once, and she had said, without hesitation, "Yes, I am that kind of girl." Ashok had overheard her on the phone with her relatives, telling them how much she missed driving.

So Ashok bought the car. He had to empty his savings account and take out a loan to do it, but *voilà*, he thought, now they had one. The Tata Nano had turned out to be too cheap—so cheap it did not work. The car they bought was squat and boxy like a golf cart, and one of the most economical vehicles on the market, at 3.3 *lakhs*. But it worked, and it was theirs. Ashok referred to it as "the poor man's Merc."

When they first got married, Ashok told Parvati he was an "amazing driver," but once they got the car, she saw this wasn't true. He was anxious and uncertain in all his movements and had no idea how to follow road signs. Sometimes, he'd freeze in the middle of the road in heavy traffic as rickshaws darted around him. Motorcycles would nearly clip the car, and giant, brightly painted carrier trucks would barrel past, their "Horn OK please" signs disappearing in the distance. A cacophony of horns would sound, until at last Ashok unfroze and crossed the intersection.

"I saw how amazing you are," Parvati told him after one such incident, laughing.

"This doesn't happen all the time, just today," Ashok protested.

"You stop saying that you are amazing, that day I'll believe you," said Parvati, and Ashok laughed with her.

❦❦❦❦❦

Ashok had a new goal: to not just finish the novel but also find a publisher. He could see the way the novel had changed with each woman he was with—from Nada, when his writing was lighter, to their breakup, when the book turned dark, to his breakup with Mallika, when his writing became despairing. Now, with Parvati, his writing had changed again. Since marriage, he wrote more authentically about relationships—about the complex power struggles, unspoken hurts, and small moments of grace between husband and wife. He also sometimes pilfered little pieces of Parvati's life that she shared with him, such as how, in her college days, she had tried to build a boat that could fly, but it never took off from the ground.

It had been six months since Parvati's break began. Ashok was now able to write more often in the mornings, though there were still many days wasted. If he were to find a publisher, he'd need uninterrupted time to write. But when Ashok asked Parvati what her plans were, she told him she was still confused. She said she wasn't sure whether to go back to school. As Ashok listened to her waver, he grew irritated with her in a way she had not seen before.

At the newspaper, a colleague had recently quoted a Marathi saying about marriage: *Love is like a scorpion's sting. At first it's painful pleasure. But as the poison begins to seep in you feel the pain more.*

"This is not the way things should be," he told Parvati, his voice severe. "You cannot indefinitely be depressed. You have to consider that there are others living with you."

Parvati was quiet. She knew he was right.

That week, she called her oldest friend from childhood, whom she had not spoken to in years. Pacing across their living room floor—from their altar with their gods by the door to her wedding photo and back—Parvati told her friend about all that had happened since they last talked. She began with Joseph and ended with Ashok and the loneliness of her long break in Mumbai, a city of eighteen million or more. A city where it seemed anyone could disappear.

Her friend listened, and at the end said, "Do you think there is any future with this guy?"

With Joseph.

"I'm married to Ashok," said Parvati. In that simple statement, she knew she had her answer.

She would give up on Joseph. She would go back to school. And she would try to love Ashok as best she should.

It was time to pick a role, pick a life.

After Parvati hung up, she felt a kind of calm she hadn't felt in a long time. And she did not cry after this, fulfilling the promise she'd made to Ashok—not until what happened with the baby.

IN TIME

Maya and Veer, 2014 to 2015

"The bite wounds on your lower lip
So distress my heart
That it seems we are still one
Though we've been so long apart?"

—*Jayadeva,* The Gita Govinda

Veer made plans to take Maya out to dinner, which he never did, at a restaurant in Juhu by the sea. But it rained so hard that day, and the night before, that the roads were flooding, and they saw Juhu would take hours to reach. The morning paper reported that the runway to Juhu's airport had turned into a lake. It warned that because of all the rain, a crocodile had walked on land and dragged a woman washing clothes into the water. And it noted that in the west-central part of the country, because of the monsoon, it "rained happiness" but "poured worry" too.

Maya and Veer decided to go to the mall for dinner instead, a common refuge when the city got too hot or rainy. On the road, motorcyclists held umbrellas, riding one-handed, or drove with plastic bags over their faces. Rickshaw drivers unfurled their rain flaps, though they never kept out all the rain. As they sat in traffic growing hungry, Veer brought up a recent visit with his aunt. "Janu told her he wanted to drink alcohol," he told Maya, dropping his voice low. "He said he wants to drink it since 'it's not a big deal, and Maya and Veer and Subal always do it.'" Maya made a face. "Now she has some *masala*," Veer said. Maya nodded; he was right. Gossip like this could lead to trouble. *Janu is too smart,* she thought, turning to look at him in the back seat. They'd have to start disguising their drinks at restaurants.

But all gossip was forgotten when they got inside the mall, which was huge and new and gleaming. Banners hung in the mall's atrium boasting of an upscale Chinese restaurant and Italian *ristorante*. As rain dripped from the ceiling, a sinewy man crouched with a bucket and rag and wiped up every drop. Maya and Veer wandered from floor to floor, Janu running with delight in front of them. He was four now, and excitable and curious about everything.

They chose an all-you-can-eat Indian restaurant, which Veer preferred, with gaudy colored pendants hanging from the ceiling. As they ate *pani puri* and other *chaat*, a DJ put on a sixties-era British love song for a couple's anniversary, and Janu begged them to dance. "Not yet," said Maya, who was busy checking and rechecking her phone, as Veer went up to the buffet for more food.

After dinner was over and Janu was allowed to get up, he ran over to a tarot card reader. The reader, who was fat and had a lazy eye, told Veer, who asked for a reading, that he should start preparing for a worsening future. Veer only laughed at this. Afterward, the DJ switched to Punjabi music, and Veer and Janu began to dance. Maya, who had gotten a text from Subal after a long silence, began to film them on her phone.

On the way home, they let Janu sit in the front of the car and put the seat all the way back. Veer sang made-up lullabies to help him sleep. "*Bana,*" he sang, "*soja bana.*" Janu's eyes began to close. It had stopped raining, and a light fog hung all around them. "*Laddoo,*" Veer sang. "*Pyaar.*"

Janu, who was old enough to sleep in his own bed now but didn't, slept that night pressed against the curve of Veer's back, clutching a piece of Maya's hair in his hand.

❦❦❦❦❦

The road to Pune was covered with a misty fog, the kind that suggested ghosts and apparitions. Maya chattered as they drove, her anticipation of the trip ahead loosening up her tongue. She had seen very little of Subal that month. His visits had become even more erratic after he quit his new job, which never paid him. To see Maya, he had to drive more than an hour in traffic. But now they'd have an entire two days together.

"I'm driving, Maya," Subal said, annoyed by her constant chatter, and reached over to slap her thigh.

The road began to wind through the mountains, from which were suspended ads for the phone company Tata Docomo and the Indian whiskey brand Royal Stag. The fog made it appear as if the letters were hanging in the sky. *T-A-T-A*, and then air. The fog thickened as they drove, and soon all Subal could see was white. Maya, who craned her neck forward, spied a mountain peak through the haze. "Look at that," she said. "Let's go up there. To the top."

Subal nodded but didn't say anything. After a few minutes, he pulled over at a rest stop known for its stale *idlis* and watery *sambar*. As she went inside, he didn't follow her and instead took deep drags of a cigarette.

When they reached Pune, a city polluted by scooters and motorbikes, Subal let Maya out of the car. He had a business meeting and didn't want to be late. After he'd quit his job, his usual bluster had disappeared, along with his proclivity for jokes, and his baritone voice had become strained. But he had an idea for a new business venture, and the meeting was to raise money for it. He tried not to think about how much depended on it going well.

When they met up in a café later, Subal told Maya the man had promised him a five *crore* investment, a sum so sizeable it gave him pause. Instead of excitement, he felt only worry, a pit in his stomach like the stone of a mango. And Maya was so congratulatory it made him feel worse. She also had a business meeting that afternoon, with an engineer to troubleshoot an app she'd bought for her preschool. As she pulled out her phone to confirm the time, Subal stared at her.

"Why can't you get the problem fixed over the phone, Maya?" he asked, his voice edged with suspicion. "I don't understand."

Maya explained that she had tried that already, and it hadn't worked. Subal was not convinced.

"Do you like someone there?" he said, his voice getting louder as they walked out to the car. "Is that why you're going?"

"What? No. No." Maya dropped her phone into her purse as if it was hot.

As Subal got in the front seat, he told Maya that she would have to hail a rickshaw to her meeting. "Good-bye," he said, and shut the door, leaving her standing in the middle of the road, motorcycles and scooters whizzing past her. Maya steeled herself not to cry.

When she messaged Subal later, he told her he would sleep at a cousin's house and she would have to find her own accommodation. *What did I do wrong?* she thought. *I haven't done anything.*

Last-minute bookings for hotels in Pune turned out to be pricey, or the hotel had no vacancy, or it was in a dangerous part of town. As Maya kept searching, she began to feel anxious. It wasn't safe for women to roam alone after dark. She ended up asking for help finding a hotel from the engineer, whose name was Mohan. Mohan was several years younger than Maya and drove a Royal Enfield motorcycle. He wore a soul patch and an earring and had an open, boyish face. Maya wouldn't allow herself to think he was good-looking.

For several hours that night, Mohan drove Maya from hotel to hotel to check prices and vacancy. He kept apologizing that he couldn't let her stay at his home, which would not be appropriate for a woman traveling alone. At last, they found a reasonable hotel in the shopping district. Maya thanked him profusely for his help. In his formal, polite way, Mohan told her it was nothing and waited outside until she got up to her room.

Upstairs, Maya flopped, exhausted, onto her hotel bed and ordered room service, Indian-Chinese. She thought of how Subal loved Indian-Chinese, and then she could not stop thinking of him. She checked her phone, but he had not messaged her. She tried hard not to get upset. She pictured herself standing like an idiot in traffic and grew angry. Veer had not messaged her either. When she fell asleep, her teeth were clenched.

The next morning, Subal came to pick up Maya at the hotel and acted as if nothing had happened. He was smiling and talkative and told her all about his visit to his cousin's. Then he peppered her with questions. But Maya wouldn't answer. As he got onto the highway, she refused to answer, sitting still in her seat. Eventually, he fell quiet and pulled over at the same rest stop with the watery *sambar*. As Maya went to the bathroom, he sucked down another cigarette.

Back in the car, Subal asked how Maya had found her hotel, and she told him about the night's adventure. She said there had been almost nowhere to stay and that she had asked the engineer for help.

Subal let loose. He called Maya stupid for not booking a hotel in advance. He told her it was unsafe to roam around the city at that hour. He implied she was a *randi*, a prostitute, for calling the engineer.

He saw on her face that he had gone too far. "Okay, Maya, I need to close my mouth."

"You need to use your head and then maybe you wouldn't use your mouth," she snapped back. Her voice was bitter, but then it faltered. "Your behavior, the things you say, you can't keep doing them and expect me not to break," she said, and began to cry.

"Okay, Maya," Subal said. "I am wrong . . . Okay, Maya, I am wrong. Okay, Maya, I am wrong." He went on like this, like a broken record on a British-era gramophone, while Maya said nothing. Finally, he stopped talking. The car was silent as they passed back into Mumbai city limits.

When Subal dropped her off at home, he said he would understand if she "walked out" of what they had. Maya didn't answer and slammed the car door behind her.

Later that week, she was at school, trying not to think about Subal, when the phone rang. It was Veer, calling in the middle of the day, which he never did.

"Mayu," he said, "I'm on my way back from the factory. Are you home? I thought we could have tea."

Maya held the phone away from her, astonished, and brought it back up to her ear.

"No, *Kancha*. I'm at school," she said. She was always at school at this time. "I—I need to stay here. But Pallavi is at home. She can make you tea."

There was a pause, and the silence seemed to stretch for a long time.

"No, that's okay," Veer said. "I only wanted it if you were there."

♥♥♥♥♥♥

In the weeks after the Pune trip, Veer—who saw Maya was upset over something she would not share—began to pick fights with her at home. He asked why she was always on her phone at night, out with friends after work, and why they never went on vacation. After Maya finally agreed to plan a trip, they settled on Alibaug, an old, dusty coastal town a few hours away.

On the way there, Veer drove fast, though the roads were winding. As they approached Alibaug, he hit a stray dog as it ran in front of their car. He said it could not be helped and did not stop. He said he was sure the dog kept running after it was hit. Many people hit dogs and kept going. Maya and Janu did not look back. It was better not to spoil the day.

They checked into a guesthouse that was cheap and basic, but the outside was lovely, with hammocks, tall trees painted red, white, and yellow, and palm trees that hung very low. The coast was not far away.

When they reached the beach, the sun was falling deep in the sky. Janu ran onto the sand and begged to ride a pony. The horse was pure white with a colorful saddle and was making trips up and down the beach. They gave Janu a few rupees and told him to go ahead. After the pony ride, Janu dug deep holes in the sand, and Maya walked toward the surf. Veer started to follow her but hesitated. He had always been afraid of the water. The force around the ocean was not good for epileptics, or so he believed. He feared another seizure. When Maya turned back and saw his trepidation, she took his hand in her own.

Together, they walked toward the water, navigating around shells and fallen coconuts. The sun was setting now, and the surf was frothy. The tide was coming in, the water covering their feet. As they looked out at the sea, Veer let his hand drop from hers, and they turned back toward the sand.

"*Bana*—" they called, and Janu came running.

♥♥♥♥♥

As Janu had gotten older—he was now almost five—he had grown very close with his mother. At home in the mornings, while she was reading the paper, he often sat on her lap until she scolded him to go get dressed for the day. When they were riding in the car to school with their driver, Maya would lean on Janu's shoulder and say, "I love you," pouting her lips into a kissy face. Janu would always say "I love you" back, and squish his lips the same way. He'd often wrap his arms around her face and draw her close until they got to school.

Over time, they had developed a kind of sympathetic relationship. If Maya stayed home from work because she was feeling sick, Janu insisted he was sick and couldn't go to school either. If she stayed out at night, he couldn't sleep. He'd toss and turn and even wet the bed. If she ate nonvegetarian food, Janu insisted he also had to eat it, though Maya made him promise not to tell his father. Janu called his father, who was in Africa for work again. On WhatsApp, his father's away message was "DND"—Do Not Disturb. But Janu wanted to disturb him. He called and called and got his voice-mail. "Papa, family," Janu said into the phone, his voice serious, his long eyelashes flapping. "Family means relationship. Relationship with Mama, Papa, Grandma, Grandpa, all. Work in this country. A family means a relationship. And you don't leave the people you love. You work in the same country. Where you live. Not another country."

While Janu was close to Veer, he could also be distrustful of him. On the rare times Veer watched him, the day would always start out well. They'd often practice exercises together. "First exercise continuously begin," Veer would call out, like they did at school, and Janu would show off a somersault or jumping jack, wearing only his white undershirt and *chaddis*. "Wahhhahahah. Tom Cruise or Salman Khan," Veer would say, grinning, and Janu would giggle.

Or Veer would help him with his homework, or they'd drive around their suburb and Veer would buy Janu gifts—a giant Spider-Man balloon or an Avengers or Minions toy. But inevitably Veer would get distracted by a work call, and Janu would be left to play by himself, his balloon deflated on the floor. Veer was working harder than ever again, and it showed on his body. He had lost weight, but his paunch had come back. His hair had grown long, he had a scraggly beard, and he'd developed dark circles under his eyes.

On these days, by the time Maya got home from work or errands, both of them might be in a bad mood and fighting. Veer had been trying to work or read the newspaper, and Janu annoyed him. Or Veer had flicked Janu's ear in an awkward attempt at play, and Janu had recoiled, saying, "Hey, don't disturb me, Pop." Or Janu had been allowed to play with his dad's phone as a distraction, but then the battery ran down and Veer tried to take it back. "Dirty, dirty fellow," Janu shouted one night, with startling intensity. "Liar on a fire." *"Matkar,"* Veer shouted back. On these days, when Maya walked in the door, both seemed relieved to have her home.

Still, at night, it was not Maya but Veer who rubbed Janu's feet, singing him old Bollywood tunes or made-up lullabies. *"Bana,"* he'd sing, *"soja bana . . . Laddoo . . . Pyaar."* When Janu got overtired, it was often Veer and Maya together who got him to stop crying. While he remained a good-humored, independent child, he still got fussy at nighttime. When he cried like this, Maya would lift him up off the couch, and Veer would take him into their bedroom, patting him on the back, saying, *"Bash, bana, bash bash bash."* And if they ever asked Janu whom he loved more, the old, joking question they had first asked when he was a baby, he would still raise both arms in the air.

ლლლლლ

By September, several months after the Pune trip, Maya and Subal had stopped talking for good, and Veer began to ask where he'd gone.

Perhaps he'd noticed that Maya no longer went out with him or was on her phone far less at night. She had even unpinned the photo of Subal from her office wall. "He's busy," Maya said.

A few weeks later, he asked again. "He's busy," she repeated.

It happened in fits and bursts, but when Subal and Maya finally ended things, Maya had cried for days. One of the last times she saw him, they had lunch, and as Maya followed him out of the restaurant, she fell down the stairs and hit her arm on the wall. On the floor, she clutched her elbow in pain. "Tell me what happened," Subal said, sitting beside her, his voice soft. "How did you hurt yourself?"

By then they'd both known they were over.

He struck me to my core, Maya thought now. *I feel wrecked, snapped like a tightrope.* But after a few weeks, she decided she couldn't keep crying and that she would not think of him again. She blocked him by phone, on Facebook, and WhatsApp. For months, Subal tried different ways of reaching her, until Maya asked Ashni at work to send him a message: "Maya has taken really long to get over you and she has suffered enough and so have you. It's time you move on." Maya had not gotten over him but thought she had to pretend.

It was worse for Subal. He had stopped sleeping at night. *It's like I have fallen on my head,* he thought. *Or like she has shut a door on me, locked it, and thrown away the key.* He wondered if she had written him off as a fat, old man; he had always worried that she was younger and so beautiful. He had several boxes of belongings at Maya's preschool, and he called her and threatened to come to her school and burn them. He said he'd walk off into the woods and never come back. He knew he was acting like a fool. *But in her, I found the best in life,* he thought.

Maya thought otherwise. She could see that Subal came into her life for a reason, to teach her how to love again. But in the end he had shown his true self, and she didn't like what she saw. And now, it was all over.

After a month, Veer asked Maya again, "Where is Subal?"

"We don't talk that much anymore," she said. "We've had some disagreements."

After that, Veer didn't ask again.

♥♥♥♥♥

Veer called Maya from Africa to tell her that his father was buying them a giant flat. Or multiple giant flats. A three-bedroom-hall-kitchen for Maya, Veer, and Janu, another for Veer's brother, and a third for himself and his wife. All in the same apartment building. Veer's parents would be just a few floors away.

Veer tried to sell Maya on the benefits. The house would be closer to her preschool. It would be far fancier and larger than what they had now. And Maya could design and decorate it any way she wanted. Still, Maya thought it sounded like hell—or a trap. She couldn't imagine living in the same building with her in-laws again. When she had visited them recently, they'd been cold to her, and Veer's father said she did not come to see them enough. She told Veer she'd move into the apartment on one condition: "If you don't get me out of the house in the next two years, I'm going to walk out of it."

Veer had expected this kind of response from Maya and didn't let it worry him much. He was thrilled about the flat. *A 3BHK, 1,800 square feet*—three times the size of their current apartment. It would be evidence they'd made it beyond middle class, that perhaps they were even rich. It would show off the money he had worked so hard with his father and brothers to make. And now that a new house was within reach, Veer focused on his goal of having Maya open her own school. Not a franchise, but a school she ran—a school from which only she took money. If Maya did that, she could live independently of him at last. And perhaps he could retire alone to the shack by the sea, which he still dreamed of, selling beer, whiskey, and coconut water on the first floor to keep busy, and living alone on the floor above.

Maya went to see her astrologer. On this visit, the astrologer told her she would not leave Veer. He said they would continue to live unhappily together and never get divorced. At least for now, Maya thought the astrologer was right. There was something about Veer that wouldn't let her leave him, some vestige of the man she'd fallen in love with on the banks of the Musi River and promised herself that she'd marry.

After she and Subal ended things, Maya had begun to think about trying to kill herself again. She thought about jumping off a ledge. The astrologer knew this, even though she hadn't mentioned a word about it. "Don't do that," he told her sternly. "If you think about it again, you tell me." She promised him she would.

With Subal gone from her life, Maya had begun going out with other men. Married women in the city, it seemed, were no longer out of reach. She went out with Mohan, the engineer from Pune. She texted with a man she had gone to school with, who now lived in Berlin. And she Facebooked with a philosophical motorcyclist from New Delhi. Each of these men provided her with a kind of companionship Veer didn't, and she only occasionally thought about *hisaab*, and whether her behavior was about a debt to repay.

As if she had a sixth sense, Maya's mother called around this time to ask what was going on in her daughter's marriage. But she could tell something was wrong because Maya was never with Veer when she called. Maya decided not to lie to her. "If someday I get up from this marriage, I don't want you to be shocked," she told her mother.

"It's very easy to get up and leave," her mother said, "but what are you going to do next?" Maya was quiet. Her mother continued, "All relationships are the same. They might be in different degrees. But they all require the same amount of work and understanding." Her mother had been married to Maya's father for thirty-five years. She implied that there were almost always other people in a marriage, and that this was something you got over.

❦❦❦❦❦

In January, when Janu turned five, Maya wrote him a long, mushy letter, telling him that he taught her "what it meant to love someone more than I could ever love anyone else." Veer's hardworking, hard-drinking cousin gave Janu a gift of four lovebirds. The birds were chartreuse and russet brown and aquamarine blue. They had beady, watchful eyes, short beaks, and downy bodies. She and Janu named them Eenie, Meeny, Miney, and Moe. Janu liked the blue lovebird best. The blue lovebird was the smartest and soon learned how to open the cage with its beak. "You are very naughty," Janu told the bird. But Janu liked that his bird was so smart.

Maya started coming home to find all the lovebirds out in the house. Pallavi had to catch them one by one and put them back in their cage.

One day, a lovebird went missing, and then another. Maya realized it was because Pallavi was leaving the door to the porch open when she took the clothes out to dry. On another day, they came home to find them all gone.

On the day Janu had turned five, Veer had turned thirty-nine. He was now working so hard his family, friends, and colleagues began to worry about him. He kept saying he wanted to make enough money for Maya to start her own school, and so that Janu didn't want for anything. He hoped to be able to give away money like his grandfather had. He felt exhausted and drained but told himself he was fine. *I am a Marwari, I am never exhausted from work,* he thought. He told himself he had to surrender his emotions, including the emotion of being tired. *My DNA is muted,* he thought. *I am more of a robot now.*

But Veer did get emotional sometimes. He couldn't always be a robot. He felt this way when Maya didn't give him any time or when she stayed up late typing on her phone, which she had recently resumed doing. Sometimes, Veer snapped at her: "Are you going to take a sleep or just check your Facebook all night?" When he did this, Maya waited a few minutes so she wasn't giving in so easily, and then quietly followed him to bed.

Maya was also working harder. Her preschool had expanded, and she had had to hire a babysitter for Janu. The school continued to attract new students every month, but she still knew every child's name; this was important to her. She often made spot visits to the classrooms to talk with the children. Whenever parents of prospective students visited, Maya or Ashni gave them a speech about how the school would change their child's life. Though Maya didn't like the performative nature of this, she believed in what she was saying. "You will feel good when the child comes home and you see them doing things they couldn't do before," she or Ashni promised, and by the end of their speech, the parents were hooked. Any good parent in Mumbai now wanted their child to learn English, and at an international-style school, which would ensure a high-paying job in their child's future.

Over the years, Maya had grown into a tough but fair principal. During meetings with the teachers, she spoke in a no-nonsense tone: "Nobody is taking a leave on that Saturday. Check *karo. Chutti nahi milega.*" The girls listened with serious expressions, arms folded behind their backs. Maya told a girl who had begun coming late to work that it could not continue. When the girl made excuses, Maya cut her off: "I understand, but other girls will do it and it will become a trend." The girl promised not to come late again. Another teacher asked for a salary increase, and Maya explained when and why she would get it, or not. At the end of meetings she asked: "Any doubts?" There weren't any.

But Maya was also their friend. She ate lunch with her staff every day, which her father taught her to do so that they would respect and work harder for her. At lunch, the younger teachers told Maya and Ashni about their love lives and problems with their parents when they tried to date across community lines. "This is a boyfriend-friendly workplace," Maya said, and she and Ashni sometimes gave them advice. But when one girl showed Maya and Ashni a sexy selfie, Maya drew the line. "Don't show that to the boss," she said.

That year, Maya and Ashni decided to put on a huge Annual Day celebration for the school, for which they set an extravagant budget of 1.5 *lakhs.* They hired a professional choreographer for the children, bought elaborate costumes, and rented a large auditorium.

It was not easy to wrangle 140 wailing children to sing and dance, but at least Maya had Ashni to help. The theme of the performance was "What I want to be when I grow up," and the kids danced in different costumes—policeman, artist, teacher—professions beyond the traditional careers of lawyer, doctor, and engineer. At the end of the song the kids said in unison: "Whatever I want to be at the end of the day, I want to be a good human being." Many of the parents cried.

At the very end, the teachers performed a surprise skit for Maya, a tribute to how she had started the preschool from nothing, conducted the office with resolve and fairness, and how they were all one big happy family. As Maya watched the women sing and dance, she also began to cry. Though it had been a hard year—perhaps a hard stretch of years—she felt content knowing she had created the school she'd always wanted.

It was not long after Annual Day that Ashni let Maya know that she was leaving the preschool. Her husband told her she had to quit to run his family business, which was a women's clothing shop, so that he could take a job he liked better. At first, Ashni resisted. She was not a woman to give in. But Ashni's husband and his parents kept pressuring her, and eventually she gave her notice, like all the timid girls from conservative families had done. Maya was upset over losing Ashni, who was smart and frank and confident and had become her closest friend. They had become even closer after Ashni confided to Maya that she was seeing another man.

The man was from the village where Ashni was born and someone she knew from her school days. Ashni said he treated her like a princess. He told her he loved everything about her. Any time Ashni went home to see family, she now made plans to see him too. Soon, she began flying home just to see him. She even got a tattoo for him, after seeing Maya's treble clef. Ashni's tattoo said *ishq*, which was Arabic for "love," but a selfless kind, a love without lust. She told Maya she felt guilty that she needed both a man who obsessed over her and the man who was the father of her child.

But Maya told her not to, because she was not the only one.

❦❦❦❦❦

Maya and Veer's ninth wedding anniversary came and went. Veer didn't come home until very late from work and didn't mention the day. But this year, Maya didn't let it bother her. Her teachers held a little celebration. Friends commented on their Facebook walls, and both she and Veer thanked them. It was enough. She no longer needed Veer to pretend that they were something they were not. She had other friends, other men, who told her that she was smart and beautiful and gave her nicknames like *rani*, or "queen."

She couldn't tell these men everything, though—not the secret things from her childhood that she'd never been able to tell Veer. She knew they wouldn't understand. And so instead she told them to Ashni, who remained her close friend.

It had first happened when Maya was between six and eight years old, with the man who worked at the stationery store. Her mother used to give her two rupees to buy paper or a pencil there. Several times, the man tried to kiss and grope her, and Maya didn't know what to do. Once, when she had been gone a long time at the store, her mother came and brought her back home. "Next time there's a stranger, you be careful," her mother said, and didn't give Maya two rupees for the store again.

When Maya was a little older, eleven or so, a neighbor who was fifteen or sixteen touched her on the terrace of her house. The other kids were playing downstairs. Again, Maya didn't know what to do. This time, Maya's grandmother came to check on her, saw what was happening, and stopped it. Afterward she told Maya, "Any time you do anything like that, I'm going to tell your father." Maya was confused. She didn't think she had done anything wrong; the boy had. But now it seemed it was her fault, and that she could not tell anyone if it happened again.

The next time was with a family friend. There was a couple who lived nearby, and when the husband went out of town, Maya's parents often sent her over to their house to keep the wife company. They even had her spend the night to help the woman fall asleep. Sometimes, the husband came home very late at night, and Maya woke to find him trying to put his hands up her shirt or down her pants. She was not yet fourteen. When this happened, Maya stayed frozen; her bones felt like they were made of lead. She was certain his wife was awake and knew what was happening. And yet his wife still asked that Maya come over when her husband was away.

Finally, Maya told her parents she was not comfortable going to their house anymore. Then the man came to Maya's house instead and groped her when her parents left the room. After several visits like this, Maya got up the courage to tell him: "Don't touch me. *Bas ho gaya, abhi*, if you do it again I'm going to go and tell someone." He stopped touching her after this. She never told anyone else about it. She was sure that if she had, she would have gotten in trouble.

"Maybe it's why I go from man to man," Maya told Ashni after she finished her story. Maybe it's why she had been attracted to Subal, then left him, and was now drawn to other men. It was her *hisaab* to fulfill, or it wasn't.

Maya needed someone to tell her that she did not owe a debt— that it wasn't her fault what happened. And that perhaps she was attracted to other men for other reasons. But Ashni was quiet. These were things people didn't talk about.

❦❦❦❦❦

Just after the fourth anniversary of Maya's preschool, Veer was diagnosed with diabetes, type 1. Previously, he had been diagnosed with type 2, which was caused primarily by being overweight or lack of exercise. But now his doctors told him they'd been wrong. They said his diabetes had become so bad that his "pancreas was basically dead." The word *dead* was not lost on him, or on Maya. They told him he'd need to change his diet and life if he wanted to make it to old age.

I need to make myself a little more healthy, Veer thought after the diagnosis, trying to keep himself calm, *so I can live enough to have some wonderful time with Janu.*

Veer went away to a diabetes camp for four days, and after coming back made more dietary changes. He arrived home with bags and bags of groceries, much of it fresh produce. He said that he could no longer drink milk and that he was going to become a vegan. He asked if Maya could prepare him a raw diet.

And he vowed he would no longer work so hard. He had never felt so happy as he had at camp, because—for the first time in a long time—he had had time to sleep, work out, and eat well. He had had time to think over many things. "You know, Maya, when you take out the *T* in *trust* it becomes *rust*," he joked.

Maya laughed. The diagnosis had washed away much of her resentment. At least for now, when he needed her, and maybe couldn't live without her. She told herself she had been silly to be so angry. And they were moving to the new house soon.

A few weeks later, as Veer snacked on *namkeen*, him on one couch, Maya on the other, they discussed the move. "This is not how we should eat, without drink," he said, and went into the linen closet, which doubled as a liquor cabinet.

"Where will we hide the liquor in the new house?" Maya asked, taking a sip of the whiskey he'd brought out, which she did not like. She preferred sugary rum with sweet lime, the drink she and Subal used to have together. But Veer kept only scotch at home, favoring the expensive stuff.

"It's okay, it's kept inside the cabinet," said Veer.

"But if your parents find it, they will throw me out," Maya said. "And they will kick your bum so hard you will not walk." They both laughed and then fell quiet. "Even my dad would be upset if he knew I drank," she said.

"Oh, yeah?" Veer got a mischievous look on his face. He sat up, put down his drink, and took out his phone. Maya watched him, waiting for the joke. "Actually," he said, "I will call your father and tell him you are drinking."

Maya raised her eyebrows at this.

Veer began speaking into his phone, in the accent of a busybody neighbor, the kind who gossiped while chewing *paan* tobacco, so that it sounded like he had marbles in his mouth. "Hello, Uncle, how are you? . . . *Haan, toh,* do you know what your daughter is doing here?" Veer was chewing so much pretend *paan* he could barely be understood.

"Yes," said Veer, putting on a different accent, that of Maya's father, proper and refined. "She works for an international preschool."

"She is doing VERY international all right." Now Veer was practically spitting the imaginary *paan*. "Drinking ALL the international drinks."

"Ah?"

"ALL the pubs of Bombay exist ONLY because of her. And she is eating chicken *tikka* BESIDES."

"Nahi!" said Veer, as Maya's father, scandalized.

"HAAN."

Maya laughed so hard she almost fell off the couch, and Veer was glad he could still make her laugh.

At first, the new diabetes diagnosis made them fight less often and without bitterness. But this didn't last long. Soon, Veer told Maya that he could not eat the food she made, and Maya told him that Pallavi would make his dinners from here on out.

As life became unsettled at home, Pallavi became unpredictable in her work. She would show up in the morning but not at night. She would wash the dishes but not clean or start the laundry and then rush out the door. Or she wouldn't come at all, saying she had something else she had to do. It turned out life was also unsettled in her home.

After a few months, Pallavi told Maya what was going on: her husband was having an affair with her sister-in-law, and her sister-in-law had gotten pregnant. "Leave him," Maya told her. But Pallavi couldn't. All the money she'd saved cleaning houses was in a bank account in his name, as was her family land back home.

Pallavi seemed most distraught that the affair was out in the open. The whole family knew, which was shameful. Even the brother—the husband of the sister-in-law who was sleeping with Pallavi's husband—knew and didn't seem to care. Maya was sure it was because they all wanted access to Pallavi's money, little as it was. And now, in some twisted way, the sister-in-law and her husband could claim it.

That Sunday, Pallavi didn't show up to work or call. Her phone was switched off, as was her husband's. Her two sons showed up at Maya's door to ask if she had come to work, which worried Maya. She waited all day for Pallavi to come, and the next morning went to Pallavi's shanty, but the shanty was locked and no one seemed to be at home. In the afternoon, Maya sent Janu's babysitter to look for Pallavi, but she could not find her either.

When Pallavi finally reappeared two days later, she said her husband had been fighting with her. She said he would not let her leave the house or make a call. That was why the shanty was locked and her phone was switched off. Perhaps the boys had been locked outside. The fight was about the other woman, because the illegitimate baby was due soon.

Still, Pallavi did not leave him. It wasn't just the money—she also said it would be hard on her boys. Maya was thankful Pallavi did not have a girl child to complicate matters. If a woman left her husband, it was often hard to get a daughter married. But a divorce wouldn't affect the boys much. Boys were privileged. No matter how rich or poor, this held true.

Maya had seen it in her own life. Though she had been smarter than her brother, getting far better marks in school and continuous praise from her teachers, her parents sold land so that he could have an education in the United States. Maya, meanwhile, was sent to the local college.

"Leave him," Maya said again. She urged Pallavi to move houses when she and Veer moved and bring her two boys with her. Maya said she could start anew. Pallavi told her she'd consider it and began showing up on time again.

Despite the diagnosis, Veer soon returned to his old work schedule. His businesses depended on it. "I have taken too much of rest," he said. He also began to worry about Africa, where in one country a new government had made business uncertain and a businessman owed him twenty-two *lakhs*. "I will block him," Veer announced one day, with uncharacteristic bitterness. "And I will make him bleed from his neck."

Veer's pants were falling off him now.

♥♥♥♥♥

In the new apartment, there would be three bedrooms: one for Janu, one for Veer and Maya, and a third bedroom for guests. Or one bedroom each for Veer and for Maya.

Maya learned that Veer's father had given the other wives in the family 50 percent ownership of their apartments, while she had been given 10. Her father told her he wouldn't attend the housewarming unless Veer's father invited him, which Maya knew would never happen. All these years later, the two men still didn't get along. Veer's goal in marriage of bringing two Marwari business families together had never materialized. And Veer's father had said recently that he still believed daughters-in-law required discipline. He said he and Maya were bound to fight again in the new house. *No,* thought Maya, feeling anxious. *I don't want to fight. I don't want to move there.*

But in a strange way she also looked forward to the new apartment and its certainty of conflict. Maybe the fights would get so bad she'd work up the courage to leave Veer. *Only if he gets better,* she thought. Only if it seemed like the right thing to do. Her feelings toward the new house, like everything with Veer, were convoluted. Since he had become sick, she did not know what to think.

Though she feared the new apartment, she threw herself into the decorating, picking out color palettes and window designs and Western-style furniture. She dreamed of floor-to-ceiling bookshelves and walk-in wardrobes and a superhero theme for Janu's room. When she visited the apartment, she saw how posh the building was, though it was still under construction. There was already a security guard, bamboo plants lining the entrance, and glass doors and marble everywhere. The apartment itself had giant windows that looked out onto the city. She could see palm trees and pink buildings and the wavy hills beyond, though there were no nearby apartments with windows like tiny plays. It would be a dream home for most women.

Before the move, Veer's old friends Raj and Anika, one of the couples who had been witnesses at their wedding, came for a visit.

Raj and Anika lived a quiet life in Jaipur, where they ran a small shop together, from which they sold Rajasthani clothing. They were kind, down-to-earth people—Anika in her motherly way, though they had never had children, and Raj with his wide-set face and intense, perceptive stare.

They had not seen Maya and Veer much since their wedding.

But after spending several days with them, they were convinced the marriage was in trouble. Maya and Veer did not seem to see each other. When they spoke, they often seemed on the edge of a fight. Raj and Anika agreed they had to intervene. One night, Raj stayed up late drinking scotch with Veer—though Veer wasn't supposed to drink with his diabetes—and after an hour of talking, Raj took his chance. He asked why Veer seemed not to care about Maya anymore.

"See, I don't have affection for anyone," Veer told him, with unconvincing bluster.

"This is BS," said Raj. Among all his friends, Veer had always been the most affectionate.

"I am only into work," Veer said, and took a swig.

Years ago, after the other Maya had ended things, Veer made two promises to himself. One: he would work day and night going forward, to prevent another crash of the family business, like the one that happened decades ago. And two: he'd stop keeping many friends. He would stop making birthday calls, or sending cards on special occasions, or writing poetry to friends like Raj. He would stop getting so attached to people.

It is better not to keep too many friends, he had told himself. *If somebody like her could walk out, then anybody else could.* After losing his mother and the other Maya, he thought perhaps it was better not to love anyone at all. But this was not something he could tell Raj.

The next day, after Veer went to work, Raj and Anika sat Maya down to ask her about the marriage. Raj began by telling her what Veer had said.

"Hmmm, well, *Kancha* is detached," Maya said, as she served an elaborate lunch she had prepared for them of *roti*, rice, and different *subzis*. She thought there was no use pretending to some of their oldest friends.

"No, Maya," said Raj, dissatisfied with her answer. "*Kancha* is not the type to get detached. He is very attached. He used to write cards to me with poems inside."

Maya nodded. *That was the old Veer,* she thought.

"*Kya hua*, Maya? What happened?"

"Things started getting bad in 2008," said Maya, speaking carefully now. "It's . . . partly due to the political movements of his father and family—"

"They are crooks actually," said Anika.

"Crooks," echoed Raj, who had known Veer's family since he and Veer were young.

As they spoke, Raj remembered how happy Veer's father had been when he'd gone to talk with him about Veer and Maya's marriage. Too happy, in hindsight, that his son was going to elope. "I believe now the reason he was so happy was because it would upset your father and bring you shame," Raj said, thinking of how the two Marwari men had once done business together. Perhaps for Veer's father the union was a kind of revenge.

"Hmmm," said Maya, nodding.

"His wife is even worse."

"Hmmm," Maya said again. She had always wondered how much the actions of Veer's father were shaped by the talk of his wife—the stepmother with the cruel lips who neither Veer nor his brothers had taken to. Maya remembered something that Veer's grandmother had once told her. She said that if Veer's real mother had been alive, everything would be different. Veer's mother had always talked about wanting daughters she could treat as her own. Perhaps his mother would have helped Maya and Veer connect and would have worked to keep them together. If his mother were alive, maybe Veer would have worked less. But Veer's mother wasn't here, and Maya knew it wasn't worth thinking about what could have been.

When lunch was over, Maya served green tea and milky *chai*, and the conversation moved on to astrology. They all remembered how Maya was said to have the *mula nakshatra*, a star that was inauspicious for girls. Girls with this star were passionate but also felt restricted by conventions. They wanted to rebel. They easily grew resentful or felt betrayed. Girls with this star also had calamitous love lives and problems with their fathers. They were questers, always on a search. Even if Maya didn't fully believe in astrology, it was remarkable how much this star reflected her life.

And they all recalled how Maya and Veer's stars had not matched. "Remember, all the unbelievable things happened on the night of their wedding?" said Anika. The rain. The lateness of the hour. The eight times around the sacred fire instead of seven.

"A few years back I even changed my married name," said Maya.

"We are very worried about you," said Anika. "We would not have put our hands there and helped with the wedding if we had not believed and been committed to helping you in your marriage."

"What is *Kancha* doing?" said Raj. "I don't even know."

Maya nodded, but her enthusiasm for the conversation was waning. *Where were they years ago, when the marriage first began to go bad?*

"Maya," said Raj, perking up. "At least go see his parents once in a while, go with *Kancha*."

"No, I won't," said Maya, putting down her cup with finality. "Any woman would react this way under the circumstances and wouldn't see them."

"What about divorce?"

No. They all agreed it wasn't an option, because Veer's parents could try to take Janu away.

"There's no solution, then," said Anika.

"I will talk to *Kancha* again," said Raj.

"It's my mistake," said Maya, who began to clear the teacups. "Because I knew who *Kancha* was and married him anyway."

Anika and Raj looked at her helplessly. That night, in the middle of the night, Janu fell sick, and in the morning he vomited up his chocolate milk.

❦❦❦❦❦

The next evening, Maya and Anika took Janu to Aksa Beach just before sundown. As Janu built castles from the hard-packed sand and men hawked fresh lime soda behind them, Anika asked Maya if she was seeing another man.

"No," said Maya, her voice tight. She was losing patience with this intervention now. It felt as if Raj and Anika were now considering her as perpetrator and Veer as victim. If Veer was sick, then perhaps she was the one to blame. *They think that* Kancha *is in this state because of me, that I have to set him right,* she thought. *How am I going to do that? He's not a child. And I'm not a god. I'm human.*

Back at home, Veer arrived late from work to find Maya, Raj, and Anika sitting at the dinner table talking. Janu was already in bed. As Veer walked into the room, he began singing an old Bollywood ballad, the kind he used to sing to his grandfather. He danced past them into the kitchen and brought out four glasses, along with a bottle of Johnnie Walker Double Black.

"You can't drink that," said Maya.

"Doctor said I could have ninety milliliters," said Veer.

"Sir," Raj said, "you are lying."

Veer changed the subject. He began singing boisterously, though there also seemed to be an edge to it. He looked tired and frail. When he stopped singing, Maya was afraid of what he might say. He drained his glass and began talking of his trips to Africa.

"It's the best thing in the world," he told Raj and Anika. "The best." He paused and turned to look at Maya. "People who travel in cattle class like her would never understand."

The room was quiet. Maya looked at her lap. Raj opened up a star sign application on his phone.

"Read our stars," said Maya.

Raj entered in Maya's and Veer's details—when and where they were born—and a wheel on the app turned around and around, calculating. The app delivered its finding: for this couple, there was no compatibility and no love. Maya and Veer both laughed, perhaps bitterly. Raj continued to read aloud. "It seems you should have a separate house and a separate car," he said. Maya doubted this was the real reading. *He is just trying to save our marriage,* she thought.

Raj closed the app, and the room fell quiet again, save for the ticking of the Hindi-script clock. "Ask Maya why she married me," Veer said. He seemed drunk from the whiskey now.

"Because I was in love with you," said Maya.

"Was?" asked Anika.

"You asked about the past, so I am answering in the past tense."

"And why did you marry Maya?"

"This is a bullshit question, actually," Veer said, standing up unsteadily. "Time for another drink."

That night, Maya went to bed upset. The next morning, she cried as Veer got ready for work. "Why don't you just leave me?" she said. "Everyone thinks I'm responsible for your health problems or tries to blame me, so why don't you just leave?"

"Do you have a problem with me?" Veer asked.

"No," she said, in tears.

"And I don't have a problem with you. You live your life and I'll live mine."

After Veer went to work, Raj and Anika sat Maya down again. But Maya was in no mood to be lectured. "Stop blaming me," she shouted at them, and slammed the door as she left for work.

When she came home for lunch, she found that Raj and Anika

had gone, leaving behind a note of apology. As Maya read it, she thought: *I'm tired of this life, of this crap, of enduring this.*

Have a nice flight, she texted them.

Nine years of damage cannot be undone by one day of talking.

❦❦❦❦❦

That week, Veer told himself: *If Maya leaves me, it's okay.* It would be okay. *Because I have seen that my mother has left me and it is okay. Two people have left me and it's okay.* If this Maya also left him, he would be all right. His businesses would keep going, and he would keep bringing in money. He told himself that as a Marwari that was all that mattered.

Maya changed her profile photo on WhatsApp to an image of a semicolon, with text that read: "Choose to keep going." Then she changed it to a Charles Bukowski quote about a woman that was "mad" but "magic," there was "no lie in her fire."

She changed her Facebook photo to a seductive photo of herself, wearing party *jhumka* earrings and a silk *sari*, staring at the camera, with *kajal* lining her eyes.

She talked to some of her male friends over text and planned to meet one of them at a motel for lunch but didn't follow through. The next day it came out in the papers that Mumbai cops had raided the motel and harassed the couples they found inside. They charged some of them under the country's old morality laws, holding them for "obscenity in public," though all of them had been indoors.

The Mumbai High Court said it was shocked by the raids and that the police needed to understand that the city was changing. But Maya knew it hadn't changed that much.

❦❦❦❦❦

Later that month Navratri approached, the festival for the Hindu goddess Durga, the mother goddess, the power of all gods combined.

Durga was creator, preserver, and destroyer. Durga was evidence that the supreme being was a woman. And Durga was related to the concept of Maya—the belief that the world was an illusion—because it was said that Durga was Lord Krishna's illusory energy. Durga helped Krishna confuse the living beings who fell into attachment and believed that temporary attractions brought them happiness. The ones who did not understand that life, like marriage, was both magic and illusion. Durga was one of Maya's favorite gods. To celebrate her, she decided to host a Navratri celebration for her preschool and invite all the students, teachers, and parents.

On the day of the party, Veer surprised Maya by coming home from work on time. As he got dressed in a fancy red *kurta*, Maya put on a flowing tie-dyed dress she had handmade from Ashni's shop, which was prospering ever since she had taken over for her husband. Maya dressed Janu in a pink *kurta* that matched her own and combed his hair to one side, like his father's. The three of them drove to the hall together and Veer helped Maya set up.

The event began with an *aarti*, during which Maya and the teachers passed around a lamp with a candle, clapping as they sang a chant to Durga: "Creative, creative, mother of the world . . ."

Afterward, parents, teachers, and children began dancing the *dandiya raas*, a devotional dance inspired by Krishna, and also the *garba*, in celebration of the female form. They twirled and clapped in a giant moving circle. The men wore colorful *kurtas*, and the women had on heavy gold jewelry and makeup and *chaniya cholis*, dresses that spun out like upside-down teacups. The toddlers wore *kajal* on their eyes, and bangles and colorful caps, and held tiny *dandiya* sticks. Everyone sweated in the October heat.

Maya, who preferred to watch, sat on the sidelines holding one of the youngest students. When Ashni arrived, she hugged Maya hello. "Take my photo, *nah*?" Ashni said. She wore tight leggings and a deep blue and turquoise top from her shop. She looked at the photo Maya took and shook her head. "Take another?" The photos were for her lover. Her husband had not come to the party.

Maya stood up and tapped the microphone. It was time to give out prizes. Ashni gave out awards for best dancers and best dressed, and then Maya took the mic again. "And now, the last ten minutes of the party will be reserved for freestyle dancing," she said.

Veer, who had been missing during the *dandiya raas* and *garba*, now appeared on the dance floor to move to music he knew. As he danced in his long red *kurta*, he didn't seem sick at all. He seemed like his old self: the carefree, affectionate boy his childhood friends had all known. The man Maya first met at a wedding, who had joked and made the entire wedding party laugh. Maya gestured toward Veer and said into the microphone: "For freestyle we will have my husband. This is my husband, Veer. I know you've rarely seen much of him."

Veer didn't react to the jab and kept dancing. He was here now. Maya turned to the DJ. "Turn up the music," she said. The song was "DJ Wale Babu," an addictive new pop song that sounded nothing like the old songs Veer loved. Still, he danced. *"Duniya rakhun jooton ke niche . . ."* "I keep the world under my shoes . . ." *"Baki puri kar dunga me koi kasar jo reh rahi hai,"* "The rest is left to chance." Veer began clapping his hands, and Janu danced beside him, giggling. Maya put down the microphone and began to dance along with them. As the song ended, Veer threw his arms toward Maya, the gesture of a Bollywood hero toward his heroine. Maya moved toward him, in time.

MOVING HOUSE

Shahzad and Sabeena, 2014 to 2015

> *"The heart is like a bird: love as its head,*
> *and its two wings are hope and fear."*
>
> —*Scholar Ibn al-Qayyim*

It was May, and Mumbai's savannah climate did not disappoint. The air in the city was hot and sticky as Narendra Modi, from the pro-Hindu Bharatiya Janata Party, or BJP, assumed power as prime minister, and as Shahzad went to see the doctor again. As chief minister of Gujarat, Modi had failed to prevent, and possibly encouraged, days of communal violence and rioting in the state, which had left close to eight hundred Muslims dead. Since then, his whispered nickname had been "the Butcher of Gujarat." But Modi had also turned around the state's economy, the kind of turnaround many thought India needed. Especially after the country had not leapfrogged China the way economists had predicted it would. And so Modi was elected in a landslide, with the help of the RSS, the group whose march to the Babri Masjid had led to the mosque's demolition, which led to the riots in Mumbai. India's Muslims, who, though they were growing in number, represented only 13 percent of the population, saw once again that they had little say. Shahzad arrived at the doctor's office feeling fearful and angry.

"Doctor, you are doing nothing for me," Shahzad said. He was tired of showing up and leaving empty-handed. "What can I do for you?" said the doctor. "Nobody in the world can do what you want." But Shahzad reminded him he did not want pills to have children anymore. "At least I can have proper sex with my wife.

At least that." "All right," the doctor said, and gave him pills for performance, to be taken twice a day. Shahzad decided to double the dose.

The tablets made Shahzad sweaty and fuzzy-headed and upset his stomach—though perhaps some of that had to do with the election. His performance barely improved, but he permitted himself to believe that the heavy sensation in his testicles meant he was getting better.

"Something is happening," Shahzad told the doctor, breathlessly, on a second visit. The doctor indulged his delusion and prescribed him another round.

After Modi's election, Shahzad and Sabeena's friends and family and neighbors began to worry that steps would be taken against them on a grander scale. In the run-up to the election, Modi had made anti-Muslim statements, which leaders of the Indian National Congress, the party previously in power, would not do. The Congress party had its own problems, of course; since its glory days of helping lead the independence fight against the British, the party had become riddled with nepotism and corruption. It had also failed to root out poverty or deliver enough economic growth or reforms. And it had looted the country of thousands of *crores*, which was its own kind of murder. So it was no surprise that Congress had been voted out, even in favor of the Butcher of Gujarat.

Shahzad and Sabeena felt fearful in a way they hadn't in years. Even if Modi didn't institute anti-Muslim initiatives, they knew his legions of *bhakts*, or devotees, would do his work for him.

Achhe din aane waale hain. "The good days are coming." This was Modi's campaign slogan. But Shahzad and his friends did not believe it applied to them.

In June, the month after Modi's win, Ramadan approached, along with Shahzad and Sabeena's two favorite holidays. Sabeena loved the Night of Forgiveness best, the evening on which Allah decided the fortunes of all people: who would live, who would die, and what would or wouldn't happen during the year. On this night, Muslims prayed for good days ahead and for all their sins to be forgiven. Those who prayed hard and lamented their failings would be forgiven.

Shahzad preferred the Night of Power, which marked the day that the Prophet Muhammad went to meet Allah, the Quran was revealed, and the angels descended, bringing heaven to Earth. From this meeting the Prophet also brought *namaaz* to men. It was said that the Night of Power was better than one thousand nights combined, and that any man who prayed on this evening received the power of praying on all one thousand. Shahzad often prayed until morning, despite his exhaustion from Ramadan fasting. It made him feel close to God. This year, he decided he would ask Allah for good luck in Dharavi and to help him perform for Sabeena.

But when Ramadan started, Shahzad had to stop taking his pills. *If I continue to take them and also fast, I will become mad,* he thought. He promised himself he'd resume when the holiday was over.

Sabeena, meanwhile, devoted herself to her holiday cooking, preparing *gulab jamun*, *firni*, pudding, custard, *halwa*, and other sweet dishes for the family, which she loved to do. She put on her special *salwar kameez* and best gold. While Nadine complained that Farhan did not give her anything, Shahzad had begun to surprise Sabeena with expensive gifts. When she wore the jewelry, the gold shimmering on her neck, ears, and wrists, it made her feel as if everything in their marriage was all right.

⹀⹀⹀⹀⹀

Ever since Modi had assumed office, many Muslims held tighter to their faith. Shahzad prayed harder to Allah than before and placed more faith in the Quran, which he had started questioning after he learned it prevented adoption. But Sabeena had never doubted that

Islam was the superior religion. For her, the first evidence of this came in the Neil Armstrong story, which she had heard when she was young. The story went that when Armstrong landed on the moon, he heard a sound like music. It was a haunting, beautiful, and somehow familiar sound, so he taped it to listen to later. When Armstrong went to Cairo, he heard the exact same sound. It was the *azaan*—the Muslim call to prayer. That very day, Armstrong converted to Islam.

It did not matter that there was no evidence for the Neil Armstrong story or that sound could not be heard on the moon. In her bones Sabeena felt the story was true. The moon was a powerful force in Islam; without it there would be no calendar or way to measure time. Islamic months always began with the sighting of the moon. When Ramadan began, Sabeena sometimes went up to their rooftop to view the moon's sliver, a gleaming crescent in the polluted night sky.

For Shahzad, better proof of Islam's superiority came from the scholars of religious texts who read the Bible, Vedas, and Quran and decided the Quran was the most lucid among them. These scholars included *firangis* like the British novelist Marmaduke Pickthall, who converted to Islam from Christianity and later translated the Quran into English. They also came from the United States, United Kingdom, France, and Germany.

In recent years, though, there had been some troubling events. There was news of increasing incidents of Islamic terrorism. Shahzad had been startled by the 9/11 attacks in the United States, and then the nightmare continued with Muslim extremist groups like the Taliban, al-Qaeda, and ISIS, and the terrorist attacks on India, supposedly from Pakistan. These attacks only bolstered leaders like Modi. But these terrorists weren't real Muslims. Sabeena saw them as cowards who killed innocents, which Islam never instructed anyone to do. Shahzad thought they'd misinterpreted the Quran's meaning of *jihad* as being a physical struggle for believers. To him, *jihad* meant the simple duty a man had to spread the religion.

Shahzad despised the terrorists for what they were doing to Islam, transforming it from a religion of beauty to one of violence. In the Quran, heaven was described as more gorgeous than the human mind could fathom: with flowing milk, gardens, and angels everywhere. Everyone was young and happy. If you drank the water, you could see it flow through your body, because in heaven your skin was translucent. Shahzad thought that when it came time to die, it was better to die a Muslim.

But Shahzad did not want to feel old. He wanted to feel young—and he still wanted to be a father. At the very least, he wanted to be able to perform so he could feel some measure of strength and dignity. As a Muslim in Modi's India, having power seemed more important than ever. And in many ways, the land in Dharavi felt like his last hope.

That winter, several of Shahzad's aunts and cousins threw a wrench in Shahzad's plans for Dharavi by accepting checks for the land from the local goon. He was furious. *Some money in hand now always seems better than more money later,* he thought.

Afterward, the goon called Farhan, who had begun helping Shahzad protect Dharavi, and said, "Don't go to Dharavi now. If you do I'll break your legs."

Shahzad knew this was an important moment and that they could not back down. He told Farhan that it would be better to make a show of force than retreat, and Farhan agreed. And so the two men broke open a lock the tannery owner had placed on their property's entrance, which took almost two hours, plus some greasing oil, and the help of a stocky builder friend. They were surprised to find that no one bothered them, not even the baby-faced security guard.

Shahzad thought that perhaps it was because of the appearance of his builder friend, who was very fat, with a hard, dark face and thick mustache. The builder wore tight jeans, floral shirts, and gold rings and rode a Royal Enfield motorcycle. He carried a glitter-encrusted phone. In short, he looked like a Bollywood gangster.

After they finished building a new door, for which they would have the only key, Shahzad and the builder went to go get lunch, ordering plates piled high with chicken, mutton, and gravy. Mid-meal, Shahzad got a call.

"What are you doing in that property?" a voice said. It took him a minute to realize it was the police.

"This is our property," Shahzad said. "That's why we are here."

"You're making a riot there. You've punched the security guard of the tannery and forcibly gone in."

"No we haven't," said Shahzad. "That is a false story."

"Come to the police station right now."

Shahzad covered the receiver and told the builder what the police officer had said. "Let the police come here," the builder said, chewing his meat. "I am eating."

But they've made a false complaint, Shahzad worried, and hung up the phone. *It's a criminal case now. We are in trouble.*

Shahzad next got a call from Farhan, who had stayed back at the property. "Come quick, the police are coming." The tannery owner and his men had arrived too. The builder, annoyed, agreed to accompany Shahzad back to the property. In Shahzad's memory, when they arrived, the police pushed them into the back of a police van, along with the tannery owner and his men. At the station, the police said it was a riot case and charged them all with section 149 of the Indian Penal Code: unlawful assembly. For six hours, they were held in the detention room.

"We are not *goondas*, we are builders," the builder said. "And it's our property," Shahzad added. It didn't matter. Lawyers would have to be hired. Money would have to be spent. Palms would have to be greased. And Shahzad knew who was behind the scenes, pulling all the strings: the local goon.

But several weeks later, the local goon quit his political party. It came on the evening news. The line was that he resigned because he was unhappy with how the party, which supported Modi, had begun treating Muslims. Shahzad knew better than to believe this. The goon was pushed out. There were many maneuverings within political parties, and even big men sometimes had to fall. This meant the tannery owner no longer had protection. Though they would still have to go to court, Shahzad knew that now fate was on his side.

ᵥᵥᵥᵥᵥᵥ

In April, it was announced on the news that Yakub Memon, an alleged participant in the 1993 bomb blasts, and a Muslim, was to be hanged. Shahzad, and many other Muslims in the city, thought he did not deserve it. Shahzad knew he should have expected this news under Modi. But the excitement over Dharavi must have clouded his vision.

The story went that Memon had been near Byculla Market when the riots happened. There, it was said he had witnessed violence— women raped, men killed, or shops and houses burned—and that this experience had motivated his involvement in the bombings.

Shahzad had seen firsthand what happened to men who were on hand for the worst of the riots. They went insane, or killed themselves, or perpetrated other acts of violence. But Memon was different. He was an accountant whose role in the blasts had been only financial, or so he said. He insisted he had masterminded nothing. He had also already served two decades in prison, cooperated with authorities, and surrendered himself to police. *How could they hang such a man?* Shahzad thought.

The year before, a prominent former Hindu politician, a woman convicted of an active role in another city's riots, which killed nearly one hundred Muslims, had been let out of jail without a murmur of protest. But Shahzad knew consequences were different for Muslims, and especially for Muslims without power.

A report commissioned by the previous prime minister had confirmed that Muslims were at the bottom of the heap in everything: in literacy, schooling, jobs, earnings, and political power. Shahzad had always known this. He remembered the childhood taunts, and the saying he had learned in adulthood when Muslim groups around the world had begun committing so many acts of terror: *All Muslims are not terrorists, but all terrorists are Muslim.* Yakub Memon, Muslim accountant, was as good as a dead man.

After it was announced that Memon would hang, Shahzad felt that there was a kind of invisible gallows hanging over his own neck. For the first time since his father's death, and since inheriting the Dharavi land, he felt diminished. He was not a big man after all. He was just another powerless Muslim.

The country heatedly debated Memon's hanging. There was a final plea to stay the sentence. But the Supreme Court rejected it in the end. When Yakub Memon was hanged, Shahzad sat alone in his room and cried.

Sabeena tried to comfort her husband. These larger forces could not be controlled, she said. *Allah determines everything.* She reminded him that he still had Dharavi, and her, and Mahala and Taheem. He had a good family and a good home. And in fact, after decades in the dingy and overcrowded joint family home, they were moving soon, to a bigger and better apartment. Muslims still held land in Mumbai; Modi had not taken that away. And in Mumbai, land was a kind of power.

A month or so later, Shahzad began talking about buying a big new office space in Colaba, in the tony part of downtown. He would conduct his brokerage business from there and use it to meet with big Dharavi builders. Colaba was at the very tip of Mumbai, on a little finger of the island that curled out into the sea. It was close to the city's main government buildings, courts, and the Bombay Stock Exchange. It was filled with European-style restaurants, cafés, and bars. It was where all the *firangis* came to stay. A man who owned land or operated an office there was a man of power and prestige. But Colaba was also prohibitively expensive.

Shahzad was certain that with the Dharavi money he could someday pay off the office. Sabeena urged him not to be rash and to think of their future. If he bought the office, they'd have very little savings left. Shahzad said she didn't understand.

On the day Shahzad was to make a down payment, Sabeena stood, arms crossed, in front of their home safe. "You're not taking the money," she said, and told him she'd hidden the key. "Then I'll just break the cupboard and take everything inside," Shahzad said, his voice rising. "You go and do that," said Sabeena. "But nothing is there."

Earlier that day, Sabeena had removed all the money, five *lakhs* of it, along with their gold. Shahzad left the room, stewing, and, when he came back, saw Sabeena was gone. He called her again and again on her cell phone, to no answer.

As Sabeena sat inside her family apartment in Bhendi Bazaar, she felt calm about her act of sedition. She spent the whole day playing with her brother's children. Her little niece reminded Sabeena of herself. The girl was not allowed to roam outside, and her father never took her to the movies. She lived a cloistered life, though fewer girls in Mumbai lived like this now. Sabeena tried to keep her entertained by telling her all about her childhood, and what her grandfather had been like.

Sabeena knew she would not have stolen from the safe years ago. But the world had changed, and women were different now. They were *mazboot*; they were strong. They left the house when they wanted. They ate first instead of second. They challenged men when they needed to be challenged—about money, food, in-laws, even sex.

But after a day, Sabeena was ready to go home. She knew Shahzad would need her for his meals and *chai*, as would his mother. It was her duty to be there, and she could not abandon them. She wanted Shahzad to learn a lesson so that their future would be secure.

At home, Shahzad hadn't been able to sleep without Sabeena. All night, he had been up whispering to himself, "What to do, what to do, what to do?" In the morning, he could not eat. He felt more anxious than he had in a long time and decided not to buy the office in Colaba. *What a foolish idea,* he thought. There was no way he could afford it. He decided not to act *bimar* anymore. He told himself that any illness, even madness, could be cured. After a day had passed, he called Sabeena again, and this time she answered.

"Come home, *baba*," he said, "and see that everything is right."

❦❦❦❦❦❦

On a blistering hot day in June, Shahzad, Sabeena, and the entire joint family moved into their new flat, leaving behind the old apartment that three generations had inhabited.

They were all relieved to leave the apartment, which over the years had become dingy. The paint on all the walls was peeling. The shelves in the bedrooms were cluttered with old medicines, used beauty products, and broken electronics. And the furniture was tattered and worn. All twelve people had shared one Indian-style toilet.

The move, though, had not been their idea. A developer had approached them, asking if they would be willing to leave their home for a new luxury tower around the corner. The terms were favorable: they'd pay two *lakhs* for a property expected to be worth five *crore* soon. Because Shahzad was a broker, he knew deals like this were happening all over Mumbai. Developers were moving rent-controlled tenants in low-rise, British-era buildings into new luxury towers, razing the beautiful old buildings—many of which were up for a heritage designation—and building more luxury towers in their place. Both the tenants and developers walked away happy.

The new apartment promised a new life. The luxury tower, with its ornamental moldings and accents, signaled wealth and prestige. Inside, the apartment had shiny white floors, granite countertops, and fresh plumbing. They purchased all new furniture and threw away the shabby beds, tables, and chairs of their past. They bought elaborate wall hangings—including a few of the six *kalimas*, reminding them of the fundamentals of Islam—to decorate the smoothly painted walls. The toilets were all Western. One family member even bought an AC.

Moving was an ordeal for Sabeena, who spent an entire twenty-four hours packing. She kept their clothes, their wedding album, and some essentials, but she threw away much of what they owned. It was also difficult for Shahzad's mother, who had not left the apartment in years. After moving, she spent an entire day in the hospital recovering from the stress. Once all twelve members stood inside the new apartments—they had not one but two flats in the new building—they agreed it had been worth it.

The evening of the move, the family called several boys from a nearby *madrasa* to read verses from the Quran to bless their new home. Shahzad and Sabeena distributed sweets to everyone who came. As they did, it felt a little like the day they had agreed to marry.

The new house also shifted certain feelings in them. Maybe it was the new furniture, which was clean and plush. Maybe it was the clear sound of *namaaz* that they could hear from their window. Or maybe it was just the change in scenery, to an apartment that did not carry memories of the hurt that came before.

Sabeena liked one part of the new house best: the bedroom window, which served as kind of a gallery to the city. In the distance, she could see the railway tracks that led to the train station, the nearby *chawls* where people hung clothes on the line, and the cranes lined up behind them for new construction. She still had a view of the Haj House, where pilgrims stayed en route to Mecca, with its shiny marble terrace where crows liked to land. Close to her window, she could see a cluster of trees that bent toward the earth. On one branch two green parrots often came to sit and sing or talk to each other, urgent hums followed by softer ones.

To Sabeena, the window contained the whole city in one shot: humans, animals, traffic, trains, industry, and religion. And she almost always spotted something new as she sat in her favorite peacock blue *salwar kameez*, letting her hair down and taking in the view. As the sun dropped in the sky, she loved watching the city go dark.

Now, Sabeena went out as she pleased, because Shahzad's mother was bedridden and could not stop her. In the new house, Sabeena no longer spoke of marriage as a *laddoo* or heavy sweet but instead of the sweet dish she was excited to make for the family. She tried to look her best, trading her faded brown *kurtas* for her best *salwar kameez*, even when it wasn't a holiday. She dyed her hair with henna, so often that she caught cold. She applied French cream beneath her eyes to get rid of her dark circles and wore gold heart-shaped earrings every day. And she became obsessed with Pakistani serials, especially one called *Humsafar*, which meant "soul mate," about the life of a young married couple.

One night after moving in, Sabeena surprised Shahzad by climbing on top of him. They were lying side by side in their new twenty-thousand-rupee bed, with fresh sheets printed with bright flowers. She spent most nights in the new apartment sleeping on a mat on the floor, despite the expensive new bed, saying it was cooler underneath the fan. But tonight she got into bed, straddled Shahzad, and *took her pleasure*, or so he remembered it. In the new house it was like they were newlyweds or reacquainting after a long time. To Sabeena, it did not feel like the same old thing. Shahzad, who could not finish, did not know whether to be surprised and grateful at the change in his wife or embarrassed at how he, as usual, fell short.

☙☙☙☙☙

In the new home, the two apartments were divided this way: one for Sabeena, Shahzad, his mother, and his brother, for when he came to visit from Qatar; and one for Farhan, Nadine, Mahala, Taheem, and a few other family members. There were also two maids, one for each apartment, both of whom were good-natured and hardworking. One maid was pale-skinned and one was dark; this was sometimes how they were distinguished, instead of by name. The pale maid worked in Sabeena's home, and as she worked she told Sabeena all about her home life. She said she had been forced to marry a mute and deaf man, with whom she had six children, and that she had to work doubly hard because he couldn't get a job. The darker maid told Nadine about how her two sons were at home in a faraway village, because blue films were shot in her neighborhood in Mumbai—not a suitable place to bring up children. She said her husband had come from the village and secured a job but quit because he said he didn't like to travel in the city. Now that he had gone back home to their village, she was living here alone.

It was a truism in Mumbai that all maids had their sob stories, working hard to support big families and degenerate husbands. Still, their stories had an impact on Sabeena. Listening to them, she felt a kind of pride in Shahzad she hadn't felt before. She knew that he never stopped working. Instead he ran from Dharavi to court to neighborhoods across the city to show flats, and back to Dharavi again.

Like the old apartment, the new flat was near Crawford Market, which Sabeena could now visit regularly. If she wanted, she could also stock up for the month ahead, buying chicken, mutton, bitter gourd, and okra, because the new apartment had a big fridge and fancy elevator. Today Crawford Market offered far more variety than when Shahzad's mother had shopped there, and it had a new emphasis on presentation: pomegranates were lined up like pool balls, peaches stacked in perfect pyramids, and apples lined up in rectangular boxes padded in soft foam. The market now was also filled with the fruits of economic liberalization and what came after: German chocolates, American diapers, French shampoos, fake designer perfumes, Kashmiri walnuts, imitation purses made in China, even foreign lingerie.

But vestiges remained of the old Crawford Market: the *"shee shee shee"* of a man trying to push his cart through, the shopkeeper shouting *"aao, aao"* as he called the stray cats for crabs and shaggy dogs for leftover chicken legs, the vendor yelling *"gandu"* at another man unloading his wares incorrectly, the many women in *burqas* shouting to negotiate for bras and hankies, and the dirt-stained children juggling rocks until they were shooed from the market. There was still the pungent smell of body odor, raw chicken, curry, and must. And there were still birds for sale, and not just pigeons. Now, the market sold owls, peacocks, parakeets, weaverbirds, and starlings.

Mahala and Taheem did not usually go inside Crawford Market, but since moving into the new apartment they loved to frequent the lane beside it, where cars and motorcycles rarely drove. After school, the neighborhood children gathered in the lane to ride bikes, play cricket, and talk in clusters: girls on one side, boys on the other. They'd play for hours, until it was dinnertime, and then they'd run upstairs, stopping at Shahzad and Sabeena's apartment first to call out: "Hi, *buddhi baba. Buddhi ma*, what are you having for dinner?"

ღღღღღ

The bill passed in March of that year, but it wasn't until the summer that the impact of the Maharashtra Animal Preservation amendment became clear. Effectively, a ban on beef. Far-right Hindus had been trying to pass the bill for years, and now, under Modi, it became a reality. Shahzad knew that many Muslims who sold beef would lose their jobs. Muslims who ate beef because it was inexpensive would have to find something else to eat. Perhaps they'd eat mutton, but then the prices of mutton would rise. Some Muslims might actively protest the ban, but that would inspire Hindus to fight back. If the city was unlucky, it would lead to violence.

Through the beef ban, Shahzad saw how Modi, or at least his *bhakts*, intended to hurt Muslims: by hitting their purses and stoking community tensions. As always, it was the big people who started the problems and the small people who felt the effects. And yet Shahzad was surprised to find he did not fear Modi anymore, because Modi had begun to disappoint the country. Both Muslims and Hindus were asking why food prices were rising and when the good days were going to come. They were asking when Modi's magical economic turnaround would take effect. And they were making fun of his many international trips; he had already gone on twenty this year. Now, when Shahzad or his friends or neighbors watched the news, they called Modi the "tourist-in-chief," who was "always in flight mode." They joked that he was going to change his name from Modi to *"achhe din,"* so that when he arrived anywhere, the people would say: "Look: the good days have come."

People in the city had always talked about the differences between Hindus and Muslims. There wasn't a time that anyone— even the hunched old men and women in the market with their canes and *lathis*—could remember when that hadn't been the case. This had been true even centuries ago, under the early Hindu and Muslim kings. But while there had been battles, there had also been intermarriage. The peak of the violence was undoubtedly Partition;

nothing before or after was so bad, though there had been eruptions of violence since.

Now, after the beef ban, journalists warned the country could erupt again. Conversations took on a different quality; people said hateful things aloud they would have only thought privately before, and said them louder. They no longer seemed ashamed of their prejudice.

It wasn't like that with Christians. Hindus mostly found Christians unobjectionable, and Muslims like Shahzad and Sabeena saw Christianity and Islam as close cousins. After all, both faiths descended from Abraham, believed in one God, and saw Jesus as a prophet.

But, like many Muslims, neither Shahzad nor Sabeena could wrap their mind around Hinduism, with its earsplitting holidays and many gods, though they knew that Hindus and Muslims shared some practices and beliefs. Among them was the idea of the *nazar*, or the evil eye. To get rid of the *nazar*, Hindus burned chiles, while Muslims read the Quran. But Sabeena warned Shahzad that the *nazar* was far more important to Hindus. She reminded him that they had received a *fatwa* from the leadership in Saudi Arabia instructing them not to worry about superstitions anymore. Putting the right foot in front of the left, for example, which was said to be a tradition of the Prophet, was no longer compulsory. What was important was to attend to *namaaz* five times a day.

But Shahzad had always been unable to resist the pull of superstitions. He had always worried about some black mark on his life and felt that the many healers and *hakims* in the city could help him. For years, he had gone to see a black magic priest at Khar Station named Mamoo, who had studied in the jungle for thirty-six years, and who was said to have special powers. Years ago, Shahzad was certain Mamoo had cured his sister of stomach cancer with water he'd blessed. Next month, for the first time, Shahzad was going to

see the old priest at his home, to talk about Dharavi and his performance problems. *The home of a priest.* He could hardly believe his
good fortune. But since he'd moved into the fancy new apartment,
he had almost begun to expect the extraordinary.

When Shahzad arrived at Mamoo's apartment, he was amazed
at the humble surroundings. The old priest lived in two small, bare
rooms in the Byculla neighborhood, not far from the market. *If he
took money for his services, he would be rich,* thought Shahzad. Instead,
the priest worked as a tomato seller by day, not caring that few people knew of his powers.

Though he was older now and a little bent, Mamoo still wore his
trademark beard without a mustache, a black *topi*, and white *kurta
pyjamas.* And though he was unwell, his calm, warm demeanor had
not changed. Only his teeth had drastically altered since Shahzad
first met him. They had become darkly stained by *paan*.

Shahzad had come to ask Mamoo for good luck before a final
meeting with the builder in Dharavi. It looked as if the deal would
be finalized, but still Shahzad wanted the priest to bless and give
him water, from which he could draw power. But the old man had
other plans.

Sitting on his bed, Mamoo motioned for Shahzad to sit across
from him. He took out a stack of tiny pieces of paper, each covered
in Arabic script. For several minutes, he wordlessly shuffled through
them.

"Kya hai?" Shahzad finally asked, impatient.

Mamoo did not look up. The papers, he said, had writing on them
from a *djinn*.

"From a genie?" Shahzad asked. *Djinns* had extraordinary powers; the Quran said they were supernatural creatures created "from
the fire of a scorching wind." It was also said that *djinns*, which were
born good or evil, could alter the course of human lives. Though
they were invisible and lived far away, sometimes men could contact

them. Shahzad assumed Mamoo had learned to reach the other-worldly while studying in the jungle.

Finally, Mamoo chose a slip of paper. He studied it for a long moment and, shutting his eyes, blew on it. After a beat, he handed it to Shahzad.

"What does it say?" Shahzad asked.

"Hold it in your hand," Mamoo said, "and close your fist."

Shahzad obeyed. A minute passed in silence, and then another. Mamoo got up from his bed, spit some *paan* juice out the window, and came back. He watched Shahzad until suddenly Shahzad's whole body shook. His eyes opened wide. "I felt it." Shahzad's voice cracked with elation. "A burst of energy. It was trying to move upwards in my palm."

Mamoo nodded in approval.

"Now will my property be a success?" Shahzad asked.

The priest shook his head noncommittally. "I'm praying that everything goes all right." He got up again and spit more *paan* juice out the window. He slapped Shahzad on the head, twice, and ushered him toward the door. Shahzad held the paper tight.

"Thank you," he said, pressing a pile of rupees into Mamoo's hand. The old man nodded, took them, and shut the door.

That afternoon, Shahzad took a taxi to Bhendi Bazaar to buy a pouch for the paper. He wanted to wear it around his neck like a *tawiz*. Among dozens of drabber styles of pouches, he chose a gold, glittery one. *This is a magical blessing,* Shahzad thought, *and deserving of a beautiful vessel.* He thought even Sabeena would approve.

❦❦❦❦❦

It was pouring the night of Mahala's ninth birthday, the kind of slanting rain that rendered umbrellas useless and sent the city's stray cats hiding, mewing, under the tarps of shanties all night. Farhan and Nadine prepared for a big turnout anyway, putting up streamers, strings of glitter, and a Barbie-themed "Happy Birthday" sign. Mahala danced around the room in excitement, wearing a tulle dress, heavy earrings, and a little makeup she'd begged her mother to let her put on. Her head was uncovered, because she hadn't reached puberty yet. But at school, even some of the older Muslim girls were choosing to go without headscarves.

As the last decorations were hung, Shahzad and Sabeena arrived, and then Mahala's cousins, the neighborhood children, and her school friends. Despite the rain, everyone had dressed in their best *kurta pyjamas* and *salwar kameez*. The girls told Mahala she looked just like a princess.

Farhan put on old Hindi music, and the adults murmured in appreciation. But the kids soon shouted, "Turn it off, this is *bakwaas* music." Farhan distracted them with party masks, hats, chips, candy, and cake. "Happy Birthday Mahala," the cake read in curving letters, thick white icing on milk chocolate.

After cake, the kids commandeered the computer. Mahala changed the music to Honey Singh, a Punjabi rapper whose lyrics many parents disapproved of but whose music every child in Mumbai seemed to know. The children tried out the latest gyrations from Bollywood and looked to Mahala for approval. Taheem sprayed Silly String on his sister, and the girls giggled with delight. Farhan soon changed the music to "Ring Around the Rosie."

Some of the adults joined the children in dancing, but not Shahzad, who had been tasked with videotaping the party, and stood smiling shyly in the corner. And not Sabeena, who sat on the couch silently watching. When Mahala tried to get her to dance, she only shook her head. Women were not supposed to dance in front of men.

"Come on, *buddhi ma*."

"No, no," said Sabeena, smiling, and folded her arms across her chest.

Sabeena had never understood celebrating birthdays. *Every person has a limited time on Earth, given by God,* she thought. *Why celebrate one year reduced?* Sabeena believed that people should celebrate only weddings and births and engagements—the beginnings of things, not the endings. But she couldn't help smiling at her niece's antics.

When the party finally wound down and most of the guests left, Mahala was not ready to stop dancing. "Come, come," her father said, gently. He turned the music off and cleared his throat. Only the immediate family was left.

"Actually, as you know, celebrating birthdays is a Christian tradition," Farhan said. "And some hard-liner Muslims said we shouldn't do it."

"Here he goes, giving *gyaan*," said Nadine.

Farhan continued, "But they're just trying to ruin things. Our family is liberal. Why not provide fun for the kids?"

He added that when he was young his father would bring home a small cake and watermelon juice for his birthday. Now, birthday celebrations were much larger. But that was okay. "Actually, there used to be many more guests at these parties, before our property dispute."

"Bas, bas," said Nadine, hushing him.

For months, Farhan had been upset about the situation in Dharavi and the divisions in the family. That afternoon, though, a check from the builder had cleared. The deal had gone through. It was an advance on the money, not a life-changing amount, but enough to feel like celebrating.

And there was much to celebrate in their beautiful new flat, on Mahala's birthday, surrounded by family. Even Shahzad's mother had come to the party and clapped her hands to the music from her wheelchair. Everyone had seemed in good humor: Farhan's wife, Nadine, who put aside her usual criticisms for the day; Shahzad, holding the camera like a shy new father; and Sabeena, who didn't approve of these celebrations but was smiling as she left the party.

Sabeena had begun to notice the many changes taking place among Muslim women in the city—that women were choosing to work and not to wear the veil, that some were even choosing not to marry. She thought they must be getting their ideas from TV and online. Maybe even Mahala wouldn't marry. Shahzad's niece in Qatar, a successful doctor, had no interest in a husband. And a client of Shahzad's named Zora, who was fair and beautiful and ran a successful hair salon downtown, was forty and still unmarried.

Zora was modern in other ways. She wore T-shirts and jeans and kept her head uncovered, with a dyed streak of purple in her hair. Her salon was unisex, which meant men came there for treatments and were also employed as beauticians. Sabeena did not know what to make of this. Zora's landlady, a Wahhabi, or fundamentalist Muslim, had a stronger opinion. When she visited Zora at her flat, she liked to comment on her wayward lifestyle, saying, "Men should not touch or see women's hair," or "Going without the *hijab* is like germs getting into uncovered fruit. This is like how men pollute women by looking at them." When the landlady visited, she wanted Zora's TV switched to the Islamic televangelists from the Gulf.

Zora would listen politely to this criticism but then say, in an even tone: "This is my business and I cannot pick and choose."

Shahzad was helping her find a new flat for her and her mother. *Her and her mother,* Sabeena thought, with some measure of pity. Zora was going to be an old maid. Sabeena thought any husband was preferable to living and dying alone. Even a husband who was *bimar* in the head and the heart. The Quran told her: "And of everything We have created pairs." To Sabeena, an unmarried life was not a life at all.

And though Shahzad still made silly mistakes, like pressing the up button on the elevator to go down or leaving his medical documents on the floor like trash, he was much better than he used to be. People commented about him less. He spent less time washing his hands. Sabeena saw clearly now that life went up, went down, and came up again. The key was to accept this. And since moving into the new apartment, it seemed that their fortunes were picking up. There was an Arabic proverb that went: *Contentment is an inexhaustible treasure.* Now, she thought she understood what it meant.

And soon it was Bakri Eid, and all the excitement that came with it, the holiday that celebrated Abraham's willingness to sacrifice his son.

As the story went, God had asked Abraham to offer up his most beloved possession. Though it pained him greatly, Abraham agreed to give up his son for sacrifice. At the last minute, the boy had vanished, and a goat appeared in his place. It had been a test of Abraham's love for God, who never intended to take his son away.

Shahzad loved the Bakri Eid story, in part because Abraham's wife had reportedly given birth to her son when Abraham was one hundred years old. *One hundred!* Shahzad thought. *Wah, incredible.* It gave Shahzad hope he could still be a father, perhaps after all the Dharavi money came through. After all, he was only fifty-five.

He also loved the holiday because of the sacrifice of the goats. Killing the goat was difficult, especially if the children of the family had grown attached in the weeks they cared for and fattened the animal. Last year, Taheem had sobbed for a whole day after the cutting. Shahzad thought this was why the slaughter was important. It was what true sacrifice felt like.

This year, they received their goats only a few days before Bakri Eid. Their new apartment building, which was populated almost entirely by Muslims, had set up a dedicated space in the courtyard for cutting. In India, a Hindu-dominated country, a country of many vegetarians, it was important that the slaughter not take place outside. It was even more important this year, when Bakri Eid happened to coincide with one of the immersion days of the Ganpati festival. The same week that thousands of Hindus would walk toward the sea with their Ganesh idols, thousands of Muslims would slaughter goats as a sacrifice and distribute the meat to family and friends. To both faiths, it was a time of great religiosity. And with tensions growing under Modi, there were fears that violence would break out.

Before Bakri Eid, the priest at Shahzad's mosque told the congregation, "When you cut the animal, and Ganpati is also there, don't go showing everybody, saying, 'We have cut the animal, and here is blood.' Don't go showing, and saying, 'We are Muslims, we have cut the goat, today is our Eid.' We are not in a Muslim state. We are in the power of another state. So we should respect them also."

The night before the cutting, the goats bleated and cried so loudly that they could be heard upstairs. They stomped their hooves. They swiveled their heads back and forth nervously in the wind. There were more than a dozen goats tied up in the courtyard, all with different-patterned coats: splotched tan and white, black with white spots, white with black spots, or the color of *café au lait*. They had straight horns and curled ones, big eyes and small ones, thick beards or no beards at all. They were almost all a little fat. As they cried through the night, Shahzad thought it was as if the goats knew what was going to happen. He was glad they lived in a Muslim neighborhood, so that the Hindus could not hear. Their crying lasted all the way until morning.

The next day, everyone in the joint family rose early. The men went to the mosque for prayer, and the women prepared a light breakfast of toast and butter and jam. Taheem and the other children in the building grew boisterous, jangly with anticipation.

It was the first year Shahzad's family could afford to get two goats, each for a hefty twenty-one thousand rupees, plus three thousand more to pay the butcher. Some families did the butchering themselves, but Shahzad and Farhan both thought that was not right. The slaughter must be done swiftly and properly so that it did not hurt the animal. The man wielding the knife also had to be careful with the intestines. One wrong cut and it could ruin all the meat. Only a butcher knew the proper way.

Outside in the courtyard after prayer, Shahzad and Farhan waited with the other men for their butcher and their goats' turn. Some were kind to their goats, petting them soothingly, while others were rough, pulling them hard by the ear. Several children tried to bring their goats inside, but an adult tsked them, saying, *"Saf nahi, jao."* "It's not clean, go away." There were three sections in the court-yard: a tarp-covered area at the back to cut the goats, a roped-off section to skin them, and an open area at the center where the men could stand and watch. Taheem, who had come down after break-fast, walked nervously from one section to the next.

As they waited, a fat, sweating man announced that he wanted to kill his own goat. He had only a dull knife. As he started, he cut the wrong part of the neck. It was clear he did not know what he was doing. Farhan, who stood nearby, admonished him: "Cut the heart." When the man did not, Farhan took the knife to finish. The goat died slowly, making a bleating sound that turned into a squawk and, after much gasping, into nothing at all. "The whole point is that the animal should not feel any pain," Farhan said later, his voice tinged with regret. "That's the way the cut should be done."

Shahzad was also disappointed in the man. It seemed to him that there were an unfortunate number of Muslim men like this who didn't understand religion. At Mecca the day before, hundreds of people had been killed in a stampede. It had been a hot day, and many people had pushed and shoved to throw the stones that hit Jamarat—pillars that represented the devil. After that, the stampede had begun. Shahzad thought that people sometimes became excited because they wanted to be seen as the most religious. *That was not the way to show your love to Allah,* he thought. When he read about extremist Muslims, he thought their problem was much the same. But perhaps these people had not had the benefit of growing up the way he did.

Many extremists, he knew, were not raised in a multicultural, multireligious country like India, a democracy with a free media that showed ads with Hindus and Muslims eating side by side. Most did not grow up in a mostly tolerant, cosmopolitan city like Mumbai either. And it was unlikely their priests were becoming more liberal or flexible the way his were. For all his concerns about being Muslim in India, he was often grateful he lived there instead of the Gulf. He was especially glad he did not live in Pakistan or Saudi Arabia, where he had heard rich men paid huge sums to take young girls as their wives. He heard that after they fulfilled their lust and desire with them, they said *talaq* three times and moved on.

At last, it was their turn to cut the goats. Farhan's was first. It was agreed that Farhan would make the initial quick slice and then pray from the Quran as the butcher finished. Taheem stood anxiously beside Shahzad as his father made the cut. Then Farhan began praying, and Shahzad and Taheem held the goat down, their knees on the animal's chest. The thin, wiry butcher cut the goat's neck as it writhed. Blood streamed onto Shahzad's sandals and Taheem's shorts, and then down an open drain. The killing was done quickly. Taheem allowed himself to look at the goat's eyes, which were rolled back in its head, its neck turned out at an unnatural angle. And then he quickly looked away. On one side, an already-cut and skinned goat's body parts were being divided into buckets. On the other, a live goat was bleating as he was led to the tarp. Taheem did not allow himself to cry.

Upstairs, Mahala watched from a window. She could see only a sliver of what was happening: a hoof, a tarp. But she knew. After their goat was cut, she cried in her bedroom. She took out her father's cell phone, on which she'd taken a picture of the goat, and kissed the photo. "I love you, I love you," she told the goat, clutching the cell phone tight.

While Mahala thought of the goat, Shahzad thought of his father, who used to eat the goat's eyeballs every Bakri Eid. He said it gave him better eyesight. Shahzad laughed at the memory as he walked upstairs with the butcher. Shahzad had never liked the taste of eyeballs, with their long, thin tissue of retina the consistency of chewing gum. But the memory made him miss his father. Meanwhile Sabeena, who was sitting on her haunches before a spit in the apartment, preparing to cook the first pieces of liver, thought of her own father. Out of all the people she distributed meat to, she had always enjoyed bringing it to her father most. These days, she only gave it to her sister and brother and his children. Bakri Eid had never felt the same.

Taheem had changed clothes after the cutting. Now, he wore a T-shirt with American-brand motorcycles on it and acid-washed pants, free of blood. He ran up to Shahzad and said, "Hey, *baba*, I held the feet," though Shahzad had been there to see it. "Ah, very good," Shahzad said, and patted him on the shoulder.

It was a few minutes before anyone noticed the young street girl standing at the door, looking around nervously. The women were busy making packages of meat in the kitchen to distribute to family, neighbors, and the poor. "Is auntie here?" the girl finally called into the living room, her voice high and tentative. She had a sad, round face and a purple and pink–colored veil over her *burqa*.

"*Andar*," Shahzad said and pointed to the kitchen. The girl tiptoed inside. After a minute, she came out, grasping a few rupees and a package of meat. She tiptoed back toward the door. "Hey," Shahzad said in a friendly voice. "I think I saw you before in the mosque. No?" The girl giggled and nodded. Her nervousness disappeared. "Very good," Shahzad said, and smiled at her. The little girl skipped out, bag swinging, the first of many street children who would visit them that day.

❦❦❦❦❦

In the days after Bakri Eid and the Ganpati festival, a thick smoke descended over the city, a by-product of the pollution and festival fires. The weather forecast did not say "rainy" or "foggy" or "clear," just "smoke." It often rained so hard during Ganpati that the streets began to flood—what some in Mumbai called *"haathi kabana,"* or "elephant rainfall." But this year, there had been no thud of rain on roofs. In the late September heat, the taxi and bus drivers began to fight with customers over rigged prices and where they would or would not go. Or they fought with each other. *"Madarchod,"* motherfucker, *"bhenchod,"* sisterfucker, they called back and forth, Hindu driver to Muslim driver, or one religion against itself, while the high-pitched playback singers on their radios wailed in the background. Anger did not always discriminate. Not always. On the television, there was news of a Muslim man who had been lynched by a Hindu mob in northern India after rumors spread that he had eaten beef. Afterward, journalists, artists, actors, and even politicians spoke out about the growing intolerance in the country. Modi himself said nothing for a week, until he finally made a speech saying the lynching was *dukhad*. But though it was sad, he said, he was not to blame. "What is the role of the central government in these incidents?" he asked. When Modi talked like this, Shahzad switched off the TV.

September yielded to October, and Sabeena's birthday came. She was turning fifty-two. At her request, they didn't celebrate much, but as a birthday gift Shahzad gave her seventy-five thousand rupees, a large sum, to get new gold bangles made. It was money he would have spent on the new Colaba office.

People said that Mumbai was at its worst this time of year, after several of the major holidays were over but before winter and its festivals came, including Diwali and the Prophet's birthday. It was the time when the city felt heaviest. Even the new apartment felt stuffy. And that month a poor Muslim man in their building—a man with ten children and little money to feed them but who all his neighbors said was doing "so well"—announced to Shahzad that his wife was pregnant again.

With the holidays over, Shahzad went to visit the family doctor, who knew him almost better than anyone. Recently, Shahzad had begun seeing a sexologist, who had put him on another medication. He now took five different pills every day—pills he had begun to worry weren't actually helping. He still washed his hands too much, still felt anxious at night, and still sometimes thought obsessively about having a child. He hoped the family doctor would give him some kind of conclusive answer as to why the medications weren't working.

Shahzad spent a long time in the waiting room of the private hospital, amid people with broken legs and boils. When the doctor finally let him in, Shahzad was surprised to find the man had white-gray hair, just like Shahzad did beneath his henna. They had grown old together, though it seemed no time had passed since that first visit, when Shahzad had just gotten married.

"Oy, don't come and see me when you are healthy," the doctor said, as Shahzad walked in. "But, Doctor, I'm not," Shahzad said. The doctor peered at Shahzad over his glasses and waited for him to continue.

Shahzad told the doctor what he already knew: that he was still childless, and that he could not perform, despite all the medications. But he also told him he was worried about all the pills he was on. He asked for a list of them, which the doctor wrote down carefully, from memory: one pill for blood pressure, one antidepressant, one to help him sleep, two for anxiety, plus the pill for erectile dysfunction. It was a lot, the doctor said, but they were not to blame for his problems.

"Then?" Shahzad asked.

The doctor was quiet. He looked Shahzad in the eye. "Just . . . try to relax. You have so much anxiety," he said. "It is common in joint families."

More people, more stress. He had seen this in many of his patients.

Shahzad was not satisfied. "But—"

"Sabeena, she is still very cool about everything, yes?"

"Yes," said Shahzad.

"Then?"

Shahzad nodded. There didn't seem to be anything more to say. He looked down at the list of medications, which seemed like evidence of all his problems, and put it in his bag.

On the rickshaw ride back to the train, Shahzad thought about what the family doctor said. Sabeena was *cool*, Sabeena was kind, Sabeena never judged him. It wasn't about the pills or his inability to have a child. It was about him and his anxiety and *bimari*, just like his father, and perhaps his grandfather before that. It was about the domino effect of pain and hurt in families, until someone made it stop. Until someone stood up straight.

In the weeks after the visit to the family doctor, Shahzad's father came to him in his dreams. They were vague dreams, hard to pin down or remember. Shahzad was unsettled and told his mother about them. "What to do?" he asked.

"Pray for him," she said, and also urged him to go feed the poor, the way his father used to do when no one was looking. Shahzad remembered how his father would always feed the beggar, street boy, or madman on the road. "Feed on his behalf, and then God will be happy," she said.

Shahzad nodded, and walked down the road to a cheap hotel. Out front, he found many hungry people. Some were sitting on their haunches begging, hands outstretched. Others had that gauntness in their cheeks or vacant look in their eyes. He wasn't sure why he hadn't noticed them before; he knew half the country was hungry. He gave them each fifty rupees. And for the first time, as he thought of his father, he felt good.

♥♥♥♥♥

At the end of the month, Shahzad went to Chor Bazaar, the so-called "thieves market" downtown, to find a DVD of *Mughal-e-Azam*. It had been a long time since he'd seen it, and he wanted to watch it now. On his way he stopped at Byculla Market, where most of the shopkeepers were still the same. "Where have you been all this time?" they asked. Shahzad told them about Dharavi, and they clapped him on the back, saying to one another, "See what has come of the landlord's son?"

Shahzad continued on, feeling energized as he entered the inner bylanes of Chor Bazaar. He passed the skinny *bidi-wallahs*, hacking up a lung, and the old men selling broken shortwave radios. He passed the fake-antique sellers hawking what passed as old British snuffboxes, chalices, lanterns, ship relics, clocks, coins, and rotary phones. He passed the shops with the windup gramophones, printed with the image of the dog listening to His Master's Voice. After this came the clusters of sitting Buddhas, standing Krishnas, rose petal rosaries, and imitation Mughal vases. Then came the rows and rows of rusty car parts and tailors with signs in bad English. He passed several women, who never used to come to Chor Bazaar, at least not dressed in clothes like that. Finally, he came upon the movie sellers. There, at a makeshift wooden stall, beside a motorcycle with a baby goat standing with wobbly legs on top, was a copy of *Mughal-e-Azam*.

After Shahzad got home, he asked to borrow Farhan's speakers so that he could watch the movie in their bedroom on his laptop. He could recall every scene, song, and line of dialogue of the film, but still he looked forward to the moment that dinner was over and his mother had gone to bed.

The movie opened, as Shahzad remembered well, with Emperor Akbar walking through the desert to the tomb of a saint to beg for a son. Still, Shahzad leaned forward, entranced as if for the first time. "I have everything in life, but I don't have a son," the king said. Before long, the saint granted his wish, and the queen gave birth to a naughty but good-looking baby boy.

After a little while, Sabeena, who was in the living room watching her Pakistani serial, turned off the television. She came into the bedroom just as the court dancer, Anarkali—played by Madhubala—came on screen. "Oy, Madhubala," Shahzad said to her, looking up from his spot on the bed. "Mmmm," Sabeena said, without taking her eyes off the screen. This was the part where Anarkali appeared as a statue and came to life after the prince almost shot her with an arrow. Moving closer, Sabeena leaned on Shahzad's shoulder and then drew up a chair beside him.

Almost three hours later, after the emperor had gone to war with the prince over his love of Anarkali, Shahzad and Sabeena watched as father and son confronted each other. It was the film's most quoted scene. "I am bound by my empire," the emperor told his son. "And I am bound by my love," the prince responded. Shahzad inhaled sharply. Sabeena leaned in close. Neither of them spoke. The emperor would let Anarkali live, but she and the prince could never be together.

As the credits rolled, Sabeena lay down in bed, where she didn't often sleep. Through the window, she could see the railway tracks, the Haj House, and the nearby trees where the two parrots sang to each other, as if they were in love. After a minute, Shahzad switched off the light and sat down close beside her in the dark.

THE FAMILY LINE

Ashok and Parvati, 2014 to 2015

> *"I am a million, million births*
> *Flushed with triumphant blood, each a growing*
> *Thing . . .*
> *I am a million, million silences*
> *Strung like crystal beads*
> *Onto someone else's*
> *Song."*
>
> —Kamala Das, "Someone Else's Song"

Diary, June 2014:

I have joined back to complete PhD. I feel daily log is not required. But now I can write my positive thoughts. I don't want them to go to waste.

By June, when Parvati rejoined IIT Bombay, the city had become hot and sticky, and everyone said rain was on the way. The puppies in the lane had grown so big the building's security guards now shooed them away with *lathis*. Their suburb was also growing, and getting richer, or so it seemed as the parade of residents in fancy *saris* and Western-style suits filed in and out of the Starbucks and tony Hiranandani apartments. Traffic into downtown Mumbai should have waned a little as overpasses, tunnels, and bridges were built and roads repaired. But people kept moving to the city, some five hundred a day at least, and so the traffic and road accidents only multiplied. There were twenty million people in the city now.

Everything seemed to be growing. The economy was expanding. Life expectancies were extending. And it was a young population and getting younger; most of the city's inhabitants were now under thirty-five. In their suburb, there were more cars, more birds, more crocodiles along the lake, and more lovers walking hand in hand. The suburb seemed a new place to Parvati, and she told herself this year at school would be different.

Since rejoining IIT Bombay, Parvati had become a model student. She got up on time, cooked *dal* and rice and *subzi* for lunch, did laundry, and boiled the day's water. When she walked out the door for school in her neatly ironed *kurta*, she said good-bye to Ashok with a smile. If her father called, she'd tell him in Malayalam: "It's going fine, *Appa*." She spent long hours at the lab. She hardly Gchatted Ashok now, because she was too busy. She even made friends on campus with a group of Malayali boys who reminded her of home. After school, she walked in the gardens, ate a light dinner, took the laundry off the line, and went to sleep. Wash, rinse, repeat. In the morning, she got up and did it all again.

Sometimes Parvati felt content following her new schedule and sometimes she felt ill at ease. Often, she thought of a Malayalam proverb she had always hated: *What elders tell us and how gooseberries taste is similar. It's all bitter in the beginning, but later, it tastes good.*

She had wanted the chance to prove that her father had been wrong. But now it seemed he'd been right.

It was after Parvati went back to school that the pressure to produce a child also began. They had been married for over a year now and Parvati was approaching thirty, which meant that it was past time. When Parvati's father visited them in Mumbai, he brought them a white figurine of Lord Krishna as a child and said, "I want a baby like this very soon." They put the figurine on the *pooja* shelf with the other gods and goddesses but did not unwrap it from its plastic, as if to prevent its potency from escaping.

Mostly, the pressure came from Ashok's dad. At first, his comments were innocuous, a friendly add-on to his phone conversations. "So, Ashok, where is my grandchild?" he'd say. Over time, the comments became more aggressive. "It's time for the STORK," he told Parvati, so loud he was almost shouting. The old belief was that a baby was needed to keep a new couple together. The new belief was that without live-in in-laws a baby was needed more than ever.

The most embarrassing moment came when Ashok's father told her, "We'll be really happy if one day you call and say you missed your period." *A father talking about a period.* Parvati couldn't imagine her father ever talking that way.

"I worry when you get old you'll be eccentric like your dad," she told Ashok.

"Then will you hate me?" he asked, raising his eyebrows a little.

"I won't hate you," she said, with a wry smile. "I have no choice."

Parvati had always had a sharp tongue, and, with the increased confidence she gained from going back to school, her jabs became sharper and funnier. Often, they were directed at Ashok. If he bragged about his driving, which had improved somewhat since he started taking driving classes, she'd say, "Oh, wow, Ashok, you are *suuuuper* macho." If he began to tell a story for which he didn't have the facts, she'd catch him in his lie and say, squinting her left eye and raising his right eyebrow skeptically, "Ashok, you are talking just to talk." Or she'd make fun of his poor Hindi—though in truth many Tam Brahms never learned it—and how he tried to cover it up by repeating himself.

Mostly he found her digs funny. But sometimes they seemed to have an edge to them, especially when she noticed he was acting like his father. "I really hope my child is not like you," she said one day, her voice sharp, "because I can't take more than one of you." Ashok laughed at this nervously.

Not long after Parvati went back to school, Ashok was getting ready for work when there was a loud *ghaddaghaddahat* sound, like gunfire, outside their apartment. Ashok—still in the wrinkled button-up shirt and drawstring pants he wore to sleep, his hair unbrushed and ungelled—rushed into the bedroom and threw open the window. A car had burst into flames outside. Children from a nearby school—there were three in the vicinity—screamed and ran, their backpacks bouncing on their small backs. As smoke began to rise from the car, teachers shouted and hustled them away. Parvati had just left in a rickshaw for school. Ashok punched in numbers on his phone.

"*Chiboo,*" he said, and sighed with relief when she answered. "You're at the lab? Phew. *Chiboo,* you won't even believe what just happened here. There was a car here—by the school—that kind of burst into flames right now. I don't even know if there were kids inside the car or not—"

"What? Are you okay?" asked Parvati.

"I'm fine," he said. "It was like *ghadda-ghadda-ghadda.*" He switched to Tamil. "It was like a bomb blast. I went into our room and . . ."

Ashok was grateful Parvati hadn't been at home when the blast happened. She would have gotten upset. She would have wanted to call people or make him stay home from work. Or maybe he would have made her stay home from school. They were similar that way, both cautious, careful people.

Later, Ashok would learn the blast was caused by a short circuit in the car's wiring. The current had followed the wrong path. Short circuits could happen anywhere—in Mumbai, Trivandrum, or even Germany, where Ashok knew Joseph still lived. Joseph, who did not have the same gods or beliefs as Parvati. *They would have struggled with that,* Ashok thought.

But this kind of blast probably happened more often on the streets of Mumbai, a city of spontaneous combustion. The city where he and Parvati chose to live and where they'd soon have a child. The list of potential hazards for a child was long: bad water, bad food, air pollution, light pollution, car accidents, train accidents, shoddy construction, shoddy roads, religious violence, political violence, street mobs, fires, floods, Eve teasers, rapists, and pedophiles. And the bursting of a car into flames.

❦❦❦❦❦

In December, after their one-year anniversary, they had sex to try for a baby for the first time.

Parvati had always heard that trying for a baby was romantic. But instead it seemed like work. She tried to make it passionate, like she had in the early days of their marriage, yet somehow they couldn't summon the emotion. It didn't help that they had to plan sex: for after Ashok came home at night, exhausted from the office, or midday, when she rushed home from school for lunch, or in the morning, when she was trying to get out the door. For all of December, they kept trying.

Later that month, they decided to go away to Pune for the day. In the city, once a stronghold of an old Hindu empire, they visited Pataleshwar, an ancient Hindu cave-temple devoted to Lord Shiva, with a *lingam*, Shiva's phallic symbol, at the center. Shiva was known to be an ardent lover—so much that his lovemaking shook the cosmos. This was not one of Parvati's favorite stories.

As they left Pataleshwar, Parvati spotted a three-striped Indian palm squirrel outside the temple and thought of the story of Lord Ram, who built a bridge to rescue his wife Sita from a demon with the aid of birds and a particularly helpful squirrel. Afterward, Ram stroked the squirrel on the back with three fingers in gratitude, leaving the trademark stripes behind. Parvati preferred this story, though not its ending, when Ram wrongly accused Sita of sleeping with the demon and made her walk over coals to prove her purity. In the old myths, women were punished in many different ways.

The last stop they made was Parvati Hill. Parvati's namesake was said to help with fertility and birthing, because though the goddess had been cursed as barren, she ultimately gave birth to a child. On the hill there was a colorful Parvati temple, painted in bright reds and yellows. It reminded Parvati of the flamboyant domed churches in Saint Petersburg and Moscow Joseph had told her about. After visiting the temple, Ashok and Parvati stood at the top of the hill, quietly looking down at the city. The sun was just beginning to set. It was the golden hour, and the air felt very cool. Parvati took photo after photo of the city bathed in yellow light. Ashok asked her to take a photo of him and she did, laughing.

As they rode the bus home to Mumbai in their cramped but cozy seats, rain pouring down outside, it almost felt romantic. Parvati hoped that the next time they made love it would be more like the movies in the West, where a baby was conceived with passion, maybe even over a bottle of wine.

After the New Year—a holiday that passed without fanfare, though Parvati expected this now—they tried again. At the same time, Parvati's parents kept doing *poojas* for her to get pregnant and to the snake gods. In early February, when Parvati peed on a stick at home, she saw that there was a line.

She didn't believe it and took a second test with the same result. She called Ashok into the room. "Let's not get too excited," she said, though her voice said otherwise. "Let's not get too excited," Ashok said back, and kissed her on the forehead. He was already thinking of baby names. "And let's not tell this to anyone yet," she added, because she knew how much could go wrong in a pregnancy. Ashok promised her he wouldn't.

But it was hard to keep the news a secret. A Malayalam proverb went: *You can keep one* betel *nut in your pocket, but will it be possible to keep a* betel *nut tree?* Although Ashok told only his father and brother, they both told other members of the family, who told still others, until many people knew. Ashok's parents were so excited they immediately planned a trip to Mumbai.

Outside Ashok and Parvati's bedroom window, a pigeon began building a nest. Parvati saw it and thought she should remove it. It was on their air-conditioner unit, and the eggs might crack. She also didn't want the birds coming in the house. A common superstition said that a bird inside was an omen of a death to come.

Parvati tossed the sticks and twigs to the ground every time she noticed them. But the pigeon was persistent, and soon a nest was built and two eggs were laid on top of the AC. Parvati told Ashok, who agreed they should be removed, but not by them, because it could be bad luck. Ashok asked the maid to take care of it.

After that, Parvati came home from school one day to find the AC unit spotless. She hoped the maid had been careful with the eggs and also worried a little about whether the pigeon would be able to find her babies down below.

❦❦❦❦❦

At her previous appointment, the doctor had warned Parvati that miscarriages were common at this stage, especially for Indian women; about a third experienced a spontaneous miscarriage the first time. "This happens all the time," the doctor said, in a voice that sounded aggressive and loud to Parvati. "See, it's just four weeks, so you're not emotionally attached to it yet."

Who are you to say that? Parvati thought. *I know my body, and I became attached right away.*

In the month since Parvati found out, she had begun waking up nauseous in the mornings. Afterward, she felt ravenous, as if she were already hungry for two. She felt an immediate connection to the baby. *There is something alive in my body,* she thought.

Since Ashok's parents arrived in Mumbai, they had talked about nothing but the baby. Ashok's father spent most of his time online, looking up data on early stages of pregnancy. He relayed all his findings to them: *At four weeks, a baby is the size of a poppy seed. At five weeks, the beginnings of the spine, brain, and backbone begin to form. At six weeks, the average heart rate of a fetus is 120 to 160 beats per minute.*

When Parvati went to the doctor's office for her next checkup, the doctor did a scan. Afterward, Ashok and Parvati sat in the room together, waiting like Carl and Ellie in the movie *Up.* When the doctor came back, she announced without fanfare: "There is no heartbeat."

Zero beats per minute.

Her voice still seemed loud.

At home, Ashok's father opened the door, his head hanging low. Ashok had called him from the car. Parvati saw that she had to be strong for Ashok's father, who clearly could not be strong for her. "It's okay," she told him. "Next time we'll have a baby. Next time there will be a heartbeat."

"But are you sad?" Ashok's father asked.

How is this a question? Parvati thought.

"Yes," she said, and her voice felt far away. "But there is nothing we can do."

Ashok's mother, who could always be relied on to be warm and kind, came over to her. "You're like my own daughter," she said, and though she had said this before, this time Parvati knew she meant it.

Parvati called her parents in Trivandrum, who demanded she send them her medical reports so they could consult local doctors they trusted. Meanwhile, Ashok disappeared into the computer room to search for information on miscarriages. He was heartened to find that even women who had four miscarriages or more could still carry a healthy baby to term.

He came back into the living room and told Parvati, "*Chiboo,* we'll be okay."

But the fetus was still inside Parvati. The doctor had given her a pill; if not for the scan, she said, she would have had a natural miscarriage in four months. On the official paperwork, it was called an abortion.

That night, after Parvati swallowed the pill, she began to throw up violently. "Call your mom," she told Ashok. It was always a woman who helped in these situations, when women were considered unclean.

"No," he said, firmly. "I'll help you."

All through the night, as Parvati threw up, Ashok stayed awake and wiped her face with tissues. She threw up over and over again and began to bleed.

"I flushed my baby," she said, and she was crying now, for the first time since she had promised Ashok she wouldn't. "I flushed my baby."

"No, no," Ashok said, and his voice was calming. He cleaned her face again and massaged her back and feet. His touch felt so unbearably kind to Parvati that she only cried harder. A line from the movie *Up* went: "I have just met you, and I love you." As he kept kneading her feet and back, Parvati felt she had not really seen Ashok until now.

♥♥♥♥♥

After the miscarriage and Ashok's parents' departure, Parvati began to dream again of snakes. Her parents were still doing their *poojas* to the snake gods. A belief: the snake deity Naga could make a woman fertile or he could turn malevolent, depending on how he was pleased. In the nearby lake, one of the crocodiles that usually sunned himself turned up dead.

Parvati dreamed of other things, including the Jacobite boy from college. On Facebook she saw that his wife was pregnant with a second child, and in her dream, he had four children surrounding him. She messaged him to tell him about her dream, and he wrote back, "At this rate, you're right."

Parvati and Ashok visited doctor after doctor together. At each visit, Parvati asked what she'd done wrong. Ashok and the doctors told her that was silly. "Don't blame yourself," the doctors said. "The miscarriage was not in your control."

Then Parvati's sister got pregnant a second time, along with several of Parvati's cousins. It seemed like the whole country was getting pregnant. "Everyone's getting two babies and I'm not even getting one," Parvati told Ashok. "You just go sit there and watch some TV if you're going to think like that," he said, and then added, "Wait, do you mean to be funny? Or are you making a joke of being sad?"

Both, Parvati thought.

"What will happen if we don't have children?" Ashok asked the following month as they sat in their bedroom with the shades drawn.

"Well," Parvati said, and tried to envision it. "If we do not have a kid, you will withdraw into a shell. You'll spend most of the time in front of the computer writing. And over time, you'll grow indifferent to me."

"Ah," said Ashok. This sounded right. He also tried to imagine it. "*Chiboo,* you're tempestuous and you'd become more tempestuous," he said. "You will rage and rant a lot. And when my parents would come to stay with me, you will treat them badly and not be nice to them at all."

They both laughed at this.

"So we better have a kid," said Parvati.

"Right," said Ashok. "But . . . couples find ways to stay together without kids," he said. "We'd still be together. Because fundamentally there is a lot of connection, *Chiboo.*"

There was a saying Ashok had grown up hearing the elders of the family say, which had variations across India: *The family name—the* kutumpa peyar—*should continue. The family line should not end. The family line must not be broken.*

Also, in Hinduism, there were four life stages. Student, householder, retiree, renunciation. The second stage, householder, meant getting married and having children. The *Mahabharata* said the householder should take a spouse and then establish "a fire of his own." You couldn't move on to the third stage without the second.

Also, in Hinduism, only a male child can light his father's funeral pyre.

In the fall they decided to try again. Parvati's father told her to visit the campus temple to Laxmi, goddess of prosperity, to pray for a successful pregnancy. The temple was rose pink and overlooked the artificial lake and stood against a backdrop of trees. Once a week before class, Parvati dutifully visited the shrine. It couldn't hurt.

At night, she practiced her Carnatic singing, which helped keep her focus elsewhere. It also made her think of home. She thought that if she got pregnant again, the baby would hear her and feel calm.

"Go for it like it's the first time," the doctors kept telling them, but it didn't feel like the first time at all. The calendar method only increased the pressure, because there was only a small window in which to conceive. *We can't just wait for passion to arrive,* thought Parvati. Especially when it didn't seem like passion was going to come.

There were many ancient beliefs in Hinduism about what happened if you conceived without passion. Mostly it was said this would be reflected in the mental state of the child.

There were also beliefs about the best time to conceive, which was supposed to be between midnight and 3 p.m. Diti, the earth goddess, had conceived two sons out of lust and out of jealousy of her sister, at dusk, an improper time. As a result, her sons had been born wicked and immoral.

There were also beliefs about how to have a son. A husband and wife should have sex midway through the menstrual cycle and perform a special ritual.

And there were beliefs about what a pregnant woman shouldn't do. Dhanvantari, avatar of Vishnu, and god of Ayurveda, supposedly said if a pregnant woman drew *kajal* on her eyes, the baby would be born blind. He said that if a woman cried while pregnant, the baby would have bad eyesight. If she got an oil massage, then the child would have leprosy. If the woman laughed too much, then the baby's lips would be black.

Ashok and Parvati did not place much stock in the old Hindu tales. But Parvati worried about the belief about passion. It seemed only logical that a child should be conceived that way. One day Parvati suggested a solution to their problem: she and Ashok should watch porn.

Parvati didn't know much about pornography. Conservative families down south mostly didn't talk about it. The only time porn was openly discussed was when it was in the news, such as when three politicians were caught watching porn on their cell phones in the legislature. Or when actress Sunny Leone crossed over from porn films—*Goddess: Sunny's First Anal Scene*—to big-budget Bollywood thrillers. After Leone's third Bollywood appearance, a woman in Mumbai filed a police report against her for "destroying Indian culture and society." India now had among the most women watching porn of any country.

From what little Parvati knew about porn, she thought it might help them. She had watched some soft-core videos on her own on the website Dailymotion, and she knew Ashok sometimes watched more graphic films on sites like YouPorn and RedTube. Like many Indian men, he searched keywords like "boyfriend girlfriend" and "husband wife," because he liked watching couples together. Or because he didn't know there were more explicit videos out there.

Ashok was unnerved by her suggestion. He'd much rather watch porn alone. He thought that they should solve their passion problem in other ways, such as by going out with friends, which seemed to act as an aphrodisiac.

But Ashok need not have worried, because when he finally agreed, the website wouldn't load. They tried another site. Nothing. Another. It wouldn't load either. The sites all displayed the message that they were "blocked as per the instruction of Competent Authority." Later, they read in the newspaper that the central government had enacted some kind of ban on pornography, which was allegedly just for child porn but had also extended to adult sites. Some 850 adult websites in total had been found in violation of "decency or morality," which were enshrined in the constitution.

Despite the ban, she and Ashok were determined to make their sex better. One week, they had sex five times in six days, and Parvati hoped that it was with enough passion to make a baby.

♥♥♥♥♥

Ashok was also determined to get his manuscript out to literary agents. After four years, it was finally complete. The novel was very long now and filled with complex story lines. But Ashok saw it as the simple story of a man's botched efforts in marriage, work, and life—though he had tacked on a happy ending. One day, after Parvati left for school, he hunkered down to write a synopsis so he could send it off.

For nearly an hour, he tried to write on his laptop out in the living room but kept getting distracted. Across from him was the *pooja* shelf with the ceramic baby Krishna, still in its wrapping. He moved into the computer room, empty of sentimentality—just a bed, desktop computer, and books, with Jeffrey Eugenides's *The Marriage Plot* on top. Next to the desktop was a medical slip from Parvati's last visit to the doctor. On it were a few scrawled notes: "miscarriage

March 2015," "planning for a baby," and "anxious about any pre-
cautions or care to be taken."

Ashok decided to send off the book the next day.

It was around this time—after a long period of forgetting—that
Ashok thought of the incidents with the *chai-wallah* and the man in
the theater. He decided they were not significant events and that he
did not need to tell Parvati about them. He knew that many young
boys in Mumbai had dealt with worse. Many young boys had not
just been touched but had also been forced to have sex. A line from
The Marriage Plot about sadness said it was like a bruise you had to
try not to touch. The key was not to think about it.

♥♥♥♥♥

Parvati felt both hungry and nauseous, and her period was late. She
wondered if she could be pregnant again. She allowed herself to get
a little excited at the prospect.

The following night, she and Ashok went bowling at the mall,
passing a romantic fountain with colored lights at the entrance
and a lingerie store promising "lace all over . . . so, so sensual."
The city's malls were so different from the street bazaars of old—
far more sterile and orderly. They passed a kids' arcade filled with
well-dressed children and a giant Hamleys toy shop from London.
As they walked, Eric Clapton's "Have You Ever Loved a Woman"
played from the loudspeakers.

"I don't know if I have ever loved," Ashok said to Parvati in a
put-on, dreamy voice.

Parvati laughed at this. Just that week, Ashok had told her that
he loved her. He said he loved her the most in the mornings, when
she smelled just like a baby.

They went bowling and then played a game of pool—Ashok
guiding her hands on the cue stick to show her how to strike the
ball. Afterward, they walked back to the car with their arms around

each other's shoulders. Parvati kept wondering if she might be pregnant. They stopped to take a selfie by the fountain, the colors changing from purple to blue behind them.

That week, they tried sex with Parvati on top, and both thought it felt good. It felt so good that they made love for a long time.

And then it was their second wedding anniversary, and Parvati woke up feeling hopeful. In the morning, Ashok's parents had called to wish them a happy day, and she'd talked to them for a long time— even laughed at Ashok's father's jokes. While she talked, Ashok sat beside her and gently massaged her legs. Afterward, he offered to make them lunch. "Today is a special day, so I'll rustle up something, *boo boo*." He'd started calling her "boo boo" when she was crying all the time, and now he used the nickname with confidence.

"No, no," she said, laughing, "I'll help."

Together they made a giant spread of potato, okra, broccoli, and coconut curd, using fresh, hand-ground coconut. On their first anniversary, they had gone out to a nice restaurant and the mall and taken a picture to preserve the memory. But this year it was enough just to be together. As background music, Ashok put on a Carnatic song, an ode to Parjanya, the South Indian god of rain and the life-giver. After eating, they went into the bedroom to talk and agreed to try to watch porn again soon. The government, facing the outrage of the country, had lifted the ban.

That night, Parvati got her period. After she saw the blood, she sank into the couch and put on *The Holiday*, a bad American movie, and ate an entire dark chocolate bar. She called Ashok, who told her, quietly, "It's okay, *Chiboo*. It'll be okay." She nodded but thought bitterly: *I am supposed to love today, but I hated it.*

When she got her period, Parvati often used a hot water bag to ease the cramps. This time, Ashok came into their bedroom every half hour to reheat it. Parvati was surprised to find his efforts romantic.

And this time, a memory came back to her from Trivandrum. Once, many years ago, she had been on her period, and the cramps had been almost unbearable. That day, for once, though her father was supposed to consider her untouchable, he had come into her bedroom and held her hand. Parvati had forgotten this until now.

❦❦❦❦❦

The following month, Parvati's father came to Mumbai for a visit. As always, he was pleasant but proper with his daughter and son-in-law. Over lunch, he brought up Kathakali, the expressive style of dance from Kerala, and told Parvati he was glad it was becoming obsolete. He told her it was "boring" and "had no use" because the performers didn't speak. "Then what would be the use of any music or dance?" Parvati asked, incredulous. "Exactly," he said.

But after he left to go back to Trivandrum, Parvati was surprised to find she missed him. She even cried a little when he was gone. Her father was something known, and solid, after a year filled with uncertainty. She could have guessed what his opinion would be on Kathakali. She almost always knew what he'd say. And she thought that even if he was wrong about art, perhaps he had been right about other things—like marrying Ashok instead of Joseph. She fought with Ashok about little things, but they did not argue over gods or family or tradition. And when they had a baby, they would not fight over what beliefs to pass on.

After he left Mumbai, Ashok's mother also came for a visit. She did a last-ditch baby *pooja* for them, buying salt and sesame seeds and waving them over their faces. She brought the spices back home to Trivandrum and did another *pooja* at home. She put *ghee* in a bowl of fire while a priest chanted a *mantra*, and sent the *ghee* to them in Mumbai, telling them to use it to cook with for three or four days. After that, she said, Parvati would definitely become pregnant. Parvati almost believed her. *Believing can't hurt,* she thought. In hindsight, even removing the bird's nest had seemed like bad luck.

❦❦❦❦❦

Just before Parvati took another pregnancy test, certain this time it'd be positive, they made plans to have over her Malayali friends from school. Parvati cleaned the house and bought fresh vegetables, and they made a big lunch of rice and *sambar* together, which filled the house with the smells of coriander and cinnamon. Parvati dressed in a pressed white and black patterned *kurta* and tied her thick hair back.

Over lunch, the conversation with the Malayali boys turned to marriage, and Ashok asked if any of them were married yet. One said he was having trouble getting married off because the "sin" factor in his astrology chart was low. "It's bad if the guy is low and the girl is high," he said, and another boy joked, "Should not be a good guy with a bad girl." Everybody laughed at this, and then one of them brought up intermarriage, which was becoming more common in the city.

"Well, if my child wants to marry a Muslim, I'd accept it," Ashok said.

"I would too," one of the Malayali boys agreed.

"I—I don't think I would," Parvati said softly, stirring the remaining vegetables on her plate.

Ashok, startled, turned to look at her. "Really, *Chiboo*? Why not?"

"My thinking has grown more conservative over time," she said. "I've grown more like my father."

Parvati got up from the table and began clearing the dishes. There was a silence as she disappeared into the kitchen, gliding past the lunch table and the bookshelves, which contained all her old Malayali books. It had been years since she'd read *The God of Small Things*, which warned of the love laws that kept people apart. It had been years since she read Kamala Das and wanted to live as fearlessly as she had, thinking: *You don't have to just live the way your parents have told you.*

It turned out she had lived according to those laws and to her parents' wishes. She had married Ashok, another Hindu and a Tam Brahm, and it had worked out well enough. Now Parvati thought that she should push her son or daughter to do the same. He or she should marry someone who shared the same background; it was easier that way. That is, if she ever got pregnant. Pushing her thoughts aside, Parvati picked up a cake thick with icing from the kitchen counter and carried it into the living room. "Dessert," she told the Malayali boys brightly, holding the cake aloft. Ashok got up to help her cut it.

After cake, the Malayali boys asked for a concert. Parvati did not want to sing, but they pestered her, and eventually she gave in. She turned on her electric *tanpura*, which gave out a continuous drone to keep the time, so she and Ashok could play together.

"No, you sing," Ashok said, and she nodded at him.

Parvati chose a song from an old Malayalam movie called *The Colors of Love*, which she had watched as a little girl. As she began, her alto voice was certain, supple, yet also melancholy and filled with emotion. "The heart of early morning is filled with turmeric color," she sang. It was a haunting song, or hopeful, depending on how it was heard. In the song, the girl sang of her future lover without knowing all that lay ahead. As Parvati sang, she kept her eyes closed and held her hand to her ear.

When she was young, she had sung this song at parties her father held, and all the guests told her how beautiful her singing was.

Now as Parvati finished the song, everybody clapped, Ashok loudest of all.

EPILOGUE: MUMBAI, 2015

PUNE: The monsoon season ended on Wednesday . . . The weakest monsoon [in years] . . . The country has seen two back-to-back droughts . . . The India Meteorological Department (IMD) has, however, discontinued using the term "drought" because it believes an entire country never faces a drought.

The Times of India, October 1, 2015

Maya and Veer

THE SEASON after the monsoon ends in Mumbai—a monsoon that floods the city and leaves it bone dry at the end, so dry there is a water crisis and farmer suicides in the state—Maya and Veer and Janu move into their new apartment. It is in a concrete apartment building in a suburb far north of the city. It is hot, but they do not fight.

But first, they host a *gruhpravesh*, or traditional Hindu house-warming ceremony, and the invitations are sent out in Veer's father's name. On the invite Maya sends out herself, she writes: "Bless us as we enter our new home '*Sukhtara*.'"

Sukhtara. Happy star. She cannot help giving the new apartment the same name.

In the morning, they do a *pooja* with a priest in the flat, and at night they host a big dinner. Veer's family invites Maya's father to the ceremony, as does Maya, but he does not come. Veer invites many of their friends, including Subal, which surprises Maya, but Subal does not come either. Maya has begun going on her own or with Janu to Aksa Beach now. As they play together by the sea, she lets new memories paper over the old.

Guests at the *gruhpravesh* tell Maya she should have used Italian marble on the floors. *Why spend so much and not show it off?* they ask. Instead she has used wood, which feels homey to her. Veer does not care how she decorates the new apartment. But at the tile store, he says he wants to buy tile printed with images of galloping horses for his new study. He announces plans to someday own a fleet of horses, a fleet of airplanes, and a brewery. He makes these plans on a day he is feeling unwell. Maya tells him not to get the tile because it is tacky.

The first night in their new apartment, Maya cannot sleep. It does not feel like home to her. That week, Janu cycles around the flat on a bicycle because it is so big. He says he is bored, because there are no children in the courtyard to play with.

Maya throws herself into the work of decorating the apartment. She finds lovely yellow flowered chairs, pale blue couches, and an old antique clock on a trip to Jaipur, the city where she and Veer were wed. For Janu's room, she buys astronaut sheets and origami wallpaper. To his collection of toys, she adds the pink fluffy teddy bear she bought Veer after their wedding.

Almost all the furniture is new, but they keep the living and dining room tables from their old apartment. Maya does not try to replace them. "Papa won't let us give them away," says Janu, his tone serious, and Maya agrees. The tables are from Veer's childhood, from time he spent with his mother. Janu has begun eating more meat but knows not to ask for meat in their new home.

In the guest room, Maya installs bookshelves against the wall, which contain books she has bought, or that were given to her by Subal, or collected from places she doesn't remember. Among them is *Sacred Games*, the book she bought with Veer that Sunday he came to Crossword. She also hangs the painting of Radha and Krishna in the guest room and thinks that she might sleep in there sometimes.

After a few months in the new house, Maya decides to go to a session of past-life regression therapy. She wants an answer to why she moved into the new flat, even though it was an opportunity to leave Veer. Even though he is feeling better from the diabetes. And even though there are other men more suited—men who tell her how much they love her. She feels that her past must contain the answer.

The session lasts four or five hours, and in this time Maya is taken through her past lives, each of which feels like a dream. In one, she sees that she was a hippie who died in a road accident. In another, she was a Buddhist monk child. Janu also appears in several of her lives—twice or three times as her son and once as her father. The therapist tells Maya, "Janu is the one guiding your soul from birth to birth." This does not surprise Maya. She does not get an answer about why she cannot leave Veer.

At home, Veer's health has improved. He even puts on a little weight, but not too much. His pants fit him just right. He works hard, like he always has, traveling between his factories and family offices and to Africa. He does not repeat his big plans about horses and airplanes. He begins coming home early, in time to help Maya put Janu to bed.

Veer is doing better in part because their new maid cooks him the mostly vegan diet he needs. They have a new maid despite the fact that Maya tried to convince Pallavi to move homes with them. She even took Pallavi to meet a broker and look at shanties nearby. Pallavi initially told Maya she would move with them, but in the end she said she couldn't leave her husband. When she said this, Maya thought of Pallavi's two small sons, who showed up that day looking for her, anxiety on their faces. She also thought of Janu.

Around this time, Janu tells Maya that in school he has learned about Santa Claus, whom he sees as a kind of miracle. "Santa Claus, you know what he will do?" Janu tells his mother one day in a rickshaw, his voice earnest. He watches her face to make sure she is listening. "He will make one snow globe and inside will be me, and you, and Papa also, and when he shakes it all of Bombay will be covered in snow."

"*Haan, beta,*" Maya says, and ruffles his hair.

After Janu tells her this, Maya does not push the matter with Pallavi. She understands why she does not leave.

Shahzad and Sabeena

AFTER THE weak monsoon is over and the holidays have passed—the last goat slaughtered and the last stains of blood washed away in the rain—the city is left in limbo. At the downtown mosque, at the southernmost tip of Mumbai, the men who work in corporate offices still show up to prayer on time. But elsewhere men are struggling. The monsoon came and went too quickly and set off droughts across the state. In Dharavi, the slum dwellers have to wait even longer in line at a common tap and do not know if they will get water. Shahzad visits Dharavi and meets with the builder, who promises the final big deposit of money soon.

At home, with the new fans on high, Farhan helps Taheem and Mahala with their homework and their memorization of the Quran. He teaches them about world religions and how similar they all are. He tells them that Christianity and Islam are almost synonymous in their belief in one God, and that the divisions between Sunni and Shia Muslims do not matter. He tells them that terrorism is wrong. "This is ego, this is power," Farhan says. "Everyone is searching for some power." The children nod solemnly.

Someday, Farhan thinks he will also teach them what he has learned about marriage. He will tell them that it is about small things, that when you marry you are young or unthinking or both and not aware of the many problems you will face together. Money. Time. And that you will always desire more than you have.

Taheem is not focused on his tuitions today, and Nadine hits him hard on the head. "Oww," he shouts, and runs out of the apartment, over to his aunt and uncle's flat. *"Kya hua?"* Sabeena asks, as Taheem plops down beside her. "I was making too much *masti*," he says, wincing as she pats him on the head. Sabeena laughs, eyes twinkling, and tells him it will be okay. She knows that Nadine must have *fire in the heart* over her marriage again and is grateful she is old enough to be past this.

That afternoon, Shahzad lays out his prayer mat for *namaaz*. Recently, he went to see his local *imam* and asked about the old rules on adoption. The *imam* told him these guidelines were outdated. He said that Islam had no problem with adoption anymore. "You are doing a good deed by adopting a child," the *imam* told him. "You can even give the child your name."

Hearing this, Shahzad at first was excited. He told Sabeena he wanted to go visit Ajmer, where it was said that praying to the grave of a saint would magically grant you a son. But Sabeena told him she wasn't interested. She gently reminded him that it was too late. She told him to focus on helping raise Taheem and Mahala, who saw him as a kind of father.

On the prayer mat today, Shahzad does not say his usual prayer for a child. Instead, he says a *dua* of the Prophet Muhammad, which goes: "Oh turner of the hearts, make my heart firm on your *deen*." *Deen* can be translated many ways, but Shahzad understands it as "a complete way of life," which is often difficult for a man to attain. Or difficult for a man to recognize even after he has achieved it.

After Shahzad finishes his prayer, he lies down on his bed for a nap and dreams of his father. This time they are at the cold storage shop together, which always left them stinking of meat and blood. When Shahzad wakes up, he thinks, *Arey, Shahzad, your father is not here, and there is no shop. You sold it. It's finished.*

He is glad this is in the past now, and that his future is with Sabeena, Taheem, and Mahala. He is glad it is only a dream.

Ashok and Parvati

THEY DO not know if it is a boy or a girl, because it is illegal to find out, and so they choose names for both. They have moved out of their anonymous-looking cooperative apartment, not into the sky-high towers but into a small flat on the campus of Parvati's school. The new apartment is cramped and hot after the monsoon that came in fits and bursts and died out too soon. It is hard for Parvati to even steam *idlis* in the tiny new kitchen. And it is hard for her to go to school with her morning sickness or take road trips with Ashok to beautiful places like Khandala anymore. But they are too excited about the baby to care. If the baby is a boy, they have a long list of names. But if it is a girl, Ashok will name her Kavita, which means "poem" in Sanskrit. It is the name with the closest meaning to "writer" he could find.

Ashok has stopped writing ever since Parvati got pregnant again. After he sent off his book to agents, he never heard back from any of them. He tells himself he should stop trying. *I have to give this up now for the baby,* he thinks. The second stage of life: the householder, or family man. The *kutumpa peyar* should continue. The family line should not end.

Still, Ashok keeps his writer's journal. He remembers the Marathi saying about marriage, that "at first it's painful pleasure, but after the poison seeps in, it's only pain." He thinks that this maxim isn't true once you learn that you are having a baby.

Parvati makes jokes now that do not have an edge to them, and Ashok joins in. They joke that there are one billion people in India and that they should get in trouble for adding one more. There are actually 1.3 billion now. On days the baby doesn't flutter kick, Parvati jokes that she is upset she can't feel him—so upset that she might cry. But she does not have crying jags anymore, and they both know that she is better. She does not keep a journal for dark or wild thoughts, and she does not talk of her "past." Instead, they talk of how their baby will almost certainly be a boy.

Ashok's belief in a boy is based on gut feeling. Parvati's is based on the fact that boys are less work than girls, and—because Ashok came into her life, and Ashok turned out to be a husband who does not require work—then that means her baby won't either. There is also the fact that both sets of parents consulted their astrologers, and both astrologers said it would be a boy. Still, they have names for both. After the birth, Parvati plans to get the baby's horoscope written for his or her marriage one day.

Parvati does not cry anymore, but sometimes her past comes back to her. It comes and goes like she remembers the waves do on Chennai's beaches: drifting in and out again, a steady tide. But with the odd monsoon this year, the waves in the Bay of Bengal broke unusually high against the city. Chennai faced heavy floods, and many of the IIT Chennai students left school. Eventually, the floods receded. Parvati does not allow herself to think of the past for long. She does not often think of Joseph. She doesn't speak to him much either. They are both busy with their lives.

But one day, Joseph calls Parvati to tell her that his wife is also pregnant. It turns out that both women are due in mid-August. Parvati hopes, a little sheepishly, that she is the one to give birth first. Joseph tells her that his baby is a boy, which he knows with certainty because in Germany it is not illegal to learn the gender of the baby.

"If you have a girl," he jokes over the phone, "probably we can finally get together this way."

"No," says Parvati. "I'm not going to let my girl marry a Christian boy."

Joseph laughs, because he assumes that Parvati is joking. But she is serious. She is surprised at how much she has become like her father.

At night, before she goes to sleep, Parvati sings her baby a lullaby. Her belly has already become so big. She sings "Omanathinkal Kidavo," a Malayalam lullaby she learned in Trivandrum as a child, which was composed by a nineteenth-century queen to put the baby king to sleep. There had been great pressure on the queen to produce a boy, because a colonialist policy meant the birth of a girl could lead to annexation of the royal land by Britain. Fortunately, as the royal family hoped and prayed for, a baby boy was born. The lullaby is a song of relief.

"Is this sweet babe," Parvati sings in Malayalam, lying on her back in bed, her hand on her belly, "the tender leaf of the *kalpa* tree, or the fruit of my tree of fortune?" The *kalpa* tree, the wish-fulfilling tree, which once granted the goddess Parvati a child, relieving the loneliness she'd once felt. "Or a golden casket to enclose the jewel of my love?"

Parvati finishes the lullaby slowly, watching the ceiling fan spin around and around. Inside her bedroom, it is dark and cool. Outside, over the city's many millions, it is a starless night.

ACKNOWLEDGMENTS

FIRST AND FOREMOST, I am grateful to two extraordinary women: Suzanne Gluck, my agent at William Morris, who believed in this book and championed it, and Jennifer Barth at HarperCollins, who shepherded it through many drafts with a steady guiding hand. Her vision for what this book could be made it richer and better in countless ways. Thank you to everyone who touched this book at HarperCollins.

I also owe thanks to many talented people who suffered through interviews at different stages of my research, including: Anand Giridharadas, Aroon Tikekar, Mariam Dossal, Jim Masselos, Jerry Pinto, Sujata Patel, Paromita Vohra, Rhea Tembhekar, Vihang Vahia, Siddhartha Shah, Santosh Desai, Sidin Vadukut, Ramachandra Guha, Sudhir Kakar, and Wendy Doniger.

This book would not have been made without the encouragement and wisdom of my professors at New York University's Arthur L. Carter Journalism Institute, especially Robert Boynton, Brooke Kroeger, and Suketu Mehta, who understands Mumbai as no one else does. I am particularly indebted to Katie Roiphe for her mentorship, intelligence, and generosity.

I am also lucky to have had the workshops of fellow writers at NYU: Will Hunt, Laura Smith, Meryl Kremer, Alistair Mackay,

Kate Newman, Colin Warren-Hicks, and Meghan White. I am fortunate to have had the guidance of Sidharth Bhatia and Peter Griffin, who are incomparable editors and dear friends.

Joel Gunter, Imran Mujawar, Manish Alimchandani, and Madeline Gressel read sections of this book and made it far better. Daniel Stone dragged me to the library and kept me sane. Emily Brush, Stevie Dunning, Bianca Elder, Reilly Nelson, and Ali Withers kept me going, along with my DC family Sam Sanders and Zora Neale, who are my happy place.

There are a couple places and people that became my refuge at the end, including the DC Writers Room and Alexandra Zapruder there, as well as the Northeast Regional Library, whose librarians are trusty and kind.

My family was a refuge throughout, especially Jeff Flock, who believes in me and truly made this book possible, Gretchen Rubin, who edited drafts in bed and on planes, Charles Rubin, who sent butterflies to Mumbai and taught me to "accomplish the mission," Elizabeth Brack, whose words and notes sustain me, and Jane, Lucy, Claire, and Emily, who are my lifeblood.

There are a few to whom I, and this book, owe a special debt: Nick Bernel, who stood beside me when it was difficult and taught me much about love. Lance Richardson, a brilliant and generous friend, and a north star. Abhishek Raghunath and Arathi Jayaram, who showed me India and taught me to love it. And Maya, Veer, Ashok, Parvati, Shahzad, and Sabeena, who made me want to stay.

REFERENCES

There were many books that informed me on the making of this one, but those that were particularly helpful include:

Bringing Up Children in Islam, Maulana Habiibullaah Mukhtaar
The End of Karma: Hope and Fury Among India's Young, Somini Sengupta
The Essential Rumi, Jalal al-Din Rumi
Etiquettes of Life in Islam, Muḥammad Yusuf Iṣlahi
The Hindus: An Alternative History, Wendy Doniger
The Idea of India, Sunil Khilnani
Images of Asia: American Views of China and India, Harold Isaacs
India After Gandhi: The History of the World's Largest Democracy, Ramachandra Guha
India: A History, John Keay
India Calling: An Intimate Portrait of a Nation's Remaking, Anand Giridharadas
India in Love: Marriage and Sexuality in the 21st Century, Ira Trivedi
Indian Love Poems, Meena Alexander
Love Will Follow: Why the Indian Marriage Is Burning, Shaifali Sandhya
Maximum City: Bombay Lost and Found, Suketu Mehta

May You Be the Mother of a Hundred Sons: A Journey Among the Women of India, Elisabeth Bumiller

Mughal-e-Azam: An Epic of Eternal Love, Shakil Warsi

The Origin of Bombay, Jose Gerson Da Cunha

Tamil Brahmans: The Making of a Middle-Class Caste, C. J. Fuller and Haripriya Narasimhan

I also relied on archival material from many local outlets, including the *Times of India*, the *Indian Express*, *Tehelka*, *Caravan*, the *Hindu*, *Outlook*, and *FirstPost*.

I referenced a number of government and nongovernmental documents, including from the Indian Council of Social Science Research, the Office of the Registrar General and Census Commissioner, the Indian Chamber of Commerce, the Mumbai Port Trust, and the All India Muslim Personal Law Board. I also relied on reports from the Office of the United Nations High Commissioner for Human Rights, the United Nations Department of Economic and Social Affairs, the US National Center for Biotechnology Information, and the US Department of State.

I am grateful to have been able to use the poetry of Kamala Das, with the permission of her book's editor, Dr. Devinder Kohli, and Penguin Books India.

ABOUT THE AUTHOR

ELIZABETH FLOCK is a reporter for *PBS NewsHour*. She began her career at *Forbes India Magazine*, where she spent two years as a features reporter in Mumbai, and has worked for *U.S. News & World Report* and the *Washington Post*. She has also written for major outlets, including the *New York Times*, the *Atlantic*, *Al Jazeera*, *Hindustan Times*, and the *Hindu*. She lives in Washington, DC. *The Heart Is a Shifting Sea* is her first book.

About the author

About the book

Insights,
Interviews
& More . . .

Read on

An Interview with Elizabeth Flock

"Hey Can I Sleep In Your Room?": Studying Love with Elizabeth Flock

ELIZABETH FLOCK ON THE YEARS
SHE SPENT STUDYING OTHER
PEOPLE'S MARRIAGES IN MUMBAI

In her recently published book, *The Heart Is a Shifting Sea*, Elizabeth Flock aims to tell authentic stories of love in the city of Mumbai. But in a place where the notion of flashy Bollywood romance is ubiquitous, Flock went about her mission as a diligent reporter, spending close to a decade observing the daily lives of married couples in the eighth-largest city in the world—interviewing them, living with them, even sleeping on their bedroom floors.

Flock, who spent two years in Mumbai in her early twenties, returned in 2014 to embed with her book's subjects—three couples she had previously met. "I liked them because they were romantics and rule breakers," Flock writes. "They dreamed of being married for seven lifetimes, but they didn't follow convention."

The deeply reported chronicles of these

middle-class Mumbai couples depict the sometimes painful push and pull between love, breaking convention, and the ingrained duty to generations of tradition.

True to the diversity of the city, the book follows three couples from different religious and cultural backgrounds: Maya and Veer are Marwari Hindus, Shahzad and Sabeena are Sunni Muslims, and Ashok and Parvati are Tamil Brahmin Hindus.

But as Flock's writing illustrates, these backgrounds were contextual and monumentally significant to their circumstances, but not even close to wholly representative of their identities.

Although Flock removes herself from these narratives, the stories feel complete and candid in a way that seems remarkable considering they are told by an outsider. The years' worth of trust she built with her subjects—at times even babysitting their children—led to revealed secrets and emotions that take the accounts from ordinary to captivating.

Some of the obstacles these six people face—religious restrictions, gender expectations, antiquated laws and practices— are unique to their cultural environment. But what all of them are after—a successful marriage—is universally relatable.

Flock took the time to speak with Longreads about her reporting process, the state of marriage in India, and how love does or does not transcend culture and region.

JONNY AUPING: *You mention in the author's note that you moved from Chicago to Mumbai at the age of twenty-two "in search of adventure and a job." Why Mumbai? Was there something specific that drew you there?*

Elizabeth Flock: I'd studied and read about India for years, but I think it was Mumbai in particular that attracted me because it's this incredibly frenetic, fast-changing, romantic, but also really difficult city. It's sort of a city of extremes. I was really interested to find out more.

There's also this apocryphal tale of my great-grandmother moving to India by herself that I'd grown up hearing so maybe that had a part in it.

The common experience of people who love Mumbai is that when they're not there, they're having dreams about it and want to get back, and the second they're back they hate it, and they can't wait to get out. ▶

An Interview with Elizabeth Flock*(continued)*

Has that been the case for you?

Very much so. And it plays out in the realities of everyday life. It's this incredibly romantic city. It's called the City of Gold and it's wrapped up in Bollywood romance. People go there with the idea that you can be anything in Mumbai. You can come as a street sweeper and become a Bollywood star or a CEO or politician or whatever it is you want to be, and that dream can be made overnight. But at the same time, it's this incredibly harsh city with a huge divide between rich and poor. It's incredibly difficult to live there. It's incredibly polluted. Communal violence can break out at any time.

I think for me, I've always been fascinated by this collision between our romantic ideals and real life. That's very much a part of Mumbai.

Did you find work there? Aside from the reporting that constituted this book, what was your life like in Mumbai?

I worked for *Forbes India* as a young reporter learning how to report. I didn't make much money, so I did dubbing for Bollywood films. And a whole lot of side jobs for money, some of them really embarrassing. I was a beer girl. I dressed up for rich Indian family parties. Really absurd things. But the main one was dubbing for Bollywood films where I was often the white-girl voice. That paid more in an hour than my reporter job did in like a month.

I'm actually glad that I wasn't getting paid a lot. There are a lot of expats that come to India and they get an air-conditioned car and make a lot of money, and they're just miserable because they're looking at Mumbai through their car window and seeing the poverty and all the really difficult things about Mumbai through an outsider's gaze. So they want to leave Mumbai. I felt like, because journalists are really underpaid, I was sort of forced into the thick of it. In hindsight I'm grateful for it. At the time, it was really difficult.

How did you come in contact with the six people who were chronicled in this book? Were they all pure happenstance or had you set your mind to writing a project about marriage in Mumbai and you were looking for the right subjects?

No, very much not the latter. I lived with Indian families—a whole bunch of them because I didn't have much money, and there were a lot of generous families that took me in.

It was only after living with those families that I started getting interested in the Indian marriage. Of course, only when you're behind closed doors do you start to actually understand what's going on in a marriage. So I started to see the realities of that and I had a million questions.

But at first it was very informal. I was just curious. I was [thinking], "Maybe I'll write a novel about India. Maybe I'll try to write a script." So it was a long process toward this becoming a more formal project. Years later, I [said], "I want to sit down and do formal interviews with these people," and I narrowed down the many couples I'd met to these three. That was because I had stayed in touch with them, and I kept going back to them, and I was having dreams about them. I was really compelled by them and their stories and their marriages.

How did you convince them to agree to this project and open up their lives to you to the extent that they did?

I think the main thing was time. I met them a decade ago, and I'm still hanging around. That builds trust that you aren't just going to parachute in and try to tell their story without a lot of information.

One of them texted me the other week asking who I thought would play him in a movie [laughing]. So I think some of them were motivated by the excitement of it, but I think others really just trusted me, and I hope I honored that trust.

At times, I felt like a therapist, and there really isn't a form of common therapy in India. Unfortunately it's still really taboo and there's a huge crisis of people with mental health issues that aren't getting help. It's not like I'm qualified to be a therapist, but I do think a lot of people want to talk about their stories and their issues.

Tell me a little bit about the interview process. How much of the process was formal interviewing versus just being around them and picking up as many stories as you could?

It was a combination of many things. We did formal sit-down interviews with the couples together and separately over hours and hours. ▶

An Interview with Elizabeth Flock *(continued)*

You mean each individual spouse separately?

Yeah. I definitely wanted to ask them questions together and apart. And more, to be honest, apart. Because I wanted to know how they really felt about a particular situation. On each reporting trip I would spend a month living with each couple and go to work with them, travel with them, take care of the kids, whatever I could do to spend as much time with them as humanly possible. I would be like, "Hey, can I sleep in your room?"

It was a mix of that and the art of hanging out. I just tried to be present in their lives as much as they would allow me to be. Then sometimes something would happen, like they would get into a big fight. The next morning, I would try to interview them separately about it, and ask, "What was going on? What were you thinking?" Whenever someone's [dialogue] is in italics in the book that's because they told me, at the time, they were thinking *I hate you*. Or *I want to divorce you*.

I know memory is fallible. Parts of the book were reconstructed. There are parts that took place in the seventies and eighties and nineties and I wasn't there for it. I'm totally aware, of course, that the way I reconstructed that scene is probably not exactly the way it really happened. But I think the narratives that these people, and all of us, tell ourselves are really important, particularly with marriage. However you remember that fight happening affects how you're going to act toward your spouse going forward.

It does read like you were there reporting from the day they met. In the reconstruction, there really were so many details, from the weather to what they were feeling or wearing. Were you surprised by the depths of their memories at times?

I had some things that helped me out. Some of them kept diaries and journals. I used a lot of photographs so I could really accurately say what they were wearing or what was happening in the room as much as I could. And medical documents and legal documents and sometimes I interviewed a dozen people at an event.

There are some extremely personal accounts in this book: sexual anxieties, religious doubts, impotence, even molestation. People in any culture are hesitant to talk about these things. It requires a level of trust that would seem very hard to attain to get people to open up about.

I think one of the more difficult ones was, one of the people in the book, Shahzad, is a really conservative Muslim man and he has struggled with impotence, and just talking about sex and Islam and his community in the same sentence was really difficult to begin with. I think it was something that I worried about: how to write about that without upsetting him and his community. But this was also on his mind and dictated every day of his life. He wanted desperately to have a child and then couldn't.

Where did anonymity come into play? The characters' names were changed. Was that decision made as soon as you started the project?

Not immediately, but as soon as I found out that there was more happening than I anticipated. I said, "I will change your name for this project. Would that make you more comfortable?" Nothing else has been changed in the text, but I left out very specific locations where I could to try to protect their anonymity as well.

That's so important because I was following the middle class, and there's this idea of middle-class morality where people *will* talk. The wider community will talk. Your neighbors will talk. Your in-laws will talk. People out in the general world could know who you are and know that you're an Indian woman who had an extramarital affair. There will be consequences for you.

Bollywood films are a recurring point of reference for all of these couples. What role does Bollywood have in India's, or specifically Mumbai's, image of love?

Oh my God, it's huge. It's everything.

I asked Suketu Mehta, the author of *Maximum City*, "What books do you think are most essential to read about love and marriage in India?" He said, "Forget books. You don't need to read books. Just watch every Bollywood movie and you're fine." I think he's right. ▶

An Interview with Elizabeth Flock *(continued)*

Movies are such a part of everyday life. The expectations that are in Bollywood movies and the high level of romance—this showy imaginative kind of love, the idea of obsessive love, the idea of over-the-top displays of affection—are so ingrained in Bollywood, and I think [it impacts] how people love. The idea of love where you can't be with the one you love is such a huge part of love and marriage in India because there still is such a stigma to interfaith and intercaste marriages. Bollywood shows how difficult that can be, how people defy those expectations, and how important family is in the end.

But there is also, more problematically, in Bollywood, this long history of no means yes. Where the heroine says no no no to the man and in the end she says yes. People have written theses about how this encourages sexual assault. *Just try hard enough and eventually the girl gives in.*

So anyway, yes, in every possible way Bollywood has a huge influence on it.

You also have this Western influence seeping through. There's Parvati, who's an engineering student who passes the time drawing "Jennifer Lawrence, Emma Watson, and the cast of Friends." Do you think this book would look drastically different if written about three couples in Mumbai ten years in the future?

Yes.

It's hard to really know because there's such a rapid pace of social, political, and economic change in India. I was actually just talking to a CNN India reporter about this and she said, "There's all these Indian women who are watching *Friends*, they're maybe watching pornography, they are consuming social media like American teenagers, but then they're getting into these really traditional marriages." So I think it's really hard to say because it can be two steps in one direction and one step in the other.

There's this rapid change happening, but ideas of how love and sex and marriage happen are so entrenched in India. Any time I would expect the images that they're seeing from the West are going to change things super rapidly I would be proven wrong. Like Parvati: after desperately wanting to have a "love marriage" and her parents forcing her not to do that, in the end she wants her own daughter to have an arranged marriage. I was shocked by that. In the space of five years you went from the person who was going to defy your parents and run away with the person you loved, to now you're pregnant and you're going to force your daughter to have an arranged marriage. That just shows that this change is happening, but not as quickly as people think it is.

It felt like that push and pull was at the core of the book.

Yeah. Absolutely. 100 percent.

Family is probably the most consistent point of conflict in these stories. The looming father or mother-in-law is a constant presence. They seemed to represent the literal enforcement of cultural and religious traditions. Even if well intentioned, is that level of pressure coming from family nearly too much for any modern relationship?

It's extremely difficult. I interviewed a therapist in India who said that something like 90 percent of people that came to see him with mental health difficulties were there because of joint family stress. He said it's *incredibly* stressful to have the overlay of parents and family members and in-laws. In-laws are difficult in any culture, of course. The mother-in-law/daughter-in-law relationship in India has historically been extra fraught.

This is coming from a Western perspective, but I think some people seek out relationships because they want their lives to hit all the traditional milestones like job, marriage, kids, etc. But a lot of other people see the basic expected structure of society explained to them and then they become drawn to partners who are willing to break out of or circumvent that structure with them. Do you think there's something in people's lives that leads them to being in one category or the other?

That's an interesting question.

    If I think about the people in the book, there are characters who go from one category to the other within the space of a few years, like Parvati maybe. If I think anecdotally about my ▶

friends here, there's an idea in the U.S. that I hear people say and that's that when we look for someone, it's not really about *them,* but it's about the us that we see reflected in that person when we're with them. And that's what we're looking for: someone who will make us into our best self or the self that we want to become.

I think that idea is not as prevalent in India. One thing I noticed in India is that the pronouns I and me are not in people's vocabulary the way they are in the U.S. People in the U.S. will say *I'm tired. I'm hungry. I'm upset. I want to do this. I want to do that.* Obviously, India is a much more communal culture and less individualistic, and I think that seeps into relationships as well. It's less about finding a person that will reflect your best self or make you into your best self and more about fulfilling the expectation of the community. *But* that is changing.

If you think about Maya in the book, she very much looked for someone who could push her past those boundaries and she found the opposite.

The relationship expert Ester Perel always talks about how the desire for freedom and the desire for security are in inherent conflict. That's true in varying degrees in every relationship in India and here.

That's kind of scary to think about, actually.

Yeah, it's actually *really* scary [laughing].

The strains put on these couples—the expectation of children, anxiety over sex, demanding in-laws, financial burdens, feeling a spark for someone other than your spouse—all of those things are the same kind of strains that are on Western relationships. In the process of writing it, did you get the sense that all relationships are the same?

Yeah, I think a lot of this stuff is universal. There are obviously particular problems that exist for Indian relationships that don't exist here.

But part of the motivation for writing this book was because the stories we read out of India are a very particular brand. They're either really salacious or they're about Bollywood or about a gang rape. They're just making India exotic or fantasizing about it. That wasn't my experience of India at all. Yes, all that stuff is there. It's real, for sure. But it's also ordinary people trying to make it and trying to love and how hard that is. The problems that I saw within their relationships were the same reasons that my dad got divorced three times. To me, it was really important to tell the mundane, the universal, and the extreme all together.

In your opinion, is love a product of cultural expectation or a rebellion against it?

Marriage is a product of cultural expectation and love is a rebellion against it.

In the author's note, you mentioned that your parents divorced when you were young. You wrote, "When I arrived in Mumbai after my dad's third divorce, this city seemed to hold some answers." Did that ultimately ring true? Did it provide those answers?

I'm not sure, because I think love is really difficult to pin down. It's very slippery, so I'm not sure I got any closer than when I began. But I do think I learned some things about why marriages work or fail. I learned about how many expectations we place on partners in the U.S., which I think is not as much in India. That's something we could probably learn from: not demanding that a person fits exactly our perception of what that person should be. Instead, meeting them where they're at. That's the kind of thing I learned and took away.

In the end, marriage is incredibly complicated and love is incredibly slippery. ∽

Elizabeth Flock on Writing *The Heart Is a Shifting Sea*

I have been at work on this book, in some form or another, since I moved to Mumbai in 2008, which is when I first met and lived with these couples. Like many in Mumbai, they practiced a showy, imaginative kind of love, which I was immediately drawn to. But they were also dreamers and rule breakers, and seemed impatient with the old middle-class morals. Where the established rules for love did not fit for their lives, they made up new ones. And so, informally, I began to ask them questions about their marriages. I had no defined goal, except my interest, at first. Having arrived in Mumbai after my father's third divorce, these couples seemed to have some answers. I ended up living in Mumbai for almost two years, during which time I worked at a business magazine. Ultimately, I quit the magazine to write about these couples, unable to cover Mumbai's newest entrepreneurs when these couples' stories compelled me so much more. But just after I began to write, a truck crashed into a car I was riding in along the winding roads of Goa, and my back collapsed. I was forced to leave India, and these couples, though I promised I'd come back. In the intervening years, as I worked as a newspaper reporter stateside, I kept in touch with these couples. I finally returned to Mumbai, and the project, in the summer of 2014. This time, I came armed with a dozen notebooks, a laptop, a recorder, and a clearer vision of the book I hoped to write. Over that summer and the next, I lived with these couples again, and also ate, slept, worked, and traveled alongside them. This time, I tackled the subject of love and marriage the way, as a newspaper reporter, I'd learned how: with old school, shoe-leather reporting. I interviewed each couple separately and together, formally and informally, over hundreds of hours. Even when not in India, we remained in constant touch. It has now been almost ten years since I began this project. The question I have been pursuing all this time is: Why do marriages work or fail, in any culture or context? I'm not sure I've come up with a single answer for that, but I've certainly learned much. ∾

Elizabeth Flock on Modern Love

When Your Body Tells You What Your Brain Won't

He told me he wanted to marry me in an old city by the sea.

All day we had bicycled the cobbled streets of St. Augustine, Fla., a town once invaded by conquistadors. Now the Spanish buildings stood crumbling but beautiful along the water. We had been drinking, which gave him courage.

He said he wanted to marry me, and then we calmly discussed how and when. We asked the questions you are supposed to ask about committing to a life together: money (we agreed we would never have much), location (on the road, as much as possible) and children (four or five—it would be a raucous home).

We already had planned travel the following year to Tokyo, Sydney, and Mumbai, by train and plane and bus. We had picked out a spot to build a cabin near Susquehannock State Park in Pennsylvania, for when we got back, a place with the clearest night skies. We planned to have dogs and cows and chickens.

But in the days after we returned home from St. Augustine, I flinched every time he touched me. He noticed and quietly asked why. I told him I was just a doubter, especially about the institution of marriage, and he nodded. This he already knew.

On and off for a decade, I had been working on a book about marriage, interviewing people about their own. In at least one instance, I had watched infidelity unravel a couple. Though the husband was often away, I felt on edge as I watched the hurtful things his wife did to him once she decided she wanted to be with someone else, or when she confided to me excitedly about the next time she would see the other man.

I was convinced that in my marriage I wouldn't make the same mistakes as this wife, or as my father, who had been unfaithful more than once and was now contemplating marriage No. 4. I told myself that, despite my own past struggles with fidelity, I would do it better this time.

I would get married and stay married, and when we had relationship issues we would talk about them, not stray. And I promised to take lessons from couples I interviewed, who seemed not to expect too much of their spouses or wonder if there may be someone better.

For three years, I thought I had it figured out. We lived together in a red-doored rowhouse he had built and designed himself and that I filled with my presence and my things. Though he was an architect, the house remained mostly unfinished, with no interior doors or railings. But if I ever complained about this to my mother, she would say, "You know, the cobbler's wife never has any shoes."

On the walls were maps with pins marking all the places we hoped to visit. In the mornings, our dog nudged our faces to wake us up. In the afternoons, she snored at our feet. When we lay down in our too-high bed, it seemed that nothing could touch us.

The next year, a few things changed. I got a new job and became a creature of the day. He now worked at night. He also learned that his job would prevent him from moving for several years, which meant our plans for travel and a cabin would have to wait. There was also an election, and the future suddenly seemed shaky.

I wanted to discuss it with him, but he was often tired. He had always worked too hard. At night, I fell asleep alone.

Soon I began to talk about the news and bigger worries, and ▶

dreams of other cities, with other people, which only reminded me of what he and I were not able to talk about. Early in our relationship he had forwarded me the results of a personality test he had taken as a child that warned of a lack of interest in "more searching answers" to life's bigger questions, and that " 'once over lightly' seems to be the rule."

We had joked about these results, but I also told him I thought this was how he stayed so buoyant.

Now I realized it meant there had always been a set of closed doors between us, doors I may never walk through. One night we watched a TV show about a troubled marriage. When I tried to talk about it afterward, he told me there was nothing to say. At that moment, he felt very far away.

Around this time, a man I had worked with began sending me links to music, the kind of folk-blues songs that got inside you and unsettled parts better left untouched. He and I were both anxious people, and we began having long conversations about things that worried us and places we would rather be. At night, I listened to the songs he sent me, or the music of old punk bands I used to love, with lyrics that asked me questions about freedom whose answers I didn't like.

One night, after one of these songs ended, I found myself writing a story about our story's end. I wrote it on an empty envelope that had been addressed to us as I sat by our records and the map on the wall. As I was cutting a pizza, I wondered idly who would get the pizza slicer. I thought about how I would make eggs only for one. As I wrote, I felt as if I were on the outside looking in, making a decision without being a part of it. Being on the inside would have hurt too much.

On a Friday night soon after, I kissed the man who sent me the folk-blues songs. When I came home and got in bed, my whole body itched. I thought of the unfaithful wife I had interviewed who had believed it was wrong to let the other man kiss her, but she also knew she would go wild with loneliness if she didn't.

Something came apart in me after that. In life, there are certain truths you hold on to: "I am good." "We are good." When a truth you believe in falls away, a friend told me, everything seems uncertain. I stopped eating, sleeping and caring what I wrote or what I did.

There was no outrunning pasts—that was what I saw now. There was no papering over flaws with research and interviews. When I had interviewed the wife about her infidelity, I had inwardly judged her for what she had done. Or maybe I had been judging myself, predicting all along that this would happen.

In the days that followed, I packed my books and clothing in a suitcase and then took them out again. I told myself the right thing to do was to let him go so he could build a cabin near Susquehannock State Park with a woman who kept her word, but I couldn't convince myself to leave. I kept remembering how he brushed his hair back and blinked at the same time. For some reason, this tiny movement is what I loved about him most.

The day he said he wanted to marry me, there was sand in the sheets from our day at the beach, but then I remembered (though I wanted to forget it) how that night my body had said no.

Maybe it was true what people said, that the body tells you what your head doesn't want to. Maybe, even if I hadn't figured out marriage from interviewing those who had embarked upon it, I had learned that some people are right for you and some are not.

I repacked my things in the suitcase, took a few pins out of the map on the wall. I gazed at the holes where the pins had been. I couldn't bear to remove the rest. I called a friend and made hard plans to leave, plans I couldn't undo. And I thought about another truth I held on to, which is that people are not fixed—that we're not doomed to keep repeating the same mistakes.

Months after he and I broke up, we met for a drink and joked again about the results of that personality test. We laughed about it, our incompatibility, but I also sensed how sad we thought it was.

Later, I went back to my marriage interviews, looking for an answer. I read and reread certain pages and lingered on the final ones. As I did, I saw that when I asked the unfaithful wife to describe herself in the years ahead, she described only a better version of herself and a more hopeful future, one where cheating did not play a role.

Unlikely as it may seem, I found myself believing her. ❧